COME INTO MY TRADING ROOM

A Complete Guide to Trading

BOOKS BY DR. ALEXANDER ELDER

Trading for a Living

Study Guide for Trading for a Living

Rubles to Dollars:
  Making Money on Russia's Exploding Financial Frontier

COME INTO MY TRADING ROOM

A Complete Guide to Trading

Dr. Alexander Elder
www.elder.com

John Wiley & Sons, Inc.
New York • Chichester • Weinheim • Brisbane • Singapore • Toronto

To my campers

Published by John Wiley & Sons, Inc.
Published simultaneously in Canada.

This publication is designed to provide accurate and authoritative information in regard to the subject matter covered. It is sold with the understanding that the publisher is not engaged in rendering professional services. If professional advice or other expert assistance is required, the services of a competent professional person should be sought.

ISBN 0-471-22534-7

CONTENTS

INTRODUCTION

"You can be free. You can live and work anywhere in the world, be independent from the routine and not answer to anybody." With those words I began my first book, *Trading for a Living*. One of my great pleasures in the years since its publication has been meeting and becoming friends with people who became free thanks to successful trading.

Several times a year I run a Traders' Camp, a week of intensive classes at remote resorts. I enjoy my campers' successes. A stockbroker became a full-time trader, closed his business, and moved to Rio to pursue a life-long interest in Latin women. A psychologist became such a successful options writer that she paid for an early retirement for her husband and moved with him to the Virgin Islands to become an expert in what she calls synchronous hammocking. A man bought a mountain in Vermont and trades from the house he built on its top. I wish all students could succeed, but it's not that simple.

How many psychiatrists does it take to change a lightbulb? Only one—but the bulb has to want to change.

To succeed in trading you need several innate traits without which you shouldn't even start. They include discipline, risk tolerance, and facility with numbers. A big fat guy who is often drunk and can't kick a cigarette habit is unlikely to make a good trader—he lacks discipline. A nitpicker who obsesses over each dime is too tense to live with market risks. A daydreamer who cannot do simple arithmetic on the run becomes lost when prices change rapidly.

In addition to discipline, risk tolerance, and ease with numbers, successful trading requires 3 M's—Mind, Method, and Money. Mind means developing psychological rules that will keep you calm amidst the

1

noise of the markets. Method is a system of analyzing prices and developing a decision-making tree. Money refers to money management, which means risking only a small part of your trading capital on any trade; think of the way a submarine is divided into many compartments so that it won't sink if one section becomes flooded—you have to structure your account this way. Psychology, trading tactics, money management—you can learn these skills.

How long will it take you to become a competent trader and how much will it cost? What rules do you set, what methods do you use, and how do you split your trading capital? What should you study first, second, and third? What markets should you trade, and how much money can you expect to make? If these questions interest you, you picked the right book.

You can succeed in trading. It has been done before, and it's being done right now, today, by people who started from scratch, learned to trade and are making a good living at it. The best ones make fortunes. Others fail, out of ignorance or lack of discipline. If you work through this book, ignorance will not be a problem, and you will hear me yell at you again and again, pointing you towards disciplined, responsible, professional trading.

Trading is a journey of self-discovery. If you enjoy learning, if you are not scared of risk, if the rewards appeal to you, if you are prepared to put in the work, you have a great project ahead of you. You will work hard and enjoy the discoveries you'll make along the way.

I wish you success. Now let us begin.

How This Book Is Organized

Books written from the heart acquire their own direction. They develop and change in the process of being written. You start with a plan, but the book takes over, and before you know it, you're going much farther than planned.

I began writing this book three years ago on a flight to New York, returning from a Traders' Camp in Mexico. We had more beginners than usual, many of them women. They kept asking for a book that they jokingly called *Trading for Dummies*. There were no dummies in our group. Those campers were smart, sharp, and motivated—but they needed to learn the rules and the tools. I figured I would write a brief practical introduction, call it *Financial Trading for Babes in the Woods*, and be done by Christmas.

Three Christmases passed before I completed my project. The beginner part was easy, but I kept tunneling into the depths of trading, sharing what I learned in the nine years since *Trading for a Living* was published. I developed new indicators and systems. My money management became crisper, and I designed a new approach to record keeping. My work with hundreds of traders showed me how to teach people to turn their trading lives around and move from haphazard jumping in and out to a calm professional style. Take a few minutes to read how this book is organized, so that you may get full value out of it.

Part One, *Financial Trading for Babes in the Woods*, is written primarily for those who are just becoming interested in trading. It lays out topics whose mastery is essential for success and puts up danger signs around the main pitfalls. Even experienced traders would do well to review this chapter, especially the concept of external barriers to success, which has never before been spelled out in trading literature, and the critique of the efficient market theory.

Part Two, *The Three M's of Successful Trading*, teaches you the three key aspects of trading—Mind, Method, and Money. Mind is your trading psychology. Method is how you go about finding trades and making entry and exit decisions. Money is how you manage your trading capital for long-term survival and success. Once we review the psychological rules, I'll share with you my favorite analytic tools, some of which I have never before revealed. We will cover system testing, day-trading, and a new method for placing stops. The step-by-step money management strategy has never before appeared in trading literature.

Part Three, *Come into My Trading Room*, delivers another first—a set of exact instructions for organizing your time and effort, as well as keeping good records. Proper record keeping is a hallmark of successful trading. Good records help you learn from your mistakes as well as victories. You know you should keep records, but now you'll see exactly how to do it. By the time you work through this section, nobody can call you "a babe in the woods."

Take your time as you read this book, mark it up, return to the sections that interest you most. This volume distills 20 years of trading and teaching experience. It took three years to write, and it will probably take more than one reading to get its full value. Open your charting software, pull out your trading records, test all the concepts on your own data. Only testing will make these ideas your own.

By the time you leave my trading room, you'll be in a position to take your trading to a higher, more intelligent, and successful level.

MALE OR FEMALE?

Almost every nonfiction writer faces the dilemma—which pronoun to use. He? She? He or she?

Male traders outnumber women by about twenty to one, although this ratio is rapidly becoming more balanced as more and more women come into the markets. In our Traders' Camps, which attract the more sophisticated segment of traders, we have already moved from a great preponderance of men to a near parity with women.

I find that the percentage of successful traders is higher among women. They tend to be less arrogant, and arrogance is a deadly sin in trading. The male ego—that wonderful trait that has been bringing us wars, riots, and bloodshed since time immemorial—tends to get heavily caught up in trading. A guy studies his charts, decides to buy, and now his self-esteem is involved—he has to be right! If the market goes his way, he waits to be proven even more right—bigger is better. If the market goes against him, he is tough enough to stand the pain and waits for the market to reverse and prove him right—while it grinds down his account.

Women traders, on the other hand, are much more likely to ask a simple question—where's the money? They like to take profits and focus on avoiding losses instead of trying to prove themselves right. Women are more likely to bend with the wind and go with the flow, catch trends and hop off a little earlier, booking profits. When I tell traders that keeping records is a hugely important aspect of success, women are more likely to keep them than men. If you are looking to hire a trader, all other factors being equal, I'd recommend looking for a woman.

Still, there are many more male than female traders. The English language being what it is, "he" flows better than "he or she" or even jumping between the two pronouns. To make reading easier, I'll use the masculine pronoun throughout this book. I trust you understand that no disrespect is intended toward women traders. I want to make this book easier to read for everybody, of any gender, anywhere in the world.

PART ONE

FINANCIAL TRADING FOR BABES IN THE WOODS

Are traders born or made? There is no simple answer. Both aptitude and learning are important, but in different proportions for different people. At one extreme are born geniuses who require very little learning. At the other are gamblers and dunces, whom no classes are likely to help. The rest of us are in the middle of the curve, with some aptitude but in need of education.

A genius has little need for a book because he has a fantastic feel for the market. A gambler is too busy getting high on adrenaline. This book is written for the trader in the middle.

INVEST?
TRADE?
GAMBLE?

A newcomer to the market faces three paths that lead into a forest full of treasures and dangers. The first path, for investors, goes through the sunniest areas. Most of those who take it come out alive, if not much richer. Another path, for traders, leads into the heart of the forest. Many travelers disappear, but those who come out look rich. The third is a shortcut that takes gamblers into the swamp.

How can you tell which path is which? You must choose your way carefully because if you don't, you'll end up on the gamblers' path, especially since it crosses both investors' and traders' trails. We'll return to this question in the chapters on trading psychology.

AN INTELLIGENT INVESTOR

Investors profit by recognizing new trends in the economy and buying into them before the majority wakes up to opportunities. A knowledgeable investor can earn huge percentage gains by holding his position without being terribly active.

Back in the 1970s, I bought stock in a company called KinderCare, which ran a chain of child care centers. It tried to make them as uniform and reliable as McDonalds' hamburgers. KinderCare catered to baby boomers who were having babies right, left, and center. Half of my friends were pregnant at that time. A major social shift was taking place in the United States, with women going to work in record numbers. Someone had to mind the babies of all those two-income families, and the stock of KinderCare soared on the crest of a new social trend.

AT&T used to have a monopoly on long-distance phone calls. Then in the late 1970s a tiny brash upstart called MCI won a legal dogfight, allowing it to compete with AT&T. The age of deregulation was upon us, and the stock of MCI—the first company into the breach—sold for $3 presenting another great opportunity to hop aboard a new trend.

A few years ago I flew into New York from the Caribbean with my friend George. He became a millionaire by buying $30,000 worth of Dell stock before most people had heard of the company—and unloading it at the top three years later with the help of technical analysis. Sprawled in his first-class seat, George was perusing several investment advisories, trying to lock in on the next trend in Internet technology. How right he was! Within a year Internet stocks were flying, defying gravity.

That's the lure of investing. If you can buy a chunk of Dell at $4 a share and cash out at $80 a few years later, it is easy to fly down to a resort for a week rather than sit in front of a monitor watching every tick.

What are the disadvantages? Investing requires a great deal of patience and an immense supply of self-confidence. To buy Chrysler after it was rescued from the brink of bankruptcy or Internet search engines before anyone knew what those words meant, you had to have a huge level of confidence in your ability to read the trends in society and the economy. All of us are smart after the fact; very few are smart early in the game, and only the tiniest percentage has the emotional strength to make a large bet on their vision and hold on to it. Those who can do this consistently, like Warren Buffett or Peter Lynch, are hailed as superstars.

An Intelligent Trader

Traders make money by betting on short-term price swings. The idea is to buy when our reading of the market tells us prices are rising and sell when the uptrend runs out of steam. Alternatively, we can bet on a decline and sell short when our analysis points to a downtrend, covering when the downtrend starts bottoming out. The concept is simple, but implementing it is difficult.

It is hard to become a good analyst, but harder to become a good trader. Beginners often assume they can make money because they're smart, computer-literate and have a record of success in business. You can get a fast computer and even buy a backtested system from a vendor, but putting money on it is like trying to sit on a three-legged stool with two legs missing. The two other factors are psychology and money management.

Balancing your mind is just as important as analyzing markets. Your personality influences your perceptions, making it a key aspect of your success or failure. Managing money in your trading account is essential for surviving the inevitable drawdowns and prospering in the long run. Psychology, market analysis, and money management—you have to master all three to become a success.

There are two main approaches to profiting from crowd behavior. The first is momentum trading—buy when a ripple starts running through the crowd, sending the market higher, and sell when that ripple starts losing speed. It is a challenge to identify a new trend while it's still young. As the trend speeds up and the crowd becomes exuberant, amateurs fall in love with their positions. Professionals remain calm and monitor the trend's speed. As soon as they find that the crowd is returning to its normal sleepiness, they take profits without waiting for a reversal.

The other method is the countertrend strategy. It involves betting against the deviations and for a return to normalcy. Countertrend traders sell short when an upside breakout starts running out of speed and cover when a downtrend starts petering out. Beginners love to trade against trends ("let's buy, this market can't go any lower!"), but most get impaled on a price spike that fails to reverse. A man who likes peeing against the wind has no right to complain about his cleaning bills. Professionals can trade against trends only because they are ready to run at the first sign of trouble. Before you bet on a reversal, be sure your exit strategy and money management are fine-tuned.

Momentum traders and countertrend traders capitalize on two opposite aspects of crowd behavior. Before you put on a trade, be sure to know whether you're investing, momentum trading, or countertrend trading. Once you've entered a trade, manage it as planned! Don't change your tactics in the midst of a trade because then you'll contribute to the winners' welfare fund.

Amateurs keep thinking what trades to get into, while professionals spend just as much time figuring out their exits. They also focus on money management, calculating what size positions they can afford under current market conditions, whether to pyramid, when to take partial profits, and so on. They also spend a great deal of time keeping good records of their trades.

The Efficient Market Theory

A trader strains his mind, his soul, his entire being trying to take profits out of the market when an unsettling piece of news comes down the pike—the efficient market theory. Its main adherents are academics, who are fond of pointing out that prices reflect all available market information. People buy and sell on the basis of their knowledge, and the latest price represents everything known about that market. This is a valid observation, from which the efficient market gang draws the curious conclusion that no one can beat the market. Markets know everything, they say, and trading is like playing chess against someone who knows more than you. Don't waste your time and money—simply index your portfolio and select stocks based on volatility.

What about traders who make money? The efficient market theorists say that winners are plain lucky. Most people make money at some point, before bleeding it back into the markets. What about those who keep outperforming markets year after year? Warren Buffett, one of the twentieth century's great investors, says that investing in a market in which people believe in efficiency is like playing poker against those who believe it does not pay to look at cards.

I think that the efficient market theory offers one of the truest views of the markets. I also believe it is one of the largest pieces of theoretical garbage. The theory correctly observes that markets reflect the intelligence of all crowd members; it is fatally flawed in assuming that investors and traders are rational human beings who always strive to maximize gains and minimize losses. That is a very idealized view of human nature.

Most traders can be rational on a fine weekend when the markets are closed. They calmly study their charts and decide what to buy and sell, where to take profits, and when to cut losses. When the markets open on Monday, the best laid plans of mice and men get ripped up in the sweaty palms of traders.

Trading and investing are partly rational and partly emotional. People often act on an impulse even if they harm themselves in the process of doing so. A winning gambler brags about his positions and misses sell signals. A fearful trader beaten up by the market becomes cautious beyond measure. As soon as his stock ticks down a bit, he sells, violating his own rules. When that stock rises, overshooting his original profit target, he can no longer stand the pain of missing the rally and buys way above his planned entry point. The stock stalls and slides, and he watches, first with hope and later frozen in horror, as it sinks like a rock. In the end, he can't take any more pain and sells out at a loss—right near the bottom. What's so rational about this process? The original plan to buy may have been rational, but implementing it created an emotional storm.

Emotional traders do not pursue their best long-term interests. They are too busy savoring the adrenaline rush or too twisted in fear, desperate to extract their fingers from a mousetrap. Prices reflect intelligent behavior of rational investors and traders, but they also reflect screaming mass hysteria. The more active the market, the more traders are emotional. Rational individuals can become a minority, surrounded by those with sweaty palms, pounding hearts, and clouded minds.

Markets are more efficient during flat trading ranges, when people are apt to use their heads. They grow less efficient during trends, when people become more emotional. It is hard to make money in flat markets because your opponents are relatively calm. Rational people make dangerous enemies. It is easier to take money from traders who are excited by a fast-moving trend because emotional behavior is more primitive and easier to predict. To be a successful trader you must keep your cool at all times and take money from aroused amateurs.

People are more likely to be rational when alone, and grow more impulsive when they join crowds. A trader's intense focus on the price of a stock, a currency, or a future pulls him into the crowd of all who trade that vehicle. As the price ticks up and down, the eyes, the heads, and the bodies of traders across the continents start moving up and down in unison. The market hypnotizes traders like a magician hypnotizes a snake, by moving his flute rhythmically up and down. The faster the price moves, the stronger the emotions. The more emotional a market, the less efficient it is, and inefficiency creates profit opportunities for calm, disciplined traders.

A rational trader can make money by remaining calm and following his rules. Around him, the crowd chases rallies, hard with greed. It sells into falling markets, squealing from pain and fear. All the while, the intelligent trader follows his rules. He may use a mechanical system or act as a discretionary trader, reading his markets and putting on trades. Either way, he follows his rules rather than his gut—that is his great advantage. A mature trader pulls money through the big hole in the efficient market theory, its presumption that investors and traders are rational human beings. Most people aren't; only winners are.

What Is Price?

Each trade represents a transaction between a buyer and a seller who meet face to face, by phone or on the Internet, with or without brokers. A buyer wants to buy as cheaply as possible. A seller wants to sell as expensively as possible. Both feel pressure from the crowd of undecided traders that surrounds them, ready to jump in and snatch away their bargain.

A trade takes place when the greediest buyer, afraid that prices will run away from him, steps up and bids a penny more. Or the most fearful seller, afraid of getting stuck with his merchandise, agrees to accept a penny less. Sometimes a fearful seller dumps his merchandise on a calm and disciplined buyer waiting for a trade to come to him. All trades reflect the behavior of the market crowd. Each price flashing on your screen represents a momentary consensus of value among market participants.

Fundamental values of companies and commodities change slowly, but prices swing all over the lot because the consensus can change quickly. One of my clients used to say that prices are connected to values with a mile-long rubber band, allowing markets to swing between overvalued and undervalued levels.

The normal behavior of the crowd is to mill around, make noise, and go nowhere. Once in a while a crowd becomes excited and explodes in a rally or a panic, but usually it just wastes time. Bits of news and rumors send ripples through the crowd, whose shifts leave footprints on our screens. Prices and indicators reflect changes in crowd psychology.

When the market gives no clear signals to buy or sell short, many beginners start squinting at their screens, trying to recognize trading signals. A good signal jumps at you from the chart and grabs you by the face—you can't miss it! It pays to wait for such signals instead of forcing trades when the market offers you none. Amateurs look for challenges; professionals look for easy trades. Losers get high from the action; the pros look for the best odds.

Fast-moving markets give the best trading signals. When crowds are gripped by emotions, cool traders find their best opportunities to make money. When markets go flat, many successful traders withdraw, leaving the field to gamblers and brokers. Jesse Livermore, a great speculator of the twentieth century, used to say that there is time to go long, time to go short, and time to go fishing.

An Intelligent Gambler?

Most people gamble at some point in their lives. For most it provides entertainment, for some it becomes an addiction, while a few become pros and make a living at it. Gambling provides a living for a very small minority and entertainment for the masses, but a casual gambler reaching for a quick buck has the same chance of success as an ice cube on a hot stove.

Some famous investors like betting on horses. They include Peter Lynch, of Magellan Fund fame, and Warren Buffett, who used to publish a newsletter on handicapping. My friend Lou, to whom my first book was dedicated, spent several years on the handicapping circuit and bet on horses for a living before buying an exchange seat and approaching financial markets like a cool handicapper. Some card games, such as baccarat, are based on chance alone, whereas others, such as blackjack, involve a degree of skill that attracts intelligent people.

Professionals treat gambling as a job. They keep calculating odds and act only when mathematics point in their favor. Losers, on the other hand, itch for the action and enter one game after another, switching between half-baked systems.

When you gamble for entertainment, follow a set of money management rules. The first rule is to limit how much you'll risk in any given session. On a rare occasion when a friend pulls me into a casino, I put what I am willing to lose that night into my right pocket, and stuff my winnings, if any, into the left one. I stop playing as soon as my right pocket is empty, without ever reaching into the left. Once in a while I find more money in the left pocket than I had in my right, but I certainly do not count on it.

A friend who is a successful businessman enjoys the glitter of Las Vegas. Several times a year he takes $5,000 in cash and flies there for a weekend. When his bankroll runs out, he goes for a swim in the pool, enjoys a good dinner, and flies back home. He can afford to spend $5,000 on entertainment and never blows more than his initial stake. Lounging at a pool after his cash is gone, he differs from legions of compulsive gamblers who keep charging more chips on their credit cards, waiting for their "luck" to turn. A gambler with no money management is guaranteed to bust out.

WHAT MARKETS TO TRADE?

Many people give little thought to life's important decisions. They stumble into them by accidents of geography, time, or chance. Where to live, where to work, what markets to trade—many of us decide on a whim, without much serious thought. No wonder so many are dissatisfied with their lives. You can choose your markets on a whim or pause to think whether to trade stocks, futures, or options. Each of those has pluses as well as minuses.

Successful traders are rational people. Winners trade solely for the money, while losers get their kicks out of the excitement of the game. Where those kicks land is another question.

In choosing a market to trade, keep in mind that every trading vehicle, be it a stock, a future, or an option, has to meet two criteria: liquidity and volatility. Liquidity refers to the average daily volume, compared with that of other vehicles in its group. The higher the volume, the easier it is to get in and out. You can build a profitable position in a thin stock, only to get caught in the door at the exit and suffer slippage trying to take profits. Volatility is the extent of movement in your vehicle. The more it moves, the greater the trading opportunities. For example, stocks of many utility companies are very liquid but hard to trade because of low volatility—they tend to stay in narrow price ranges. Some low-volume, low-volatility stocks may be good investments for your long-term portfolio, but not for trading. Remember that not all markets are good for trading simply because you have a strong opinion on their future direction. They also must have good volume and move well.

STOCKS

A stock is a certificate of company ownership. If you buy 100 shares of a company that issued 100 million shares, you own one-millionth of that firm. You become a part owner of that business, and if other people want to own it, they will have to bid for your shares, lifting their value.

When people like the prospects of a business, they bid for its shares, pushing up prices. If they don't like the outlook, they sell their stock, depressing prices. Public companies try to push up share prices because it makes it easier for them to float more equity or sell debt. The bonuses of top executives are often tied to stock prices.

Fundamental values, especially earnings, drive prices in the long run, but John Maynard Keynes, the famous economist and a canny stock picker, retorted "In the long run we're all dead." Markets are full of cats and dogs, stocks of unprofitable companies that at some point fly through the roof, defying gravity. Stocks of sexy new industries, such as biotechnology or the Internet, can fly on the expectations of future earnings rather than on any real operating records. Each dog has its day in the sun before reality sets in. Stocks of profitable, well-run companies may drift sideways to down. The market reflects the sum total of what every participant knows, thinks, or feels about a stock, and a declining price means large holders are selling. The essential rule in any market is "It's OK to buy cheap, but not OK to buy down." Don't buy a stock that's trending lower, even if it looks like a bargain. If you like its fundamentals, use technical analysis to confirm that the trend is up.

Warren Buffett, one of the most successful investors in America, is fond of saying that when you buy a stock, you become a partner of a manic-depressive fellow he calls Mr. Market. Each day Mr. Market runs up and offers either to buy you out of business or to sell you his share. Most of the time you should ignore him because the man is psychotic, but occasionally Mr. Market becomes so terribly depressed that he offers you his share for a song—and that's when you should buy. At other times he becomes so manic that he offers an insane price for your share—and that's when you should sell.

This idea is brilliant in its simplicity, but hard to implement. Mr. Market sweeps most of us off our feet because his mood is so conta-gious. Most people want to sell when Mr. Market is depressed and buy when he is manic. We need to keep our sanity. We need objective criteria to decide how high is too high and how low is too low. Buffett makes his decisions on the basis of fundamental analysis and a fantastic gut feel. Traders can use technical analysis.

Speaking of gut feel, this is something that an investor or a trader may develop after years of successful experience. What beginners call gut feel is usually an urge to gamble, and I tell them they have no right to a gut feel.

What stocks should we trade? There are more than 10,000 of them in the United States, with even more abroad. Peter Lynch, a highly successful money manager, writes that he only buys stocks in companies that are so simple that an idiot could run them—because eventually one will. But Lynch is an investor, not a trader. Stocks of many companies with little fundamental value can embark on fantastic runs, making heaps of money for bullish traders before collapsing and making just as much money for the bears.

The stock market offers a wealth of choices, even after we cut out illiquid or flat stocks. You open a business newspaper, and stories of fantastic rallies and breathtaking declines leap at you from the pages. Should you jump on the bandwagon and trade stocks in the news? Have they moved too far from the gate? How do you find future leaders? Having to make so many choices stresses beginners. They spread themselves thin, jumping between stocks instead of focusing on a few and learning to trade them well. Newbies who cannot confidently trade a single stock go looking for scanning software that will let them track thousands.

In addition to stocks, you can choose from their kissing cousins, mutual funds, called *unit trusts* in Europe. Long-term investors tend to put money into diversified funds which hold hundreds of stocks. Traders tend to focus on sector funds that let them trade specific sectors of the economy or entire countries. You pick a favorite sector or country and leave individual stock selection to the supposedly hot-shot analysts laboring at those funds.

Choosing a winning stock or fund is a lot harder than listening to tips at a party or scanning headlines in a newspaper. A trader must develop a set of fundamental or technical search parameters, have the discipline to follow his system, and spread a safety net of money management under his account. We will delve into all three areas in Part 2.

WHERE DO I GO FROM HERE?   *How to Buy Stocks* by Louis Engel is the best
introductory book for stock investors and traders. The author died years
ago, but the publisher updates the book every few years—be sure to
get the latest edition.

FUTURES

Futures look dangerous at first—nine out of ten traders go bust in their
first year. As you look closer, it becomes clear that the danger is not in
futures but in the people who trade them. Futures offer traders some
of the best profit opportunities, but the dangers are commensurate with
rewards. Futures make it easy for gamblers to shoot themselves in the
foot, or higher. A trader with good money management skills needn't
fear futures.

Futures used to be called *commodities*, the irreducible building blocks
of the economy. Old-timers used to say that a commodity was something that hurt when you dropped it on your foot—gold, sugar, wheat,
crude oil. In recent decades many financial instruments began to
trade like commodities—currencies, bonds, stock indexes. The term
futures includes traditional commodities along with new financial
instruments.

A future is a contract to deliver or accept delivery of a specific quantity of a commodity by a certain date. A futures contract is binding on
both buyer and seller. In options the buyer has the right but not an
obligation to take delivery. If you buy a call or a put, you can walk
away if you like. In futures, you have no such luxury. If the market
goes against you, you have to add money to your margin or get out of
your trade at a loss. Futures are stricter than options but are priced better for traders.

Buying a stock makes you a part owner of a company. When you
buy a futures contract you don't own anything, but enter into a binding contract for a future purchase of merchandise, be it a carload of
wheat or a sheaf of Treasury bonds. The person who sells you that
contract assumes the obligation to deliver. The money you pay for a
stock goes to the seller, but in futures your margin money stays with
the broker as a security, ensuring you'll accept delivery when your
contract comes due. They used to call margin money *honest money*.
While in stocks you pay interest for margin borrowing, in futures you
can collect interest on your margin.

Each futures contract has a settlement date, with different dates selling for different prices. Some professionals analyze their differences to predict reversals. Most futures traders do not wait and close out their contracts early, settling profits and losses in cash. Still, the existence of a delivery date forces people to act, providing a useful reality check. A person may sit on a losing stock for ten years, deluding himself it is only a paper loss. In futures, reality, in the form of the settlement date, always intrudes on a daydreamer.

To understand how futures work, let's compare a futures trade with a cash trade—buying or selling a quantity of a commodity outright. Let's say it's February and gold is trading at $400 an ounce. Your analysis indicates it is likely to rise to $420 within weeks. With $40,000 you can buy a 100-ounce gold bar from a dealer. If your analysis is correct, in a few weeks your gold will be worth $42,000. You can sell it and make a $2,000 profit, or 5 percent before commissions—nice. Now let's see what happens if you trade futures based on the same analysis.

Since it is February, April is the next delivery month for gold. One futures contract covers 100 oz. of gold, with a value of $40,000. The margin on this contract is only $1,000. In other words, you can control $40,000 worth of gold with a $1,000 deposit. If your analysis is correct and gold rallies $20 per oz., you'll make roughly the same profit as you would have made had you bought 100 oz. of gold for cash—$2,000. Only now your profit is not 5% but 200%, since your margin was $1,000. Futures can really boost your gains!

Most people, once they understand how futures work, are flooded with greed. An amateur with $40,000 calls his broker and tells him to buy 40 contracts! If his analysis is correct and gold rallies to $420, he'll make $2,000 per contract, or $80,000. He'll triple his money in a few weeks! If he repeats this just a few times, he'll be a millionaire before the end of the year! Such dreams of easy money ruin gamblers. What, if anything, do they overlook?

The trouble with markets is that they don't move in straight lines. Charts are full of false breakouts, false reversals, and flat trading ranges. Gold may well rise from $400/oz. to $420/oz., but it is perfectly capable of dipping to $390 along the way. That $10 dip would have created a $1,000 paper loss for someone who bought 100 oz. of gold for cash. For a futures trader who holds a 100 oz. contract on a $1,000 margin that $10 decline represents a total wipeout. Long before he reaches that sad point, his broker will call and ask for more margin money. If you have committed most of your equity to a trade, you'll have no reserves and your broker will sell you out.

Gamblers dream of fat profits, margin themselves to the hilt, and get kicked out of the game by the first wiggle that goes against them. Their long-term analysis may be right and gold may rise to its target price, but the beginner is doomed because he commits too much of his equity and has very thin reserves. Futures do not kill traders—poor money management kills traders.

Futures can be very attractive for those who have strong money management skills. They promise high rates of return but demand ice-cold discipline. When you first approach trading, you are better off with slower-moving stocks. Once you have matured as a trader, take a look at futures. They may be right for you if you're very disciplined. We return to the futures markets in Part 2 and look at the best ones for getting started.

WHERE DO I GO FROM HERE?   *Winning in the Futures Markets* by George Angell is the best introductory book for futures traders. (It is highly superior to all his other books.) *The Futures Game* by Teweles and Jones is a mini-encyclopedia that has educated generations of futures traders (be sure to get the latest edition). *Economics of Futures Trading* by Thomas A. Hieronymus is probably the most profound book on futures, but it's long been out of print—try finding a used copy.

OPTIONS

An option is a bet that a specific stock, index, or future will reach or exceed a specific price within a specific time. Please stop and reread that sentence. Notice that the word *specific* occurs in it three times. You must choose the right stock, predict the extent of its move, and forecast how fast it'll get there. You must make three choices—if you're wrong on just one, you'll lose money.

When you buy an option, you have to jump through three hoops in a single leap. You have to be right on the stock or the future, right on its move, and right on its timing. Ever tried tossing a ball through three rings at an amusement park? This triple complexity makes buying options a deadly game.

Options offer leverage—an ability to control large positions with a small outlay of cash. The entire risk of an option is limited to the price you pay for it. Options allow traders to make money fast when they're right, but if the market reverses, you can walk away and owe nothing! This is the standard flow of brokerage house propaganda. It attracts hordes of small traders who cannot afford to buy stocks but want a bigger bang for their buck. What usually gets banged is the option buyer's head.

My company, Financial Trading, Inc., has been selling books to traders for years. Whenever a person comes back to buy another book, it is a sign that he is active in the markets. Many clients buy books on stocks or futures every few months or years. But when a first-time buyer orders a book on options, he never returns. Why? Does he make so much money so fast that he doesn't need another book? Or does he wash out?

Many beginners buy calls because they can't afford stocks. Futures traders who get beat up sometimes turn to options on futures. Losers switch to options instead of dealing with their own inability to trade. Using a shortcut to weasel out of trouble instead of facing a problem never works.

Successful stock and futures traders sometimes use options to reduce risks or protect profits. Serious traders buy options rarely and only in special situations, as we will see later in this book. Options are hopeless for poor people who use them as substitutes for stocks because they can't afford the real thing.

Professionals take full advantage of starry-eyed beginners crowding into options. Their bid-ask spreads are terrible. If an option is bid 75 cents, offered at a dollar, you are 25% behind the game as soon as you buy. The expression "your loss is limited to what you paid for an option" means you can lose 100%! What's so great about losing everything?

A client of mine was a market-maker on the floor of the American Stock Exchange. She came to my classes on technical analysis because she was pregnant and wanted to get off the floor and trade from home. "Options," she said, "are a hope business. You can buy hope or sell hope. I am a professional—I sell hope. I come to the floor in the morning and find what the public wants. Then I price that hope and sell it to them."

Professionals are more likely to write options than buy them. Writing is a capital-intensive business. You need hundreds of thousands of dollars to do it right, and most successful options writers operate with millions. And even theirs is not a risk-free game. Several years ago a friend who used to be one of the nation's top money managers landed on the front page of *The Wall Street Journal* after he lost 20 years' worth of profits in a single bad day of writing naked puts.

There are two types of option writers. Covered writers buy a stock and write an option against it. Naked writers write calls and puts on stocks they don't own, backing their writes with cash in their accounts. Writing naked options feels like taking money out of thin air, but a violent move can put you out of business. Writing options is a serious game, suitable only for disciplined and well-capitalized traders.

Markets are like pumps that suck money out of the pockets of the poorly informed majority and pump it into the pockets of a savvy minority. People who service those pumps, such as brokers, vendors, regulators, and even janitors who sweep exchange floors, are paid from the stream of money flowing through the markets. Since markets take money from the majority, pay help, and give what's left to the savvy minority, the majority, by definition, must lose. You can be sure that whatever the majority of traders does, believes, and says, is not worth doing, believing, and saying. You have to stand apart from the crowd in order to succeed. Smart traders look for situations where a large majority does something one way, while a small, moneyed minority goes the opposite way.

In options the majority buys calls and, to a lesser degree, puts. The insiders almost exclusively write options. Professionals use their heads, while amateurs are driven by greed and fear. Options take full advantage of those feelings.

Greed is the engine of option-selling propaganda. You must have heard the slogan: "Control a large block of stock with just a few dollars!" An amateur may be bullish on a $60 stock, but doesn't have $6,000 to buy 100 shares. He buys some $70 calls with two months of life left in them for $500 each. If that stock rises to 75, those options will acquire $500 of intrinsic value, while maintaining some time value, and a speculator can double his stake in a month! The amateur buys calls and sits back to watch his money double.

Strange things begin to happen. Whenever the stock rises two points, his calls go up only one, but when the stock falls or even pauses, his calls fall briskly. Instead of seeing his money double in a hurry, the amateur is soon staring at a 50% paper loss, while the clock starts ticking louder and louder. The expiration date is nearing, and even though the stock is higher than it was when he bought his calls, they are now cheaper, showing a paper loss. Should he sell and salvage some money or hold and wait for a rally? Even if he knows the right thing to do, he's not going to do it. His greed does him in. He hangs on until his options expire worthless.

Another great motivator for buying options is fear, especially in options on futures. A loser takes a few painful hits—his analysis was wet and money management nonexistent. He sees an attractive trade but fears losing. He hears the siren song—"unlimited gains with limited risk"—and buys options on futures. Speculators buy options like poor people buy lottery tickets. A person who buys a lottery ticket risks 100% of what he paid. Any situation where you risk 100% looks like an odd case of limited risk. Limited to 100%!?! Most speculators ignore this ominous figure.

Option buyers have a dismal track record. They may make a few dollars on a few trades, but I've never seen anyone build equity buying options. The odds in this game are so bad that after a few trades they are sure to kick in and destroy a buyer. At the same time, options have a high entertainment value. They provide a cheap ticket to the game, an inexpensive dream, just like a lottery ticket.

You need a minimum of one year of successful trading experience in stocks or futures before touching options. If you are new to the markets, do not even dream of using options in lieu of stocks. No matter how small your account, find some stocks and learn to trade them.

WHERE DO I GO FROM HERE?   The all-time bestseller on options, and deservedly so, is Lawrence MacMillan's *Options as a Strategic Investment*. It is a veritable mini-encyclopedia that covers all aspects of options trading, better than his other book.

THE FIRST STEPS

Trading lures us with its promise of freedom. If you know how to trade, you can live and work anywhere in the world, be independent from the routine, and not answer to anybody. Trading attracts people of above-average intelligence who enjoy games and aren't afraid of risks. Before you rush into this exciting venture, keep in mind that in addition to your enthusiasm you will need to bring a sober understanding of the realities of trading.

Trading will stress your feelings. To survive and succeed, you will need to develop a sound trading psychology.

Trading will challenge your mind. To gain an edge in the markets, you will need to master good analytic methods.

Trading will demand good mathematical skills. A math illiterate who can't manage risks is guaranteed to bust out.

Trading psychology, technical analysis, money management—if you learn all three, you can make it in trading. But first, let us look at the external obstacles to your success.

The markets are set up to separate the maximum number of people from their money. Stealing is not permitted, but markets are heavily slanted in favor of insiders and against outsiders. Let us explore the barriers that prevent many traders from succeeding and try to lower them.

THE EXTERNAL BARRIERS TO SUCCESS

An investor can start with practically nothing, buying a few thousand dollars worth of shares. If he buys and holds, his commissions and other expenses will be minor factors in his success or failure. Traders have a harder task. Seemingly trivial expenses can break them, and the smaller the account, the greater the danger. Transaction costs can raise an impassable barrier to winning.

Transaction costs?!

Beginners hardly think of them, yet transaction costs are a leading cause of trader mortality. Adjusting your plans to reduce those costs gives you an advantage over the market crowd.

I have a friend whose 12-year-old daughter recently came up with a brilliant idea for a new business, which she called The Guinea Pig Factory. She ran off promotional flyers on her mom's copy machine and stuffed them into neighbors' mailboxes. Guinea pigs, popular among kids in her neighborhood, cost $6, but she could buy them at the central market for only $4. The girl dreamed of profits when her mother, who is a trader, asked how she was going to get from the Sydney suburb where they lived to the central market and back. Someone will give me a ride, answered the girl.

A child may get a free ride, but the market will not give it to you. If you buy a stock at $4 and sell it at $6, you won't make a $2 profit. A big chunk of it will go for transaction costs. Amateurs tend to ignore them, while professionals focus on them and do everything in their power to reduce them—unless they're collecting them from you, in which case they try to blow them up. Beginners get into their Guinea Pig Factories and cannot understand why they keep buying at 4, selling at 6, and are still losing money.

A new trader is like a little lamb walking into a dark forest. He is likely to be killed, and his skin—his trading capital—divided three ways, between brokers, professional traders, and service providers. Each will try to grab a piece of that poor lamb's skin. Don't be that lamb—think of transaction costs. There are three kinds of them: commissions, slippage, and expenses.

Commissions

Commissions may appear to be a minuscule expense. Most traders neglect them, but if you add them up, you're likely to find that your broker ends up with much of your profit.

A brokerage firm may charge about $20 to buy or sell up to 5,000 shares. If you have a $20,000 account and buy 200 shares of a $100 stock, the commission of $20 comes to one-tenth of one percent. When

you sell those shares and pay another commission, the cost of brokerage rises to approximately two-tenths of one percent of your equity.
Trade like that once a week, and at the end of the month your broker
will have earned one percent of your account, regardless of whether you
made money. Keep going like that for a year, and your commission cost
will rise to 12% of your equity. That's a lot of money. Professional money
managers are happy with 25% annual returns, year after year. They could
not generate them if they had to pay 12% annually in commissions.

But wait, it gets worse.

Look at a small trader who can afford only 100 shares of a $20 stock.
His purchase price is $2,000, but he pays the same $20 commission, which
eats up a whopping 1 percent of his equity. When he closes that trade and
pays another commission, he is 2 percent behind the game. If he trades
like that once a week, by the end of the month his commissions will
come to 10% of his account, more than 100% on annualized basis. The
great George Soros averages 29% annual gain. He could have never
accomplished that if he had to jump over a 100% commission barrier.

The bigger your account, the smaller the percentage eaten by commissions and the lower your barrier to winning. Having a large account
is a great advantage, but whatever your size, do not be hyperactive.
Each trade and each seemingly cheap commission raise the barrier to
your success. Design a system that doesn't trade very often.

I've met futures traders who paid $80 roundtrip commissions to full-
service brokers. That was the price of allegedly sage advice, but any dis-
interested professional will tell you that a futures trader who pays $80
roundtrip has no chance of winning. Why do people pay such exorbitant rates? Because the little lamb who ventures into a dark forest is so
afraid of the big bad wolf, the professional trader, that he hires himself
a protector to guide him, a full-service broker. Once you do the math,
it becomes clear that you're better off taking your chances on the wolf
than signing up for a guaranteed skinning by your protector.

There are full-service brokers whose advice is worth the money.
They bring good tips, get good fills, and their commissions are not
exorbitant. The catch is that they only accept very large accounts that
generate a high volume of business. Bring them a million-dollar account
with a history of active trading, and you may get their attention.

If you have an account in five or six figures and trade only a couple of times a week, do not waste your time and money looking for
false security of an expensive broker. Get a cheap, reliable, no-frills

broker that you can easily reach via the Internet or on the phone—and start looking for good trades.

Slippage

Slippage is the difference between the price at the time you placed your order and the price at which that order got filled. You may place an order to buy when a guinea pig is trading at $4, but your bill comes to $4.25. How come? Then the guinea pig goes up to $6 and you place an order to sell at the market, only to receive $5.75. Why? In our daily lives we are used to paying posted prices. Here, at the grown-up Guinea Pig Factory, they clip you for a quarter buying and another selling. It could get worse. Those quarters and halves can add up to a small fortune for a moderately active trader. Who gets that money? Slippage is one of the key sources of income for market professionals, which is why they tend to be very hush-hush about it.

No stock, future, or option has a set price, but it does have two rapidly changing prices—a bid and an ask. A bid is what a buyer is offering to pay, whereas an ask is what a seller is asking. A professional is happy to accommodate an eager buyer, selling to him instantly, on the spot—at a price slightly higher than the latest trade in that market. A greedy trader who's afraid that the bullish train is leaving the station overpays a pro who lets him have his stock right away. That pro offers a similar service to sellers. If you want to sell without waiting, afraid that prices may collapse, a professional will buy from you on the spot—at a price slightly lower than the latest trade in that market. Anxious sellers accept ridiculously low prices. Slippage depends on the emotional state of market participants.

The professional who sells to buyers and buys from sellers is not a social worker. He is running a business, not a charitable operation. Slippage is the price he charges for rapid action. He has paid a high price for his spot at the crossroads of buy and sell orders, buying or leasing an exchange seat or installing expensive equipment.

Some orders are slippage-proof, while others invite slippage. The three most popular types of orders are limit, market, and stop. A limit order specifies the price; that is, "Buy 100 shares of Guinea Pig Factory at $4." If the market is quiet and you're willing to wait, you'll get that price. If GPF dips below $4 by the time your order hits the market, you may get it a little cheaper, but don't count on it. If the market rises above $4, your limit order will not be filled. A limit order lets you control the price at which you buy or sell, but doesn't guarantee you a fill.

A market order lets you buy or sell immediately, at whatever price you can get at the moment. The execution is guaranteed, but not the price. If you want to buy or sell right away, this very moment, you cannot expect to get the best price—you give up control and suffer slippage. Market orders placed by anxious traders are the bread and butter of the pros.

A stop order becomes a market order when the market touches that level. Suppose you buy 100 shares of Guinea Pig Factory at $4.25, expect it to rise to $7, but protect your position with a stop at $3.75. If the price slides to $3.75, your stop becomes a market order, executed as soon as possible. You'll get out, but expect to suffer slippage in a fast-moving market.

You can choose what you want to control when you place an order—the price or the time. A limit order lets you control the price, with no assurance of a fill. When you place a market order, a fill is assured, but not the price. A calm and patient trader prefers to use limit orders, since those who use market orders keep losing slivers of capital in slippage.

Slippage tends to be a much bigger expense than commissions. I estimated the size of both in *Trading for a Living* and thought this was one of the most explosive parts of the book, but very few noticed. People in the grip of greed or fear want to trade at any price, rather than focus on their long-term financial interests. So much for the efficient market theory.

There are day-trading firms promising to teach traders to take advantage of slippage by trading inside the bid-ask spreads. Their technology does not guarantee success, while commissions from active trading negate any advantage. People pay a lot of money for Level 2 quotes, but I haven't noticed any great increase in performance among those who use them.

Getting into a trade is like jumping into a fast-moving river. The opportunity as well as the danger is in the water. You are safe standing on the bank and can control where and when to jump, but getting out of the water can be more tricky. You may see a spot where you want to get out—a profit target, where you can place a limit order. You may want to let the river carry you as long as the current allows, protecting your position with a trailing stop. That may increase your profits, but it also will increase slippage.

Limit orders work best for entering trades. You'll miss a trade once in a while, but there will be many others. That river has been flowing for hundreds of years. A serious trader uses limit orders to get in and to take profits, and protects his positions with stops. Anything we can do to reduce slippage goes directly to our bottom line and improves our odds of long-term success.

Expenses

Some expenses are unavoidable, especially in the beginning—you'll have to buy a few books, download trading software, sign up with a data service, and so on. It is important to keep your expenses as low as possible. Amateurs have a charming habit of paying for their trading-related expenses, such as computers, subscriptions, and advisory services, with credit cards, without taking money out of their trading accounts. That protects them from seeing the true rate at which they are going downhill.

Good traders add to profitable positions and reduce the size of their trades during losing streaks. We can apply the same sound principle to expenditures. Losers like to throw money at problems, while winners invest a fraction of their profits in their operations. Successful traders treat themselves to a new computer or software package only after they have enough profit to pay for it.

Even the best tools can blow you out of the water. At a recent seminar in Frankfurt, a trader was excited about a powerful analytic package for which he was going to sign up the following week. It cost 2,000 marks a month (almost $1,000), but it was going to give him a tremendous analytic advantage. "How much money do you have in your trading account?" I asked. 50,000 marks. "Then you can't afford it. This software will cost you 24,000 marks a year, and you'll have to generate almost 50% profit simply to pay for your signals. No matter how good the software, at this rate you'll lose money. Look for a cheaper package, something that'll cost no more than 1,000 marks per year, or about 2% of your account."

Institutional traders get support from their managers, peers, and staff, but private traders tend to feel lonely and isolated. Vendors prey on them by promising to help lead them out of the wilderness. The more overloaded you feel, the more likely you are to listen to vendors. Nine out of ten professionals in any field, be they lawyers, auto mechanics, or doctors, are not good enough. You don't trust an average auto mechanic or a doctor, but rather ask for referrals from friends you respect. Most private traders do not know who to ask and respond to advisors with the loudest advertisements, who are rarely the best trading experts.

An advisor I've known for years was recently indicted by the Feds for stealing hundreds of millions of dollars from Japanese clients. Prior to that, he cultivated a reputation as one of the most prominent market experts in the United States, constantly quoted by the media. We were introduced at a conference, where people paid thousands of dollars to listen to him. He asked me what I thought of his presentation, and I said it sounded amazingly interesting but I could not understand much of it. "That's the point," he beamed. "If my clients believe I know something they don't, I've got them for life!" I knew right away the man was dishonest, and was surprised only by the size of his loot.

Some trading advice can be amazingly good. A few dollars will buy you a book that holds the experience of a lifetime. A few hundred dollars will get you a subscription to a newsletter with original and helpful advice. But gems are few and far between, while legions of hucksters prey on insecure traders. I have two rules for filtering out the worst offenders: avoid services you don't understand and avoid expensive services.

If you don't understand an advisor, stay away from him. Trading attracts people of above-average intelligence, which probably applies to you. If you cannot understand something after an honest effort, it's probably because the other guy is giving you double-talk. When it comes to books, I avoid those written in bad English. Language is a reflection of thought, and if a guy cannot write clearly, his thinking probably isn't too clear either. I also avoid books with no bibliography. We all borrow from our predecessors, and an author who doesn't acknowledge his debts is either arrogant, lazy, or both. Those are terrible traits in a trader, and if he writes like that, I don't want his advice. And of course, I have zero respect for thieves. Book titles are not copyrighted, and in recent years a bunch of people have lifted the title of my first book, *Trading for a Living*, usually with slight variations. I am sure that some clown will steal the title of the book you're now reading. Will you want to learn from a poacher who cannot think for himself?

My second rule is to avoid very expensive services, be they books, advisory letters, or seminars. A $200 newsletter is likely to be a better value than a $2,000 one, and a $500 seminar a better value than a $5,000 one. Merchants of super-expensive products sell an implicit promise of "the keys to the kingdom." Their customers are usually desperate to dig out from under abysmal losses. Football players call this a "Hail Mary" play—when a losing team in the last seconds of the game desperately tosses the ball forward, hoping to score. They've already lost the game on skill, and now try to come back in a single desperate gamble. When a trader who lost more than half of his account buys a $3,000 trading system, he is doing the same thing.

Helpful advisors tend to be modest, and price their services accordingly. An obscene price is a marketing gimmick that conveys a subliminal message that the service is magic. There is no magic—no one can deliver on that promise. A relatively inexpensive service is a bargain when it's good, and a cheap loss when it isn't.

Someone once asked Sigmund Freud what he thought the best attitude for a patient was. "Benign skepticism," answered the great psychiatrist, and that's good advice for financial traders. Maintain an attitude of healthy skepticism. If you find something you don't understand, try it again, and if you still do not get it, it is probably not worth having. Run, do not walk, from those who offer to sell you the keys to the kingdom. Keep your expenses low and remember, any information you receive becomes valuable to you only after you've tested it on your data, making it your own.

GETTING YOUR GEAR

A successful trader is like a fish swimming upstream, against the current. Commissions, slippage, and expenses keep pushing you back. You must make enough money to overshoot these three barriers before making a dime.

There is no shame in deciding trading is too hard and walking away, just as there is no shame in being unable to dance or play the piano. Many beginners jump in without thinking and get financially and emotionally hurt. It is a great game, but if you leave, better do it early.

If you decide to trade, read on, because in the following sections we will look into psychology, trading tactics, and money management. But first, we must talk about the practical aspects of trading—how to open an account, choose a computer, and start collecting data.

Size Matters

Making or losing money in the market depends in part on how much you put into your account. Two people can take identical trades, but one will grow equity, while the other will bust out. How could this be if they buy and sell the same quantity of the same stock at the same time?

Suppose we meet and decide to pass an hour tossing a coin, playing heads-or-tails—heads you win, tails you lose. Each of us will bring $5 to the game and bet 25 cents on each flip. As long as we use a fair coin, by the end of the hour we will be about even, each with about $5.

What happens if we play the same game and use the same coin, only now you start with $5, while I bring only $1? You'll probably end up taking my money. You are likely to win because your capital provides greater staying power. It would take a string of 20 losses to bankrupt you, while for me a string of just 4 losses would be fatal. Four losses in a row are much more likely than 20. The trouble with a small account is that it has no reserves to survive even a short run of losing trades. Winning trades are always interlaced with losers, and a short losing streak wipes out small traders.

Most beginners start out with too little money. There is plenty of noise in the markets—random moves that defy trading systems. A small trader who runs into a noisy period has no safety cushion. His long-term analysis may be brilliant, but the market will do him in, because he does not have the staying power to ride out a losing streak.

Back in 1980, as a greenhorn amateur, I walked into a Chase bank around the corner and drew a $5,000 cash advance against my credit card. I needed that princely sum to meet a margin call in my depleted trading account. A beady-eyed cashier called the manager, who demanded my thumbprint on the receipt. The transaction felt dirty, but I got the money—which I proceeded to lose within a few months. My system was correct, but the market noise was killing me. It wasn't until I got my trading account into a comfortable high five figures that I started making money. I wish someone had explained the concept of size to me in those days.

Trading a small account is like flying an airplane at treetop level. You have no room to maneuver, no time to think. The slightest slip of attention, a piece of bad luck, a freaky branch sticking out into the air—you crash and burn. The higher you fly, the more time you have to find your way out of trouble. Flying at a low altitude is tough enough for experts, but deadly for beginners. A trader needs to gain altitude, get more equity, and buy some space for maneuvers.

A person with a large account who bets a small fraction on any given trade can stay calm. A person with a small account grows tense knowing that any single trade can either boost or damage his account. As the stress rises, the capacity to reason goes down.

I saw the best example of how money can twist a player's mind while teaching my oldest daughter to play backgammon. She was about eight at the time but very determined and bright. After a few months of practice she began beating me. Then I suggested we play for money— a penny a point, which in our scoring meant a maximum of 32 cents per game. She kept beating me, and I kept raising the stakes. By the time we reached 10 cents a point she started losing and soon gave back every last penny. Why could she beat me playing for little or no money but lost when the stakes increased? Because for me $3.20 was pocket change, but for the kid it was real money. Thinking about it made her a little more tense and she played slightly below her peak level— enough to fall behind. A trader with a small account is so preoccupied with money that it impairs his ability to think, play, and win.

Other beginners bring too much money to the game, and that is not good either. A beginner with too much capital goes chasing after too many rabbits, becomes careless, loses track of his positions, and ends up losing money.

How much should you have in your trading account when you start? Remember, we are talking about trading capital. It doesn't include your savings, long-term investments, retirement funds, house equity, or Christmas club. We only count the money that you want to spin in the markets, aiming to achieve a higher rate of return than you can get from Treasury bills.

Do not even dream of starting with less than $20,000. That is the barest minimum, but $50,000 provides a much safer flying altitude. It allows you to diversify and practice sensible money management. At the same time, I do not suggest starting with more than $100,000. Too much money in a trading account makes a beginner lose focus and leads to sloppy trading. Professionals can use a lot more, but beginners should stay below $100,000 while learning to trade. Learn to fly a single-engine plane before moving up to a twin-engine model. A successful trader needs to get into the habit of being careful with money.

Beginners sometimes ask me what to do if they have only $10,000 or $5,000. I urge them to study the markets and paper-trade, while getting a second job to accumulate capital. Start trading with a decent-sized account. You're going into battle, your capital is your sword, and you need a weapon that's long enough to give you a chance in combat with well-armed opponents.

Hardware and Software

Thinking about my first purchases of trading technology is pure nostalgia. I walked into a drugstore in Florida and bought a pocket calculator. A year later I acquired a programmable calculator with a tiny engine that pulled magnetic memory cards through its slot. Then I bought my first computer. It had two floppy drives—one for the program, the other for the data diskette. I upgraded it from 48K to 64K RAM (that's kilobytes, not megabytes!), and it was a rocket. My first modem collected data at a brisk 300 baud, later upgraded to a sizzling 1,200. When hard drives became available, I bought myself a 10-MB unit (they also had a 20-MB model, but who needed such a monster?). There was only one good program for technical analysis, and it cost $1,900. Today, I can buy a hundred times more powerful software for a tenth of that price.

Does every trader need a computer? My friend Lou Taylor did all his research on scraps of paper. I used to offer him computers, but to no avail. Most traders, including myself, would be lost without a computer. It expands our reach and speeds up research. Just keep in mind that computers do not guarantee profits. Technology helps, but does not guarantee victory. A poor driver will crash the best car.

To become a computerized trader, you must choose a computer, trading software, and a source of data. Trading programs tend to be undemanding and run well on older, slower machines. A good program for technical analysis must download the data, plot daily, weekly, and possibly intraday charts, and offer a multitude of indicators. A good program should allow you to add your own indicators to the system and let you scan lists of securities according to your parameters. The list of programs for traders keeps growing, so that by the time you read this book any review will be out of date. My company keeps updating our brief software guide, which we send out as a public service. To request a current copy, please contact us at the address that appears in the back of this book.

A striking development in recent years is the wealth of resources for traders available on the Internet. Today you can analyze markets without buying any software—just go to a website, key in your stocks or futures, select the indicators, and click your mouse. Some websites are free, while others are subscription-based. With all those websites, why buy technical analysis software? For the same reason that in a city like New York, with its good public transportation system, some of us own cars. Clients often ask me how to add some new indicator to their favorite website. When you travel by bus, you cannot ask the driver to take your favorite route.

Can you program your own indicator into a website and scan charts with it, posting green dots for buy signals and red dots for sell signals? When you find a website that can do it, you may no longer need software. Until that time, those of us who are serious about research will continue to buy technical analysis software. You can get a top-notch program for a few hundred dollars. A historical database with a year's worth of updates will cost a couple of hundred more. If you have a tiny account, however, use free websites. Always try to push your expenses down to the smallest possible percentage of your account.

Data

Signing up with a data service appears simple, but raises several questions that go to the heart of trading. How many markets should you follow? How far back should you go in your research? Do you need real-time data? Answering these questions takes you deep into the trading enterprise and forces you to review your decision-making process.

How Many Markets Should You Follow?   Beginners make the common mistake of trying to follow too many markets at once. Some look for software to scan thousands of stocks and quickly bog down. Serious beginners should pick no more than two or three dozen stocks and track them day in and day out. You need to get to know them, develop a feel for how they move. Do you know when your companies release their earnings? Do you know their highest and lowest prices for the past year? The more you know about a stock, the more confidence you have and the fewer surprises can jump out at you. Many professionals focus on just a few stocks, or even on a single one.

Which stocks should you track? Begin by choosing two or three currently hot industries. Technology, Internet, telecommunications, and biotechnology industries are in the forefront of the market at the time

of this writing, but the list is likely to change. It always does. Pick half
a dozen leading stocks in each of those industries and follow them
daily. That's where you'll find the highest volumes, the steadiest trends,
the crispest reversals. Several months later, after you get to know your
stocks and make some money, you may be ready to add another
industry group and pick its top six stocks. Remember, the depth of
your research is much more important than its breadth. You can make
more money from a handful of familiar stocks.

The choice is easier for futures traders—there are only about three
dozen futures, in six or seven groups. Beginners should stay away from
the most volatile markets. Take grains, for instance. You should analyze
corn, wheat, and soybeans, but trade only corn because it tends to be
the slowest and quietest of the group. Learn to ride a bicycle with training wheels before starting to race. When it comes to tropicals, analyze
all, but trade only sugar—a big, liquid, and reasonably volatile market,
leaving aside coffee and cocoa, which can move as fast as the S&P.
Needless to say, a beginner has no business with stock index futures,
whose nickname on the floor is "rockets." You may graduate to them in
a couple of years, but at this stage, if you have an opinion on the stock
market, trade SPDRs or QQQs, exchange-traded market indexes.

How Far Back Should You Go in Your Research? A daily chart on a
computer screen will comfortably show five or six months of history.
You'll see less with candlesticks (see p. 72), which take up more space.
Daily charts alone aren't enough, and you need weekly charts with at
least two years worth of history. Learning history prepares you for the
future, and it could be helpful to glance at a 10-year chart and see
whether that market is high or low in the long-term scheme of things.

Charts spanning 20 or more years are especially useful for futures
traders. Futures, unlike stocks, have natural floors and ceilings. Those
levels are not rigid, but before you buy or sell, try to find out whether
you're closer to the floor or the ceiling.

The floor price of futures is their cost of production. When a market
falls below that level, producers start quitting, supply falls, and prices
rise. If there is a glut of sugar and its price on the world markets falls
below what it costs to grow the stuff, major producers are going to start
shutting down their operations. There are exceptions, such as when a
desperately poor country sells commodities on the world markets to
earn hard currency, while paying domestic workers with devalued

local money. The price can dip below the cost of production, but it cannot stay there for long.

The ceiling for most commodities is the cost of substitution. One commodity can replace another if the price is right. For example, with a rise in the price of corn, a major animal feed, it may be cheaper to feed animals wheat. As more farmers switch and reduce corn purchases, they take away the fuel that raised corn prices. A market in the grip of hysteria may briefly rise above its ceiling, but cannot stay there for long. Its return to the normal range provides profit opportunities for savvy traders. Learning from history can help you keep calm when others are losing their heads.

Futures contracts expire every few months, making long-term charts difficult to analyze. When it comes to dailies, we look at the currently active month, but what about the weeklies? Here we have to use continuous contracts, mathematical devices that splice several contract months. It pays to download two data series—the currently active contract, going back about six months, and the continuous contract going back at least two years. Analyze weekly charts using continuous data, and switch to the front month to study daily charts.

Do You Need Real-Time Data?   Real-time data flows to your screen tick by tick, as prices change in the markets. A live screen is one of the most captivating sights on Earth, right up there with nude co-ed volleyball or a chain collision on an expressway. Watching your stock dance in front of your face can help you find the best spots for buying and selling—or make you forget reality and swim in adrenaline.

Will live data improve your trading? The answer is "yes" for a few, "maybe" for some, and "no" for most. Having a live screen on your desk, says a trader friend, is like sitting in front of a one-armed bandit. You invariably end up feeding it quarters.

Trading with live charts looks deceptively easy, while in fact it is one of the fastest games on the planet. Buy at 10:05 A.M., watch the price rise a few ticks, and take a couple of hundred dollars off the table by 10:15. Repeat several times a day, and go home at 4 with thousands of dollars and no open positions. Sleep like a baby and return in the morning. Trouble is, you need perfect reflexes to do that. If you pause to think, delay taking a profit, or quibble accepting a loss, you're dead.

Most successful day-traders are men in their early 20s. I've met very few successful day-traders over 30. There are exceptions, of course—a friend in her 70s is a fantastic day-trader, but she is an exception who confirms the rule. This game requires lightning-fast reflexes, as well as a certain thoughtless capacity to jump, that few of us preserve past the age of 30.

Beginners do not need live data because they have to put all their attention into learning to trade with daily and weekly charts. Once you start pulling money out of the markets, it might be a good idea to apply your new skills to intraday charts. When longer-term charts give you a buy or a sell signal, use live data not to day-trade but to dance into or out of positions.

Once you decide to use live data, make sure it's real and not delayed. Most exchanges charge monthly fees for real-time data, while the Internet is full of websites offering free data, delayed by 20 minutes. That delay does not interfere with the entertainment value, but trading with it is suicidal. If you need real-time data, be sure to get the best.

ANALYSIS AND TRADING

Markets generate vast volumes of information: annual and quarterly reports, earnings estimates, corporate insiders' reports, industry group studies, technology forecasts, weekly, daily, and intraday charts, technical indicators, trading volume, opinions in chat rooms, the never-ending discussion circles on the Internet. With so much data, you soon realize your analysis can never be complete.

Some traders who have lost money fall into paralysis from analysis. They develop a quaint notion that if they analyze more data, they'll stop losing and become winners. You can recognize them by their beautiful charts and shelves crammed with stock reports. They will show you indicator signals in the middle of any chart, but when you ask them what they will do at the right edge, they only mumble because they do not trade.

Analysts are paid to be right; traders are paid to be profitable. Those are two different goals, calling for different temperaments. Institutions tend to separate traders and analysts into different departments. Private traders have no such luxury.

Analysis quickly reaches the point of diminishing returns. The goal is not to be complete but to develop a decision-making process and back it up with money management. You need to develop several analytic screens to reduce a huge volume of market information to a manageable size.

Fundamental Analysis

Fundamental analysts predict price movements on the basis of supply and demand. In stocks, they study supply and demand for company products. In futures they research supply and demand for commodities.

Has a company announced a new technological breakthrough? An expansion abroad? A new strategic partnership? A new chief executive? Anything that happens to the business can influence the supply of its products and their costs. Almost everything that happens in society can influence the demand.

Fundamental analysis is hard because the importance of different factors changes with the passage of time. For example, during an economic expansion, fundamental analysts are likely to focus on growth rates, but during a recession, on the safety of dividends. A dividend may seem like a quaint relic in a go-go bull market, but when the chips are down the ultimate test of a stock is how much income it generates. A fundamental analyst must keep an eye on the crowd, as it shifts its attention from market share to technological innovation to whatever else preoccupies it at the moment. Fundamental analysts study values, but the relationship between values and prices is not direct. It's that mile-long rubber band all over again.

The job of a fundamental analyst in the futures markets isn't much easier. How do you read the actions of the Federal Reserve, with its great power over interest rates and the economy? How do you analyze weather reports during the critical growing seasons in the grain markets? How do you estimate carryover stocks and weather prospects in the Southern versus the Northern Hemispheres which are six months apart in their weather cycles? You can spend a lifetime learning the fundamentals, or you can look for capable people who sell their research.

Fundamental analysis is much more narrow than technical. A moving average works similarly in soybeans and IBM, on weekly, daily, and intraday charts. MACD-Histogram flashes similar messages in Treasury bonds and Intel. Should we forget about the fundamentals and concentrate on technicals? Many traders take the path of least resistance, but I think this is a mistake.

Fundamental factors are very important to a long-term trader who wants to ride major trends for several months or years. If the fundamentals are bullish, we should favor the long side of the market, and if bearish, the short side. Fundamental analysis is less relevant to a short-term trader or a day-trader.

You do not have to become an expert in the fundamental analysis of every stock and commodity. There are very intelligent people who specialize in that, and they publish their research. Many of them also bang their heads against the walls, unable to understand why, if they know so much about their markets, they cannot make money trading.

If we can take our ideas from fundamental analysts but filter them through technical screens, we'll be miles of head of those who analyze only fundamentals or technicals. Bullish fundamentals must be confirmed by rising technical indicators; otherwise they are suspect. Bearish fundamentals must be confirmed by falling technical indicators. When fundamentals and technicals are in gear, a savvy trader can have a field day.

WHERE DO I GO FROM HERE?   The main book on the fundamental analysis of stocks is *Security Analysis* by Graham and Dodd. Both authors are long dead, but the book is being kept up-to-date by their disciples. If you decide to study it, make sure to get the latest edition. Warren Buffett, a student of Graham, became one of the richest men in the world. There is an easy-to-read book that explains his approach to fundamental analysis—*The Buffett Way* by Robert G. Hagstrom.

The best review of futures fundamentals is in *The Futures Game* by Teweles and Jones. This classic volume is being revised and updated every 10 years or so (be sure to get the latest edition). It has a section on the fundamentals of every futures market. Whether you trade soybeans or Swiss francs, you can quickly read up on the key factors driving that market.

Technical Analysis

Financial markets run on a two-party system—bulls and bears. Bulls push prices up, bears push them down, while charts show us their footprints. Technical analysts study charts to find where one group overpowers the other. They look for repetitive price patterns, trying to recognize uptrends or downtrends in their early stages and generate buy or sell signals.

The role of technical analysis on Wall Street has changed over the years. It was very popular in the early part of the twentieth century, ushered in by Charles Dow, the founder of *The Wall Street Journal* and the originator of the Dow averages. Several prominent analysts, such as Roger Babson, predicted and identified the 1929 top. Then came a quarter century of exile, when institutional analysts had to hide their charts if they wanted to keep their jobs. Technical analysis has become hugely popular since the 1980s. Easy access to personal computers has put technical software within easy reach of traders.

The stock market has become increasingly short-term oriented in recent years. Gone are the days of "buy-and-hold" when people bought "good stocks" for the long run, put them away, and collected dividends. The pace of economic change is increasing, and stocks are moving faster and faster. New industries emerge, old ones sink, and many stocks have become more volatile than commodities. Technical analysis is well suited for those fast-paced changes.

There are two main types of technical analysis: classical and computerized. Classical analysis is based solely on the study of charts, without using anything more complex than a pencil and ruler. Classical technicians look for uptrends and downtrends, support and resistance zones, as well as repetitive patterns, such as triangles and rectangles. It is an easy field to enter, but its main drawback is subjectivity. When a classical technician feels bullish, his ruler tends to inch up, and when he feels bearish, that ruler tends to slide down.

Modern technical analysis relies on computerized indicators whose signals are much more objective. The two main types are trend-following indicators and oscillators. Trend-following indicators, such as moving averages, Directional System, and MACD (moving average convergence-divergence), help identify trends. Oscillators, such as Stochastic, Force Index, and Relative Strength Index (RSI) help identify reversals. It is important to select several indicators from both groups, set their parameters, and stay with them. Amateurs often misuse technical analysis by looking for indicators that show them what they want to see.

The main tool of technical analysis is neither the pencil nor the computer, but the organ that every analyst is supposed to have between his ears—the brain. Still, if two technicians are at the same level of development, the one with a computer has an advantage.

Technical analysis is partly a science and partly an art—partly objective and partly subjective. It relies on computerized methods, but it tracks crowd psychology, which can never be fully objective. The best model for technical analysis is a public opinion poll. Pollsters use scientific methods but need psychological flair to design questions and select polling techniques. Price patterns on our computer screens reveal crowd behavior. Technical analysis is applied social psychology, the craft of analyzing mass behavior for profit.

Many beginners, overwhelmed by the sheer volume of data, fall into the trap of automatic trading systems. Their vendors claim to have backtested the best technical tools and put them together into winning systems. Whenever an excited beginner tells me he is planning to buy an automatic system, I ask him what he does for a living and what would happen if I came to compete with him after buying an automatic decision-making system in his field. People want to believe in magic, and if that magic can also save them from working and thinking, they gladly pay good money for it.

Successful trading is based on the 3 M's—Mind, Method, Money. Technical analysis, no matter how clever, is responsible for only one-third of your success. You also need to have sound trading psychology and proper money management, as you'll see later in this book.

WHERE DO I GO FROM HERE? *Technical Analysis of Stock Trends* by Edwards and Magee, written in the first half of the twentieth century, is considered the definitive book on classical charting. Get any edition after 1955, because that was the last major revision of the book. *Technical Analysis of the Financial Markets* by John Murphy offers the most thorough review of modern as well as classical technical analysis. My first book, *Trading for a Living*, has large sections on both classical and modern technical analysis.

When to Buy and Sell

The secret of trading is that there is no secret. There is no magic password to profits. Beginners keep looking for a gimmick, and plenty of crafty vendors sell them. In truth, trading is about work—and a bit of flair. It is no different from any other field of human endeavor. Whether you do surgery, teach calculus, or fly an airplane, it all boils down to knowing the rules, having the discipline, putting in the work, and having a bit of flair.

An intelligent trader pays attention to fundamentals. He is aware of the key forces in the economy. He spends most of his analytic time on technical analysis, working to identify trends and reversals. Later in this book we will review key technical tools and put together a trading plan.

Markets keep changing, and flexibility is the name of the game. A brilliant programmer told me recently that he kept losing money but whoever was buying off of his stops must have been profitable because his stops kept nailing the bottoms of declines. I asked why he didn't start placing his buy orders where he now placed stops. He wouldn't do it because he was too rigid, and for him buy orders were buy orders and stops were stops. A high level of education can be a handicap in trading. Brian Monieson, a noted Chicago trader, once said in an interview, "I have a Ph.D. in mathematics and a background in cybernetics, but I was able to overcome those disadvantages and make money."

Many professional people are preoccupied with being right. Engineers believe that everything can be calculated, and doctors believe that if they run enough tests, they'll come up with the right diagnosis and treatment. Curing a patient involves a lot more than precision. It is a running joke how many doctors and lawyers lose money in the markets. Why? Certainly not for lack of intelligence, but for lack of humility and flexibility.

Markets operate in an atmosphere of uncertainty. Trading signals are clear in the middle of the chart, but as you get closer to the right edge, you find yourself in what John Keegan, the great military historian, called "the fog of war." There is no certainty, only odds. Here you have two goals—to make money and to learn. Win or lose, you have to gain knowledge from a trade in order to be a better trader tomorrow. Scan your fundamental information, read technical signals, implement your rules of money management and risk control. Now you are ready to pull the trigger. Go!

PART TWO

THE THREE M'S OF SUCCESSFUL TRADING

Buy low, sell high. Short high, cover low. Traders are like surfers, trying to catch good waves, only their beach is rocky, not sandy. Professionals wait for opportunities but amateurs jump in, driven by emotions—they keep buying strength and selling weakness, bleeding their equity into the markets. Buy low, sell high sounds like a simple rule, but greed and fear can override the best intentions.

A professional waits for familiar patterns to emerge from the market. He may notice a new trend with rising momentum, indicating higher prices ahead. Or he may detect the feebleness of momentum during a rally, indicating weakness. Once he recognizes a pattern, he puts on a trade. He has a clear notion of how he'll get in, where he'll take profits, and where he'll accept a loss if the market turns against him.

A trade is a bet on a price change, but there is a paradox. Each price reflects the latest consensus of value of market participants. Putting on a trade challenges that consensus. A buyer disagrees with the collective wisdom by saying the market is underpriced. A seller disagrees with the wisdom of the entire group, believing the market is overpriced. Both the buyer and the seller expect the consensus to change, but meanwhile they defy the market. That market includes some of the most brilliant minds and some of the deepest pockets on Earth. Arguing with this group is dangerous business, and it has to be done very cautiously.

An intelligent trader looks for holes in the efficient market theory. He scans the market for brief periods of inefficiency. When the crowd is gripped by greed, the newcomers jump in and load up on stocks.

When falling prices squeeze the fingers of thousands of buyers, they dump their holdings in a panic, disregarding fundamental values. Those episodes of emotional behavior dilute the cold efficiency of the market, creating opportunities for disciplined traders. When markets are calm and efficient, trading becomes a crapshoot, with commissions and slippage worsening the odds.

Crowd mentality changes slowly, and price patterns recur, albeit with variations. Emotional swings provide trading opportunities, while efficient markets chop up and down, offering no edge to traders, only piling up their costs. Technical analysis tools will work for you only if you have the discipline to wait for patterns to emerge. Professionals trade only when markets offer them special advantages.

According to chaos theory, many processes—the flow of water in a river, the movement of clouds in the sky, the changes of prices in the cotton markets—are chaotic, with transient islands of order, called fractals. Those fractals look similar from any distance, whether through a telescope or a microscope. The coast of Maine looks just as jagged from a space shuttle as it does when you drop down on your hands and knees and look at it through a magnifying glass. In most financial markets, the long-term weekly charts and the short-term 5-minute charts look so similar, you cannot tell them apart without markings. Engineers have realized that they can achieve better control over many processes if they accept them as chaotic and try to capitalize on temporary fractals, the islands of order. That's exactly what a good trader does. He recognizes the market as chaotic and unpredictable much of the time, but expects to find islands of order. He trains himself to buy and sell without quibbling when he finds those patterns.

Successful trading depends on the 3 M's—Mind, Method, and Money. Beginners focus on analysis, but professionals operate in a three-dimensional space. They are aware of trading psychology—their own feelings and the mass psychology of the markets. Each trader needs to have a method for choosing specific stocks, options, or futures as well as firm rules for pulling the trigger—deciding when to buy and sell. Money refers to how you manage your trading capital.

Mind, Method, Money—trading psychology, trading method, and money management—people sometimes ask me which of the three is more important. It is like asking which leg of a three-legged stool is the most important. Take them away one at a time and then try to sit down. In Part 2 we focus on those three foundations of market success.

MIND—
THE DISCIPLINED TRADER*

T raders come to the markets with great expectations, but few make profits and most wash out. The industry hides good statistics from the public, while promoting its Big Lie that money lost by losers goes to winners. In fact, winners collect only a fraction of the money lost by losers. The bulk of losses goes to the trading industry as the cost of doing business—commissions, slippage, and expenses—by both winners and losers. A successful trader must hop over several high hurdles—and keep hopping. Being better than average is not good enough—you have to be head and shoulders above the crowd. You can win only if you have both knowledge and discipline.

Most amateurs come to the markets with half-baked trading plans, clueless about psychology or money management. Most get hurt and quit after a few painful hits. Others find more cash and return to trading. We do not have to call people who keep dropping money in the markets losers because they do get something in return. What they get is fantastic entertainment value.

Markets are the most entertaining places on the face of the Earth. They are like a card game, a chess game, and a horse race all rolled into one. The game goes on at all hours—you can always find action.

An acquaintance of mine had a terrible home life. He avoided his wife by staying late in the office, but the building closed on weekends, pushing him into the bosom of his family. By Sunday mornings he could take no more "family togetherness" and escaped to the basement of his house. There he had set up a trading apparatus, using the equipment loaned to him by another loser in exchange for a share of future

---

*Thanks to Mark Douglas, the title of whose book I borrowed to name this chapter.

profits. What can you trade on a Sunday morning in suburban Boston? It turned out that the gold markets were open in the Middle East. My acquaintance used to turn on his quote screen, get on the phone (this was in the pre-Internet days), and trade gold in Abu Dhabi!

He never asked himself what his edge was over local traders. What has he got, sitting in a bucolic suburb of Boston, that they haven't got in Abu Dhabi? Why should locals send him money? Every professional knows his edge, but ask an amateur and he'll draw a blank. A person who doesn't know his edge does not have it and will lose money. Warren Buffett, one of the richest investors on Earth, says that when you sit down to a game of poker, you must know within 15 minutes who is going to supply the winnings, and if you don't know the answer, that person is you. My Boston buddy wound up losing his house in a bankruptcy, which put a whole new spin on his marital problems, even though he no longer traded gold in Abu Dhabi.

Many people, whether rich or poor, feel trapped and bored. As Henry David Thoreau wrote almost two centuries ago, "The mass of men lead lives of quiet desperation."

We wake up in the same bed each morning, eat the same breakfast, and drive to work down the same road. We see the same dull faces in the office and shuffle papers on our old desks. We drive home, watch the same dumb shows on TV, have a beer, and go to sleep in the same bed. We repeat this routine day after day, month after month, year after year. It feels like a life sentence without parole. What is there to look forward to? Perhaps a brief vacation next year? We'll buy a package deal, fly to Paris, get on a bus with the rest of the group, and spend 15 minutes in front of the Triumphal Arch and half an hour going up the Eiffel Tower. Then back home, back to the old routine.

Most people live in a deep invisible groove—no need to think, make decisions, feel the raw edge of life. The routine does feel comfortable—but deathly boring.

Even amusements stop being fun. How many Hollywood movies can you watch on a weekend until they all become a blur? How many trips to Disneyland can you take before all the rides in plastic soap dishes feel like one endless ride to nowhere? To quote Thoreau again, "A stereotyped but unconscious despair is concealed even under what are called games and amusements of mankind. There is no play in them."

And then you open a trading account and punch in an order to buy 500 shares of Intel. Anyone with a few thousand dollars can escape the routine and find excitement in the markets.

Suddenly, the world is in living color! Intel ticks up half a point—you check quotes, run out for a newspaper, and tune in for the latest updates. If you have a computer at work, you set up a little quote window to keep an eye on your stock. Before the Internet, people used to buy pocket FM receivers for market quotes and hide them in half-open desk drawers. Their antennae, sticking out of desks of middle-aged men, looked like beams of light shining into prison cells.

Intel is up a point! Should you sell and take profits? Buy more and double up? Your heart is pounding—you feel alive! Now it's up three points. You multiply that by the number of shares you have and realize that your profits after just a few hours are close to your weekly salary. You start calculating percentage returns—if you continue trading like that for the rest of the year, what a fortune you'll have by Christmas!

Suddenly you raise your eyes from the calculator to see that Intel has dropped two points. Your stomach is tied in a knot, your face pushes into the screen, you hunch over, compressing your lungs, reducing the flow of blood to the brain, which is a terrible position for making decisions. You are flooded with anxiety, like a trapped animal. You are hurting—but you are alive!

Trading is the most exciting activity that a person can do with their clothes on. Trouble is, you cannot feel excited and make money at the same time. Think of a casino, where amateurs celebrate over free drinks, while professional card-counters coldly play game after game, folding most of the time, and pressing their advantage when the card count gives them a slight edge over the house. To be a successful trader, you have to develop iron discipline (Mind), acquire an edge over the markets (Method), and control risks in your trading account (Money).

SLEEPWALKING THROUGH THE MARKETS

There is only one rational reason to trade—to make money. Money attracts us to the markets, but in the excitement of the new game we often lose sight of that goal. We start trading for entertainment, as an escape, to show off in front of our family and friends, and so on. Once a trader loses his focus on money, his goose is cooked.

It is easy to feel cool, calm, and collected reading a book or looking at your charts on a weekend. It's easy to be rational when the markets are closed—but what happens after 30 minutes in front of a live screen? Does your pulse begin to race? Do upticks and downticks hypnotize you? Traders get an adrenaline rush from the market, and the excitement clouds their judgment. Calm resolutions made on a weekend fly out the window during rallies or declines. "This time is different . . . It's an exception . . . I won't put in a stop now, the market is too volatile" are the giveaway phrases of emotional traders.

Many intelligent people sleepwalk through the markets. Their eyes are open, but their minds are shut. They are driven by emotions and keep repeating their mistakes. It is OK to make mistakes but not OK to repeat them. When you make a mistake for the first time, it shows that you are alive, searching, experimenting. Repeating a mistake is a neurotic symptom.

Losers come in all genders, ages, and colors, but several stock phrases give them away. Let us review some of the common excuses. If you recognize yourself, use that as a sign to start learning a new approach to the markets.

Blame the Broker

A trader hears his broker's voice at the most important and tense moments—when placing buy or sell orders or requesting information that may lead to an order. The broker is close to the market, and many of us assume that he knows more than we do. We try to read our broker's voice and figure out whether he approves or disapproves of our actions.

Is listening to your broker's voice a part of your trading system? Does it say to buy when the weekly moving average is up, daily Force Index is down, and the broker sounds enthused? Or does it simply say to buy when such and such indicators reach such and such parameters?

Trying to read your broker's voice is a sign of insecurity, a common state for beginners. Markets are huge and volatile, and their rallies and declines can feel overpowering. Frightened people look for someone strong and wise to lead them out of the wilderness. Can your broker lead you? Probably not, but if you lose money, you'll have a great excuse—it was your broker who put you into that stupid trade.

A lawyer who was shopping for an expert witness recently called me. His client, a university professor, had shorted Dell at 20 several years ago, before the splits, after his broker told him it "could not go any higher." That stock became the darling of the bull market, went through the roof, and a year later the professor covered at 80, wiping out his million-dollar account, which represented his life savings. That man was smart enough to earn a Ph.D. and save a million dollars but emotional enough to follow his broker while his life savings were doing a slow burn. Few people sue their brokers, but almost all beginners blame them.

Traders' feelings towards brokers are similar to patients' feelings towards psychoanalysts. A patient lies on the couch, and the analyst's voice, emerging at important moments, seems to carry deeper psychological truths than the patient could have possibly discovered himself. In reality, a good broker is a craftsman who can sometimes help you get better fills and dig up information you requested. He is your helper—not your advisor. Looking to a broker for guidance is a sign of insecurity, which is not conducive to trading success.

Most people start trading more actively after switching to electronic brokers. Low commissions are a factor, but the psychological change is more important. People are less self-conscious when they don't have to deal with a live person. All of us occasionally make stupid trades, and electronic brokers allow us to make them in private. We are less ashamed hitting a key than calling a broker.

Some traders manage to transfer their anxieties and fears onto electronic brokers. They complain that electronic brokers do not do what they want, such as accept certain types of orders. Why don't you transfer your account, I ask—and see fear in their faces. It is the fear of change, of upsetting the cart.

To be a successful trader, you must accept total responsibility for your decisions and actions.

Blame the Guru

A beginner entering the markets soon finds himself surrounded by a colorful crowd of gurus—experts who sell trading advice. Most charge fees, but some give advice for free to drum up business for their brokerage firms. Gurus publish newsletters, are quoted in the media, and many would kill to get on TV. Masses are hungry for clarity, and gurus are there to feed that hunger. Most are failed traders, but being a guru is not that easy. Their mortality rate is high, and few stay around for more than two years. The novelty wears off, customers do not renew subscriptions, and a guru finds it easier to earn a living selling aluminum siding than drawing trendlines. My chapter on the guru business in *Trading for a Living* drew more howls and threats than any other in that book.

Traders go through three stages in their attitudes towards gurus. In the beginning, they drink in their advice, expecting to make money from it. At the second stage, traders start avoiding gurus like the plague, viewing them as distractions from their own decision-making process. Finally, some successful traders start paying attention to a few gurus who alert them to new opportunities.

Some losing traders go looking for a trainer, a teacher, or a therapist. Very few people are experts in both psychology and trading. I've met several gurus who couldn't trade their way out of a paper bag but claimed that their alleged expertise in psychology qualified them to train traders. Stop for a moment and compare this to sex therapy. If I had a sexual problem, I might see a psychiatrist, a psychologist, a sex therapist, or even a pastoral counselor, but I would never go to a Catholic priest, even if I were Catholic. That priest has no practical knowledge of the problem—and if he does, you want to run, not walk away. A teacher who does not trade is highly suspect.

Traders go through several stages in their attitudes towards tips. Beginners love them, those who are more serious insist on doing their own homework, while advanced traders may listen to tips but always drop them into their own trading systems to see whether that advice will hold up. Whenever I hear a trading tip, I run it through my own computerized screens. The decision to buy, go short, or stand aside is mine alone, with an average yield of one tip accepted out of every 20 heard. Tips draw my attention to opportunities I might have overlooked, but there are no shortcuts to sweating your own trades.

A greenhorn who has gotten burned may ask for a guru's track record. Years ago I used to publish a newsletter and noticed how frighteningly easy it was for gurus to massage and slant their records, even if they were tracked by independent rating services.

I've never met a trader who took all the recommendations of his guru, even if he paid him a lot of money. If a guru has 200 subscribers, they'll choose different recommendations, trade them differently, and most will lose money, each in his own way. There is a rule in the advisory business: "If you make forecasts for a living, make a lot of them." Gurus offer convenient excuses to sleepwalking traders who need a scapegoat for their losses.

Whether or not you listen to a guru, you're 100% responsible for the outcome of your trades. The next time you get a hot tip, drop it into your trading system to see whether it gives you a buy or sell signal. You are responsible for the consequences of taking or rejecting advice.

Blame the Unexpected News

It is easy to feel angry and hurt when a sudden piece of bad news blows a hole in your stock. You buy something, it goes up, bad news hits the market, and your stock collapses. The market did it to you, you say? The news may have been sudden, but you are responsible for handling any challenges.

Most company news is released on a regular schedule. If you trade a certain stock, you should know well in advance when that company releases its earnings and be prepared for any market reaction to the news. Lighten up on your position if unsure about the impact of a coming announcement. If you trade bonds, currencies, or stock index futures, you must know when the key economic statistics are released and how the leading indicators or the unemployment rate can impact your market. It may be wise to tighten your stops or reduce the size of your trade in advance of an important news release.

What about a truly unexpected piece of news—a president gets shot, a noted analyst comes out with a bearish earnings forecast, and so on? You must research your market and know what happened after similar events in the past; you have to do your homework before the event hits you. Having this knowledge allows you to act without delay. For example, the stock market's reaction to an assault on a president has always been a sharp hiccup to the downside, followed by a complete retracement, so a sensible thing to do is buy the break.

Your trading plan must include the possibility of a sharp adverse move caused by sudden events. You must have your stop in place, and the size of your trade must be such that you cannot get financially hurt in the case of a reversal. There are many risks waiting to spring on a trader—you alone are responsible for damage control.

Wishful Thinking

When the pain grows bit by bit, the natural tendency is to do nothing and wait for an improvement. A sleepwalking trader gives his losing trades "more time to work out," while they slowly destroy his account.

A sleepwalker hopes and dreams. He sits on a loss and says, "This stock is coming back; it always did." Winners accept occasional losses, take them, and move on. Losers postpone taking losses. An amateur puts on a trade the way a kid buys a lottery ticket. He waits for the wheel of fortune to decide whether he wins or loses. Professionals, to the contrary, have ironclad plans for getting out, either with a profit or a small loss. One of the key differences between professionals and amateurs is their planning for exits.

A sleepwalking trader buys at 35 and puts in a stop at 32. The stock sinks to 33, and he says, "I'll give it a little more room." He moves his stop down to 30. That is a fatal mistake—he has breached his discipline and violated his own plan.

You may move stops only one way—in the direction of your trade. Stops are like a ratchet on a sailboat, designed to take the slack out of your sails. If you start giving your trade "more room to breathe," that extra slack will swing around and hurt you. When the market rewards traders for breaking their rules, it sets up an even deeper trap in their next trade.

The best time to make decisions is before you enter a trade. Your money is not at risk, and you can weigh profit targets and loss parameters. Once you're in a trade, you begin to form an attachment to it. The market hypnotizes you and lures you into emotional decisions. This is why you must write down your exit plan and follow it.

Turning a losing trade into an "investment" is a common disease among small private traders, but some institutional traders also suffer from it. Disasters at banks and major financial firms occur when poorly supervised traders lose money in short-term trades and stick them into long-term accounts, hoping that time will bail them out. If you are losing in the beginning, you'll lose in the end. Do not put off the hour of reckoning. The first loss is the best loss—this is the rule of those of us who trade with our eyes open.

A REMEDY FOR SELF-DESTRUCTIVENESS

People who like to complain about their bad luck are often experts in looking for trouble and snatching defeat from the jaws of victory. A friend in the construction business used to have a driver who dreamed of buying his own truck and working for himself. He saved money for years and finally paid cash for a huge brand-new truck. He quit his job, got gloriously drunk, and at the end of the day rolled his uninsured truck down an embankment—it was totaled, and the driver came back asking for his old job. Tragedy? Drama? Or fear of freedom and an unconscious wish for a safe job with a steady paycheck?

Why do intelligent people with a track record of success keep losing money on one harebrained trade after another, stumbling from calamity to catastrophe? Ignorance? Bad luck? Or a hidden desire to fail?

Many people have a self-destructive streak. My experience as a psychiatrist has convinced me that most people who complain about severe problems are in fact sabotaging themselves. I cannot change a patient's external reality, but whenever I cure one of self-sabotage, he quickly resolves his external problems.

Self-destructiveness is such a pervasive human trait because civilization is built on controlling aggression. As we grow up, we are trained to control aggression against others—behave, do not push, be nice. Our aggression has to go somewhere, and many turn it against themselves, the only unprotected target. We turn our anger inward and learn to sabotage ourselves. Little wonder so many of us grow up fearful, inhibited, and shy.

Society has several defenses against the extremes of self-sabotage. The police will talk a potential suicide down from the roof, and the medical board will take the scalpel away from an accident-prone surgeon, but no one will stop a self-defeating trader. He can run amok in the financial markets, inflicting wounds on himself, while brokers and other traders gladly take his money. Financial markets lack protective controls against self-sabotage.

Are you sabotaging yourself? The only way to find out is to keep good records, especially a Trader's Journal and an equity curve, shown later in this book. The angle of your equity curve is an objective indicator of your behavior. If it slopes up, with few downticks, you're doing well. If it points down, it shows you're not in gear with the markets and possibly in a self-sabotage mode. When you observe that, reduce the size of your trades and spend more time with your Trader's Journal figuring out what you're doing.

You need to become a self-aware trader. Keep good records, learn from past mistakes, and do better in the future. Traders who lose money tend to feel ashamed. A bad loss feels like a nasty comment— most people just want to cover up, walk away, and never be seen again. Hiding doesn't solve anything. Use the pain of a loss to turn yourself into a disciplined winner.

Losers Anonymous

Years ago I had an insight that changed my trading life forever. Back in those days my equity used to swing up and down like a yo-yo. I knew enough about markets to profit from many trades but couldn't hold on to my gains and grow equity. The insight that eventually got me off the roller coaster came from a chance visit to a meeting of Alcoholics Anonymous.

One late afternoon I accompanied a friend to an AA meeting at a local YMCA. Suddenly, the meeting gripped me. I felt as if the people in the room were talking about my trading! All I had to do was substitute the word *loss* for the word *alcohol*.

People at the AA meeting talked about how alcohol controlled their lives, and my trading in those days was driven by losses—fearing them and trying to trade my way out. My emotions followed a jagged equity curve—elation at the highs and cold clammy fear at the lows, with fingers trembling above the speed dial button.

Back in those days I had a busy psychiatric practice and saw my share of alcoholics. I began to notice similarities between them and losing traders. Losers approached markets the way alcoholics walked into bars. They entered with pleasant expectations, but left with mean headaches, hangovers, and loss of control. Drinking and trading lure people across the line from pleasure to self-destructiveness.

Alcoholics and losers live with their eyes closed—both are in the grip of an addiction. Every alcoholic I saw in my office wanted to argue about his diagnosis. To avoid wasting time, I used to suggest a simple test. I'd tell alcoholics to keep on drinking as usual for the next week, but write down every drink, and bring that record to our next appointment. Not a single alcoholic could keep that diary for more than a few days because looking in a mirror reduced the pleasure of impulsive behavior. Today when I tell losing traders to keep a diary of their trades, many become annoyed.

Good records are a sign of self-awareness and discipline. Poor or absent records are a sign of impulsive trading. Show me a trader with good records, and I'll show you a good trader.

Alcoholics and losers do not think about the past or the future, and focus only on the present—the sensation of alcohol pouring down the gullet or the market pulsing on the screen. An active alcoholic is in denial; he doesn't want to know about the depth of his abyss, the severity of his problem, or the harm he is causing himself and others.

The only thing that can pierce an alcoholic's denial is the pain of hitting what AA calls "rock bottom." It is each individual's private version of hell—a life-threatening illness, a rejection by family, a job loss, or another catastrophic event. The unbearable pain of hitting rock bottom punctures the alcoholic's denial and forces him to face a stark choice: he can self-destruct or turn his life around.

AA is a nonprofit voluntary organization whose only purpose is to help alcoholics stay sober. It doesn't ask for donations, advertise, lobby, or take part in any public actions. It has no paid therapists; members help each other at meetings led by long-term members. AA has a system of sponsorships whereby older members sponsor and support newer ones.

An alcoholic who joins AA goes through what is called a 12-Step program. Each step is a stage of personal growth and recovery. The method is so effective that people recovering from other addictive behaviors have begun to use it.

The first step is the most important for traders. It looks easy, but is extremely hard to take. Many alcoholics can't take it, drop out of AA, and go on to destroy their lives. The first step consists of standing up at a meeting, facing a room full of recovering alcoholics, and admitting that alcohol is stronger than you. This is hard because if alcohol is stronger than you, you cannot touch it again. Once you take the first step, you are committed to a struggle for sobriety.

Alcohol is such a powerful drug that AA recommends planning to live without it one day at a time. A recovering alcoholic does not plan to be sober a year or five years from now. He has a simpler goal—go to bed sober tonight. Eventually those days of sobriety add up to years. The entire system of AA meetings and sponsorships is geared toward the goal of sobriety one day at a time.

AA aims to change not only the behavior but the personality in order to reinforce sobriety. AA members call some people "sober drunks." It sounds like a contradiction in terms. If a person is sober, how can he be a drunk? Sobriety alone is not enough. A person who has not changed his thinking is just one step away from sliding back into drinking under stress or out of boredom. An alcoholic has to change his way of being and feeling to recover from alcoholism.

I never had a problem with alcohol, but my psychiatric experience had taught me to respect AA for its success with alcoholics. It was not a popular view. Each patient who went to AA reduced the profession's income, but that never bothered me. After my first AA meeting I realized that if millions of alcoholics could recover by following the program, then traders could stop losing, regain balance, and become winners by applying the principles of AA.

How can we translate the lessons of AA into the language of trading?

A losing trader is in denial. His equity is shrinking, but he continues to jump into trades without analyzing what is going wrong. He keeps switching between markets the way an alcoholic switches between whiskey and cheap wine. An amateur whose mind isn't strong enough to accept a small loss will eventually take the mother of all losses. A gaping hole in a trading account hurts self-esteem. A single huge loss or a series of bad losses smash a trader against his rock bottom. Most beginners collapse and wash out. The lifetime of an average speculator is measured in months, not years.

Those who survive fall into two groups. Some return to their old ways, just like alcoholics crawl into a bar after surviving a bout of delirium. They toss more money into their accounts and become customers of vendors who sell magical trading systems. They continue to gamble, only now their hands shake from anxiety and fear when they try to pull the trigger.

A minority of traders that hit rock bottom decide to change. Recovery is a slow and solitary process. Charles Mackay, the author of one of the best books on crowd psychology, wrote almost two centuries ago that men go mad in crowds, but come to their senses slowly, and one by one. I wish we had an organization for recovering traders, the way recovering alcoholics have AA. We don't because trading is so competitive. Members of AA strive for sobriety together, but a meeting of recovering traders could easily be poisoned by envy and showing off. Markets are such cutthroat places that we don't form mutual support groups or find sponsors. Some opportunists hold themselves out as traders' coaches, but most make me shudder at their sharkiness. If we had a traders' organization, I'd call it Losers Anonymous (LA). The name is blunt, but that's fine. After all, Alcoholics Anonymous does not call itself Drinkers Anonymous. A harsh name helps traders face their impulsivity and self-sabotage. Since we do not have LA, you'll have to walk on the road to recovery alone. I wrote this book to help you along the way.

Businessman's Risk vs. Loss

Years ago, when I began my recovery from losing, each morning I held what I called a Losers Anonymous meeting for one. I'd come into the office, turn on my quote screen, and while it was warming up I'd say, "Good morning, my name is Alex, and I am a loser. I have it in me to do serious damage to my account. I've done it before. My only goal for today is to go home without a loss." When the screen was up, I'd begin trading, following the plan written down the night before while the markets were closed.

I can immediately hear an objection—what do you mean, go home without a loss? It is impossible to make money every day. What happens if you buy something, and it goes straight down—in other words, you've bought the top tick of the day? What if you sell something short and it immediately rallies?

We must draw a clear line between a loss and a businessman's risk. A businessman's risk is a small dip in equity. A loss goes through that limit. As a trader, I am in the business of trading and must take normal business risks, but I cannot afford losses.

Imagine you're not trading but running a fruit and vegetable stand. You take a risk each time you buy a crate of tomatoes. If your customers do not buy them, that crate will rot on you. That's a normal business risk—you expect to sell most of your inventory, but some fruit and vegetables will spoil. As long as you buy carefully, keeping the unsold spoiled fruit to a small percentage of your daily volume, your business stays profitable.

Imagine that a wholesaler brings a tractor-trailer full of exotic fruit to your stand and tries to sell you the entire load. He says that you can earn more in the next two days than you made in the previous six months. It sounds great—but what if your customers don't buy that exotic fruit? A rotting tractor-trailer load can hurt your business and endanger its survival. It's no longer a businessman's risk—it's a loss.

Money management rules draw a straight line between a businessman's risk and a loss, as you will see later in this book.

Some traders have argued that my AA approach is too negative. A young woman in Singapore told me she believed in positive thinking and thought of herself as a winner. She could afford to be positive because discipline was imposed on her from the outside, by the manager of the bank for which she traded. Another winner who argued with me was a lady from Texas in her seventies, a wildly successful trader of stock index futures. She was very religious and viewed herself as a steward of money. Each morning she got up early and prayed long and hard. Then she drove to the office and traded the living daylights out of the S&P. The minute a trade went against her, she'd cut and run—because the money belonged to the Lord and wasn't hers to lose. She kept her losses small and accumulated profits.

I thought that our approaches had a lot in common. Both of us had principles outside the market preventing us from losing money. Markets are the most permissive places in the world. You may do anything you like, as long as you have enough equity to put on a trade. It's easy to get caught in the excitement, which is why you need rules. I rely on the principles of AA, another trader relies on her religious feelings, and you may choose something else. Just make sure you have a set of principles that clearly tells you what you may or may not do in the markets.

Sober in Battle

Most traders open accounts with money earned in business or the professions. Many bring a personal track record of success and expect to do well in the markets. If we can run a hotel, perform eye surgery, or try cases in court, we can surely find our way between the high, the low, and the close! But the markets, which seem so simple at first, keep humbling us.

Little blood gets spilled in trading, but the money, the lifeblood of the markets, has a major impact on the quality and the length of our lives. Recently, a friend who writes a stock market advisory showed me a stack of letters from his subscribers. The one that caught my eye came from a man who made enough money trading to pay for a kidney transplant. It saved his life, but I thought of what happened to legions of others who also had big needs but traded poorly and lost money.

Trading is a battle. When you pick up your weapon and put your life on the line, would you rather be drunk or sober? You have to prepare yourself, choose your fight, go in when you are ready, and quit after you've done what you've planned. A man who is cool and sober calmly picks his fights. He enters and leaves when he chooses and not when some bully throws him a challenge. A disciplined player chooses his own game out of hundreds available. He doesn't have to chase every rabbit like a dog with its tongue hanging out—he lays an ambush for his game and lets it come to him.

Most amateurs won't admit they are trading for entertainment. A common cover story is that they're in the markets to make money. In reality, most traders get tremendous thrills tossing money at half-baked ideas. Trading financial markets is more respectable than betting on ponies, but the kicks are just as good.

I tell my horse-playing friends to imagine going to a race where you can place bets after the horses are out of the gate and take your money off the table before the race ends. Trading is a fantastic game, but its temptations are very intense.

THE MATURE TRADER

Successful traders are sharp, curious, and unassuming people. Most have been through losing periods. They graduated from the school of hard knocks, and that experience helped smooth their rough edges.

Successful traders are self-assured but never arrogant. People who survive in the markets remain alert. They trust their skills and trading methods, but keep their eyes and ears open for new developments. Confident and attentive, calm and flexible, successful traders are fun to be with.

Successful traders are often unconventional people, and some are very eccentric. When they mix with others, they often break social rules. The markets are set up for the majority to lose money, and a small group of winners marches to a different drummer, in and out of the markets.

Markets consist of huge crowds of people watching the same trading vehicles, mesmerized by upticks and downticks. Think of a crowd at a concert or in a movie theater. When the show begins, the crowd gets emotionally in gear and develops an amorphous but powerful mass mind, laughing or weeping together. A mass mind also emerges in the markets, only here it is more malignant. Instead of laughing or weeping, the crowd seeks each trader's private psychological weakness and hits him in that spot.

Markets seduce greedy traders into buying positions that are too large for their accounts and then destroy them with a reaction they cannot afford to sit out. They shake fearful traders out of winning trades with brief countertrend spikes before embarking on runaway moves. Lazy traders are the favorite victims of the market, which keeps throwing new tricks at the unprepared. Whatever your psychological flaws and fears, whatever your inner demons, whatever your hidden weaknesses and obsessions, the market will seek them out, find them, and use them against you, like a skilled wrestler uses his opponent's own weight to toss him to the ground.

Successful traders have outgrown or overcome their inner demons. Instead of being tossed by the markets, they maintain their own balance and scan for chinks in the crowd's armor, so that they can toss the market for a change. They may appear eccentric, but when it comes to trading they are much healthier than the crowd.

Being a trader is a journey of self-discovery. Trade long enough, and you will face all your psychological handicaps—anxiety, greed, fear, anger, and sloth. Remember, you're not in the markets for psychotherapy; self-discovery is a byproduct, not the goal of trading. The primary goal of a successful trader is to accumulate equity. Healthy trading boils down to two questions you need to ask in every trade: "What is my profit target?" and "How will I protect my capital?"

A good trader accepts full responsibility for the outcome of every trade. You cannot blame others for taking your money. You have to improve your trading plans and methods of money management. It will take time, and it will take discipline.

Discipline

A friend of mine used to have a dog-training business. Occasionally a prospective client would call her and say, "I want to train my dog to come when called, but I do not want to train it to sit or lie down." And she'd answer, "Training a dog to come off-leash is one of the hardest things to teach; you must do a lot of obedience training first. What you're saying sounds like, 'I want my dog be a neurosurgeon, but I do not want it to go to high school.'"

Many new traders expect to sit in front of their screens and make easy money day-trading. They skip high school and head straight for neurosurgery.

Discipline is necessary for success in most endeavors, but especially in the markets because they have no external controls. You have to watch yourself because no one else will, except for the margin clerk. You may put on the stupidest and self-destructive trades, but as long as you have enough money in your account, no one will stop you. No one will say hold on, wait, think what you're doing! Your broker will repeat your order to confirm he got it right. Once your order hits the market, other traders will scramble for the privilege of taking your money.

Most fields of human endeavor have rules, yardsticks, and professional bodies to enforce discipline. No matter how independent you feel, there is always some agency looking over your shoulder. If a doctor in private practice starts writing too many prescriptions for painkillers, he'll soon hear from the health department. Markets impose no restrictions, as long as you have enough equity. Adding to losing positions is similar to overprescribing narcotics, but nobody will stop you. As a matter of fact, other market participants want you to be undisciplined and impulsive. That makes it easier for them to get your money. Your defense against self-destructiveness is discipline. You have to set up your own rules and follow them in order to prevent self-sabotage.

Discipline means designing, testing, and following your trading system. It means learning to enter and exit in response to predefined signals rather than jumping in and out on a whim. It means doing the right thing, not the easy thing. And the first challenge on the road to disciplined trading involves setting up a record-keeping system.

Record-Keeping

Good traders keep good records. They keep them not just for their accountants but as tools of learning and discipline. If you do not have good records, how can you measure your performance, rate your progress, and learn from your mistakes? Those who do not learn from the past are doomed to repeat it.

When you decide to become a trader, you sign up for an expensive course. By the time you figure out the game, its cost may equal that of a college education, only most students never graduate—they drop out and get nothing for their money except for memories of a few wild rides.

Whenever you decide to improve your performance in any area of life, record keeping helps. If you want to become a better runner, keeping records of your speeds is essential for designing better workouts. If money is a problem, keeping and reviewing records of all expenditures is certain to uncover wasteful tendencies. Keeping scrupulous records turns a spotlight on a problem and allows you to improve.

Becoming a good trader means taking several courses—psychology, technical analysis, and money management. Each course requires its own set of records. You'll have to score high on all three in order to graduate.

Your first essential record is a spreadsheet of all your trades. You have to keep track of entries and exits, slippage and commissions, as well as profits and losses. Chapter 5, "Method—Technical Analysis" on trading channels will teach you to rate the quality of every trade, allowing you to compare performance across different markets and conditions.

Another essential record shows the balance in your account at the end of each month. Plot it on a chart, creating an equity curve whose angle will tell you whether you are in gear with the market. The goal is a steady uptrend, punctuated by shallow declines. If your curve slopes down, it shows you're not in tune with the markets and must reduce the size of your trades. A jagged equity curve tends to be a sign of impulsive trading.

Your trading diary is the third essential record. Whenever you enter a trade, print out the charts that prompted you to buy or sell. Paste them on the left page of a large notebook and write a few words explaining why you bought or sold, stating your profit objective and a stop. When you close out that trade, print out the charts again, paste them on the right page and write what you've learned from the completed trade.

These records are essential for all traders, and we will return to them later in Chapter 8, "The Organized Trader." A shoebox crammed with confirmation slips does not qualify as a record-keeping system. Too many records? Not enough time? Want to skip high school and dive into neurosurgery? Traders fail because of impatience and lack of discipline. Good records set you apart from the market crowd and put you on the road to success.

Training for Battle

How much training you need depends on the job you want. If you want to be a janitor, an hour of training might do. Just learn to attach a mop to the right end of the broomstick and find a pail without holes. If, on the other hand, you want to fly an airplane or do surgery, you'll have to learn a great deal more. Trading is closer to flying a plane than to mopping a floor, meaning you'll need to invest a lot of time and energy in mastering this craft.

Society mandates extensive training for pilots and doctors because their errors are so deadly. As a trader, you are free to be financially deadly to yourself—society does not care, because your loss is someone else's gain. Flying and medicine have standards and yardsticks, as well as professional bodies to enforce them. In trading, you have to set up your own rules and be your own enforcer.

Pilots and doctors learn from instructors who impose discipline on them through tests and evaluations. Private traders have no external system for learning, testing, or discipline. Our job is hard because we must learn on our own, develop discipline, and test ourselves again and again in the markets.

When we look at training for pilots and doctors, three features stand out. They are the gradual assumption of responsibility, constant evaluations, and training until actions become automatic. Let us see whether we can apply them to trading.

1. The Gradual Assumption of Responsibility A flying school doesn't put a beginner into a pilot's seat on his first day. A medical student is lucky if he is allowed to take a patient's temperature on his first day in the hospital. His superiors double-check him before he can advance to the next, slightly higher level of responsibility.

How does this compare to the education of a new trader?

There is nothing gradual about it. Most people start out on an impulse, after hearing a hot tip or a rumor of someone making money. A beginner has some cash burning a hole in his pocket. He gets a broker's name out of a newspaper, FedExes him a check, and enters his first trade. Now he is starting to learn! When do they close this market? What is a gap opening? How come the market is up and my stock is down?

A "sink or swim" approach does not work in complex enterprises, such as flying or trading. It is exciting to jump in, but excitement is not what good traders are after. If you do not have a specific trading plan, you're better off taking your money to Vegas. The outcome will be the same, but at least there they'll throw in some free drinks.

If you are serious about learning to trade, start with a relatively small account and set a goal of learning to trade rather than making a lot of money in a hurry. Keep a trading diary and put a performance grade on every trade.

2. Constant Evaluations and Ratings The progress of a flying cadet or a medical student is measured by hundreds of tests. Teachers constantly rate knowledge, skills, and decision-making ability. A student with good results is given more responsibility, but if his performance slips, he has to study more and take more tests.

Do traders go through a similar process?

As long as you have money in your account, you can make impulsive trades, trying to weasel your way out of a hole. You can throw confirmation slips into a shoebox, and give them to your accountant at tax time. No one can force you to look at your test results, unless you do it yourself.

The market tests us all the time, but only a few pay attention. It gives a performance grade to every trade and posts those ratings, but few people know where to look them up. Another highly objective test is our equity curve. If you trade several markets, you can take this test in every one of them, as well as in your account as a whole. Do most of us take this test? No. Pilots and doctors must answer to their licensing bodies, but traders sneak out of class because no one takes attendance and their internal discipline is weak. Meanwhile, tests are a key part of trading discipline, essential for your victory in the markets. Keeping and reviewing records, as outlined later in this book, puts you a mile ahead of undisciplined competitors.

3. Training until Actions Become Automatic   During one of my finals in medical school I was sent to examine a patient in a half-empty room. Suddenly I heard a noise from behind the curtain. I looked, and there was another patient—dying. "No pulse," I yelled to another student, and together we put the man on the floor. I began pumping his chest, while the other fellow gave him mouth to mouth, one forced breath for four chest pumps. Neither of us could run for help, but someone opened the door and saw us. A reanimation team raced in, zapped the man with a defibrillator and pulled him out.

I never had to revive anyone before, but it worked the first time because I had five years of training. When the time came to act, I didn't have to think. The point of training is to make actions automatic, allowing us to concentrate on strategy.

What will you do if your stock jumps five points in your favor? Five points against you? What if your future goes limit up? Limit down? If you have to stop and think while you're in a trade, you're dead. You need to spend time preparing trading plans and deciding in advance what you will do when the market does any imaginable thing. Play those scenarios in your head, use your computer, and get yourself to the point where you do not have to ruminate about what to do if the market jumps.

The mature trader arrives at a stage where most trading actions have become nearly automatic. This gives you the freedom to think about strategy. You think about what you want to achieve, and less about tactics of how to achieve it. To reach that point, you need to trade for a long time. The longer you trade and the more trades you put on, the more you'll learn. Trade a small size while learning and put on many trades. Remember, the first item on the agenda for a beginner is to learn how to trade, not to make money. Once you've learned to trade, money will follow.

METHOD— TECHNICAL ANALYSIS

Will this stock rise or fall? Should you go long or short? Traders reach for a multitude of tools to find answers to these questions. Many tie themselves into knots trying to choose between pattern recognition, computerized indicators, artificial intelligence, or even astrology for some desperate souls.

No one can learn all the analytic methods, just as no one can master every field of medicine. A physician cannot become a specialist in heart surgery, obstetrics, and psychiatry. No trader can know everything about the markets. You have to find a niche that attracts you and specialize in it.

Markets emit huge volumes of information. Our tools help organize these flows into a manageable form. It is important to select analytic tools and techniques that make sense to you, put them together into a coherent system, and focus on money management. When we make our trading decisions at the right edge of the chart, we deal with probabilities, not certainties. If you want certainty, go to the middle of the chart and try to find a broker who will accept your orders.

This chapter on technical analysis shows how one trader goes about analyzing markets. Use it as a model for choosing your favorite tools, rather than following it slavishly. Test any method you like on your own data because only personal testing will convert information into knowledge and make these methods your own.

Many concepts in this book are illustrated with charts. I selected them from a broad range of markets—stocks as well as futures. Technical analysis is a universal language, even though the accents differ. You can apply what you've learned from the chart of IBM to silver or Japanese yen. I trade mostly in the United States, but have used the same methods in Germany,

Russia, Singapore, and Australia. Knowing the language of technical analysis enables you to read any market in the world.

Analysis is hard, but trading is much harder. Charts reflect what has happened. Indicators reveal the balance of power between bulls and bears. Analysis is not an end in itself, unless you get a job as an analyst for a company. Our job as traders is to make decisions to buy, sell, or stand aside on the basis of our analysis.

After reviewing each chart, you need to go to its hard right edge and decide whether to bet on bulls, bet on bears, or stand aside. You must follow up chart analysis by establishing profit targets, setting stops, and applying money management rules.

BASIC CHARTING

A trade is a bet on a price change. You can make money buying low and selling high or shorting high and covering low. Prices are central to our enterprise, yet few traders stop to think what prices are. What exactly are we trying to analyze?

Financial markets consist of huge crowds of people who meet on the floor of an exchange, on the phone, or via the Internet. We can divide them into three groups: buyers, sellers, and undecided traders. Buyers want to buy as cheaply as possible. Sellers want to sell as expensively as possible. They could take forever to negotiate, but feel pressure from undecided traders. They have to act quickly, before some undecided trader makes up his mind, jumps into the game, and takes away their bargain. Undecided traders are the force that speeds up trading. They are true market participants, as long as they watch the market and have the money to trade it. Each deal is struck in the midst of the market crowd, putting pressure on both buyers and sellers. This is why each trade represents the current emotional state of the entire market crowd.

Price is a consensus of value of all market participants expressed in action at the moment of the trade.

Many traders have no clear idea what they are trying to analyze. Balance sheets of companies? Pronouncements of the Federal Reserve? Weather reports from soybean-growing states? The cosmic vibrations of Gann theory? Every chart serves as an ongoing poll of the market. Each tick represents a momentary consensus of value of all market participants. High and low prices, the height of every bar, the angle of every trendline, the duration of every pattern reflect aspects of crowd behavior. Recognizing these patterns can help us decide when to bet on bulls or bears.

During an election campaign pollsters call thousands of people asking how they'll vote. Well-designed polls have predictive value, which is why politicians pay for them. Financial markets run on a two-party system—bulls and bears, with a huge silent majority of undecided traders who may throw their weight to either party. Technical analysis is a poll of market participants. If bulls are on top, we should cover shorts and go long. If bears are stronger, we should go short. If an election is too close to call, a wise trader stands aside. Standing aside is a legitimate market position and the only one in which you can't lose money.

Individual behavior is difficult to predict. Crowds are much more primitive and their behavior more repetitive and predictable. Our job is not to argue with the crowd, telling it what's rational or irrational. We need to identify crowd behavior and decide how likely it is to continue. If the trend is up and we find that the crowd is growing more optimistic, we should trade that market from the long side. When we find that the crowd is becoming less optimistic, it is time to sell. If the crowd seems confused, we should stand aside and wait for the market to make up its mind.

The Meaning of Prices

Highs and lows, opening and closing prices, intraday swings and weekly ranges reflect crowd behavior. Our charts, indicators, and technical tools are windows into the mass psychology of the markets. You have to be clear about what you are studying if you want to get closer to the truth.

Many market participants have backgrounds in science and engineering and are often tempted to apply the principles of physics. For example, they may try to filter out the noise of a trading range to obtain a clear signal of a trend. Those methods can help, but they cannot be converted into automatic trading systems because the markets are not physical processes. They are reflections of crowd psychology, which follows different, less precise laws. In physics, if you calculate everything, you'll predict where a process will take you. Not so in the markets, where a crowd can always throw you a curve. Here you have to act within this atmosphere of uncertainty, which is why you must protect yourself with good money management.

The Open   The opening price, the first price of the day, is marked on a bar chart by a tick pointing to the left. An opening price reflects the influx of overnight orders. Who placed those orders? A dentist who read a tip in a magazine after dinner, a teacher whose broker touted a trade but who needed his wife's permission to buy, a financial officer of a slow-moving institution who sat in a meeting all day waiting for his idea to be approved by a committee. They are the people who place orders before the open. Opening prices reflect opinions of less informed market participants.

When outsiders buy or sell, who takes the opposite side of their trades? Market professionals step in to help, only they do not run a charity. If floor traders see more buy orders coming in, they open the market higher, forcing outsiders to overpay. The pros go short, so that the slightest dip makes them money. If the crowd is fearful before the opening and sell orders predominate, the floor opens the market very low. They acquire their goods on the cheap, so that the slightest bounce earns them short-term profits.

The opening price establishes the first balance of the day between outsiders and insiders, amateurs and professionals. If you are a short-term trader, pay attention to the opening range—the high and the low of the first 15 to 30 minutes of trading. Most opening ranges are followed by breakouts, which are important because they show who is taking control of the market. Several intraday trading systems are based on following opening range breakouts.

One of the best opportunities to enter a trade occurs when the market gaps at the open in the direction opposite your intended trade. Suppose you analyze a market at night and your system tells you to buy a stock. A piece of bad news hits the market overnight, sell orders come in, and that stock opens sharply lower. Once prices stabilize within the opening range, if you are still bullish and that range is above your planned stop-loss point, place your buy order a few ticks above the high of the opening range, with a stop below. You may pick up good merchandise on sale!

The High   Why do prices go up? The standard answer—more buyers than sellers—makes no sense because for every trade there is a buyer and a seller. The market goes up when buyers have more money and are more enthusiastic than sellers.

Buyers make money when prices go up. Each uptick adds to their profits. They feel flushed with success, keep buying, call friends and tell them to buy—this thing is going up! Eventually, prices rise to a level where bulls have no more money to spare and some start taking profits. Bears see the market as overpriced and hit it with sales. The market stalls, turns, and begins to fall, leaving behind the high point of the day. That point marks the greatest power of bulls for that day.

The high of every bar reflects the maximum power of bulls during that bar. It shows how high bulls could lift the market during that time period. The high of a daily bar reflects the maximum power of bulls during that day, the high of a weekly bar shows the maximum power of bulls during that week, and the high of a five-minute bar shows their maximum power in those five minutes.

The Low Bears make money when prices fall, with each downtick making money for short sellers. As prices slide, bulls become more and more skittish. They cut back their buying and step aside, figuring they'll be able to pick up what they want cheaper at a later time. When buyers pull in their horns, it becomes easier for bears to push prices lower, and the decline continues.

It takes money to sell stocks short, and a fall in prices slows down when bears start running low on money. Bullish bargain hunters appear on the scene. Experienced traders recognize what's happening and start covering shorts and going long. Prices rally from their lows, leaving behind the low mark—the lowest tick of the day.

The low point of each bar reflects the maximum power of bears during that bar. The lowest point of a daily bar reflects the maximum power of bears during that day, the low point of a weekly bar shows the maximum power of bears during that week, and the low of a five-minute bar shows the maximum power of bears during those five minutes. Several years ago I designed an indicator, called Elder-ray, for tracking the relative power of bulls and bears by measuring how far the high and the low of each bar get away from the average price.

The Close The closing price is marked on a bar chart by a tick pointing to the right. It reflects the final consensus of value for the day. This is the price at which most people look in their daily newspapers. It is especially important in the futures markets, because the settlement of trading accounts depends on it.

Professional traders monitor markets throughout the day. Early in the day they take advantage of opening prices, selling high openings and buying low openings, and then unwinding those positions. Their normal mode of operations is to fade—trade against—market extremes and for the return to normalcy. When prices reach a new high and stall, professionals sell, nudging the market down. When prices stabilize after a fall, they buy, helping the market rally.

The waves of buying and selling by amateurs that hit the market at the opening usually subside as the day goes on. Outsiders have done what they planned to do, and near the closing time the market is dominated by professional traders.

Closing prices reflect the opinions of professionals. Look at any chart, and you'll see how often the opening and closing ticks are at the opposite ends of a price bar. This is because amateurs and professionals tend to be on the opposite sides of trades.

Candlesticks and Point and Figure   Bar charts are most widely used for tracking prices, but there are other methods. Candlestick charts became popular in the West in the 1990s. Each candle represents a day of trading with a body and two wicks, one above and another below. The body reflects the spread between the opening and closing prices. The tip of the upper wick reaches the highest price of the day and the lower wick the lowest price of the day. Candlestick chartists believe that the relationship between the opening and closing prices is the most important piece of daily data. If prices close higher than they opened, the body of the candle is white, but if prices close lower, the body is black.

The height of a candle body and the length of its wicks reflect the battles between bulls and bears. Those patterns, as well as patterns formed by several neighboring candles, provide useful insights into the power struggle in the markets and can help us decide whether to go long or short.

The trouble with candles is they are too fat. I can glance at a computer screen with a bar chart and see five to six months of daily data, without squeezing the scale. Put a candlestick chart in the same space, and you'll be lucky to get two months of data on the screen. Ultimately, a candlestick chart doesn't reveal anything more than a bar chart. If you draw a normal bar chart and pay attention to the relationships of opening and closing prices, augmenting that with several technical indicators, you'll be able to read the markets just as well and perhaps better. Candlestick charts are useful for some but not all traders. If you like them, use them. If not, focus on your bar charts and don't worry about missing something essential.

Point and figure (P&F) charts are based solely on prices, ignoring volume. They differ from bar and candlestick charts by having no horizontal time scale. When markets become inactive, P&F charts stop drawing because they add a new column of X's and O's only when prices change beyond a certain trigger point. P&F charts make congestion areas stand out, helping traders find support and resistance and providing targets for reversals and profit taking. P&F charts are much older than bar charts. Professionals in the pits sometimes scribble them on the backs of their trading decks.

Choosing a chart is a matter of personal choice. Pick the one that feels most comfortable. I prefer bar charts but know many serious traders who like P&F charts or candlestick charts.

The Reality of the Chart

Price ticks coalesce into bars, and bars into patterns, as the crowd writes its emotional diary on the screen. Successful traders learn to recognize a few patterns and trade them. They wait for a familiar pattern to emerge like fishermen wait for a nibble at a riverbank where they fished many times in the past.

Many amateurs jump from one stock to another, but professionals tend to trade the same markets for years. They learn their intended catch's personality, its habits and quirks. When professionals see a short-term bottom in a familiar stock, they recognize a bargain and buy. Their buying checks the decline and pushes the stock up. When prices rise, the pros reduce their buying, but amateurs rush in, sucked in by the good news. When markets become overvalued, professionals start unloading their inventory. Their selling checks the rise and pushes the market down. Amateurs become spooked and start dumping their holdings, accelerating the decline. Once weak holders have been shaken out, prices slide to the level where professionals see a bottom, and the cycle repeats.

That cycle is not mathematically perfect, which is why mechanical systems tend not to work. Using technical indicators requires judgment. Before we review specific chart patterns, let us agree on the basic definitions:

An *uptrend* is a pattern in which most rallies reach a higher point than the preceding rally; most declines stop at a higher level than the preceding decline.

A *downtrend* is a pattern in which most declines fall to a lower point than the preceding decline; most rallies rise to a lower level than the preceding rally.

An *uptrendline* is a line connecting two or more adjacent bottoms, slanting upwards; if we draw a line parallel to it across the tops, we'll have a trading channel.

A *downtrendline* is a line connecting two or more adjacent tops, slanting down; one can draw a parallel line across the bottoms, marking a trading channel.

Support is marked by a horizontal line connecting two or more adjacent bottoms. One can often draw a parallel line across the tops, marking a trading range.

Resistance is marked by a horizontal line connecting two or more adjacent
tops. One can often draw a parallel line below, across the bottoms, to
mark a trading range.

Tops and Bottoms   The tops of rallies mark the areas of the maximum
power of bulls. They would love to lift prices even higher and make more
money, but that's where they get overpowered by bears. The bottoms of
declines, on the other hand, are the areas of maximum power of bears. They
would love to push prices even lower and profit from short positions, but
they get overpowered by bulls.

Use a computer or a ruler to draw a line, connecting nearby tops. If it
slants up, it shows that bulls are becoming stronger, which is a good
thing to know if you plan to trade from the long side. If that line slants
down, it shows that bulls are becoming weaker, and buying is not such a
good idea.

Trendlines applied to market bottoms help visualize changes in the
power of bears. When a line connecting two nearby bottoms slants down,
it shows that bears are growing stronger, and short selling is a good
option. If that line slants up, however, it shows that bears are becoming
weaker.

When the lines connecting the tops and the lines connecting the bottoms
are close to horizontal, the market is locked in a trading range. We can either
wait for a breakout or trade short-term swings within that range.

Uptrendlines and Downtrendlines   Prices often appear to travel along
invisible roads. When peaks rise higher at each successive rally, prices are
in an uptrend. When bottoms keep falling lower and lower, prices are in
a downtrend.

We can identify uptrends by drawing trendlines connecting the bottoms
of declines. We use bottoms to identify an uptrend because the peaks of
rallies tend to be expansive, uneven affairs during uptrends. The declines
tend to be more orderly, and when you connect them with a trendline,
you get a truer picture of that uptrend.

We identify downtrends by drawing trendlines across the peaks of rallies. Each new low in a downtrend tends to be lower than the preceding
low, but the panic among weak holders can make bottoms irregularly
sharp. Drawing a downtrendline across the tops of rallies paints a more
correct picture of that downtrend.

The most important feature of a trendline is the direction of its slope.
When it rises, the bulls are in control, and when it declines, the bears are

in charge. The longer the trendline and the more points of contact it has with prices, the more valid it is. The angle of a trendline reflects the emotional temperature of the crowd. Quiet, shallow trends can last a long time. As trends accelerate, trendlines have to be redrawn, making them steeper. When they rise or fall at 60° or more, their breaks tend to lead to major reversals. This sometimes happens near the tail ends of runaway moves.

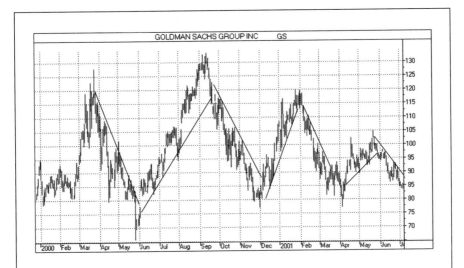

Figure 5.1   Trendlines; Kangaroo Tails

Draw uptrendlines across the bottoms to mark uptrends. Draw downtrendlines across the tops to mark downtrends. Notice that prices can briefly penetrate a trendline without breaking the trend. Observe that prices seem attached to their trendlines with rubber bands that extend only so far in any given trend. You want to establish positions in the direction of the slope of a trendline, entering reasonably close to it. By the time the trend reaches a new high or low, that swing away from the trendline is getting old—there is not much life left in the old dog. At the right edge of this chart the trend is down and the swing has fallen as far below its trendline as any since May. If you are short, it is time to start thinking of taking profits.

   Notice several bars that stick out of the tight weave of prices at the bottoms in May, November, and April, as well as the latest top in May. Those are kangaroo tails, which tend to mark turning points. The market tests a new high or a new low with a bar that is much taller than the preceding and following bars, and then recoils from that price extreme. You can recognize a tail during the bar that follows, and trade against it.

You can plot these lines using a ruler or a computer. It is better to draw trendlines as well as support and resistance lines across the edges of congestion areas instead of price extremes. Congestion areas reflect crowd behavior, while the extreme points show only the panic among the weakest crowd members.

Tails—The Kangaroo Pattern   Trends take a long time to form, but tails are created in just a few days. They provide valuable insights into market psychology, mark reversal areas, and point to trading opportunities.

A tail is a one-day spike in the direction of a trend, followed by a reversal. It takes a minimum of three bars to create a tail—relatively narrow bars in the beginning and at the end, with an extremely wide bar in the middle. That middle bar is the tail, but you won't know for sure until the following day, when a bar has sharply narrowed back at the base, letting the tail hang out. A tail sticks out from a tight weave of prices—you can't miss it.

A kangaroo, unlike a horse or a dog, propels itself by pushing with its tail. You can always tell which way a kangaroo is going to jump—opposite its tail. When the tail points north, the kangaroo jumps south, and when the tail points south, it jumps north. Market tails tend to occur at turning points in the markets, which recoil from them like kangaroos recoil from their tails. A tail does not forecast the extent of a move, but the first jump usually lasts a few days, offering a trading opportunity. You can do well by recognizing tails and trading against them.

Before you trade any pattern, you must understand what it tells you about the market. Why do markets jump away from their tails?

Exchanges are owned by members who profit from volume rather than trends. Markets fluctuate, looking for price levels that will bring the highest volume of orders. Members do not know where those levels are, but they keep probing higher and lower. A tail shows that the market has tested a certain price level and rejected it.

If a market stabs down and recoils, it shows that lower prices do not attract volume. The natural thing for the market to do next is rally and test higher levels to see whether higher prices will bring more volume. If the market stabs higher and recoils, leaving a tail pointing upward, it shows that higher prices do not attract volume. The members are likely to sell the market down in order to find whether lower prices will attract volume. Tails work because the owners of the market are looking to maximize income.

Whenever you see a very tall bar (several times the average for recent months) shooting in the direction of the existing trend, be alert to the possibility of a tail. If the following day the market traces a very narrow bar at the base of the tall bar, it completes a tail. Be ready to put on a position, trading against that tail, before the close.

When a market hangs down a tail, go long in the vicinity of the base of that tail. Once long, place a protective stop approximately half-way down the tail. If the market starts chewing its tail, run without delay. The targets for profit taking on these long positions are best established by using moving averages and channels (see "Indicators—Five Bullets to a Clip," page 84).

When a market puts up a tail, go short in the area of the base of that tail. Once short, place a protective stop approximately half-way up the tail. If the market starts rallying up its tail, it is time to run; do not wait for the entire tail to be chewed up. Establish profit-taking targets using moving averages and channels.

You can trade against tails in any timeframe. Daily charts are most common, but you can also trade them on intraday or weekly charts. The magnitude of a move depends on its timeframe. A tail on a weekly chart will generate a much bigger move than a tail on a five-minute chart.

Support, Resistance, and False Breakouts　When most traders and investors buy and sell, they make an emotional as well as a financial commitment to their trade. Their emotions can propel market trends or send them into reversals.

The longer a market trades at a certain level, the more people buy and sell. Suppose a stock falls from 80 and trades near 70 for several weeks, until many believe that it has found support and reached its bottom. What happens if heavy selling comes in and shoves that stock down to 60? Smart longs will run fast, banging out at 69 or 68. Others will sit through the entire painful decline. If losers haven't given up near 60 and are still alive when the market trades back towards 70, their pain will prompt them to jump at a chance to "get out even." Their selling is likely to cap a rally, at least temporarily. Their painful memories are the reason why the areas that served as support on the way down become resistance on the way up, and vice versa.

Regret is another psychological force behind support and resistance. If a stock trades at 80 for a while and then rallies to 95, those who did not buy it near 80 feel as if they missed the train. If that stock sinks back near 80, traders who regret a missed opportunity will return to buy in force.

Support and resistance can remain active for months or even years because investors have long memories. When prices return to their old levels, some jump at the opportunity to add to their positions while others see a chance to get out.

Whenever you work with a chart, draw support and resistance lines across recent tops and bottoms. Expect a trend to slow down in those areas, and use them to enter positions or take profits. Keep in mind that support and resistance are flexible—they are like a ranch wire fence rather than a glass wall. A glass wall is rigid and shatters when broken, but a herd of bulls can push against a wire fence, shove their muzzles through it, and it will lean but stand. Markets have many false breakouts below support and above resistance, with prices returning into their range after a brief violation.

A false upside breakout occurs when the market rises above resistance and sucks in buyers before reversing and falling. A false downside breakout occurs when prices fall below support, attracting more bears just before a rally. False breakouts provide professionals with some of the best trading opportunities. They are similar to tails, only tails have a single wide bar, whereas false breakouts can have several bars, none of them especially tall.

What causes false breakouts and how do you trade them? At the end of a long rise the market hits resistance, stops, and starts churning. The professionals know there are many more buy orders above the resistance level. Some were placed by traders looking to buy a new breakout, and others are protective stops placed by those who went short on the way up. The pros are the first to know where people have stops because they are the ones holding the orders.

A false breakout occurs when the pros organize a fishing expedition to run stops. For example, when a stock is slightly below its resistance at 60, the floor may start loading up on longs near 58.85. As sellers pull back, the market roars above 60, setting off buy stops. The floor starts selling into that rush, unloading longs as prices touch 60.50. When they see that public buy orders are drying up, they sell short and prices tank back below 60. That's when your charts show a false breakout above 60.

S&P 500 futures are notorious for false breakouts. Day after day this market exceeds its previous day's high or falls below its previous day's low by a few ticks (a tick is the minimum price change permitted by the exchange where an instrument is traded). This is one of the reasons the S&P is a difficult market to trade, but it attracts beginners like flies. The floor has a field day slapping them.

Some of the best trading opportunities occur after false breakouts. When prices fall back into the range after a false upside breakout, you have extra confidence to trade short. Use the top of the false breakout as your stop-loss point. Once prices rally back into their range after a false downside breakout, you have extra confidence to trade long. Use the bottom of that false breakout for your stop-loss point.

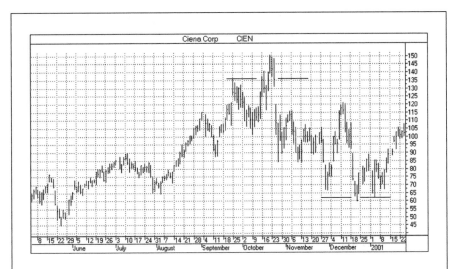

Figure 5.2 Support, Resistance, and False Breakouts

In September CIEN reached a peak below 140, then attacked that level in October and rallied above 150, only to sink below the old peak a few days later. Some poor guy actually bought above 150—he really needed that stock! The false upside breakout marked the end of the bull market.

The bear market established a bottom just near 65 in December, but in January some desperate sellers dumped enough stock to briefly push CIEN near 60. At the right edge of the chart prices are rallying above the level of their old bottom. The bear trap has slammed shut, with a 50% rally in just one month. Such signals are much easier to recognize using technical indicators, to be discussed later.

If you have an open position, defend yourself against false breakouts by reducing your trading size and placing wider stops. Be ready to reposition if stopped out of your trade.

There are many advantages to risking just a small fraction of your account on any trade. It allows you to be more flexible with stops. When the volatility is high, consider protecting a long position by buying a put or a short position by buying a call. Finally, if you get stopped out on a false breakout, don't be shy about getting back into a trade. Beginners tend to make a single stab at a position and stay out if they are stopped out. Professionals, on the other hand, will attempt several entries before nailing down the trade they want.

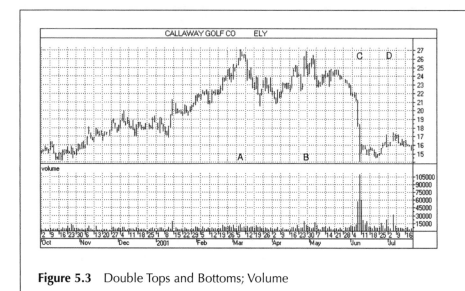

Figure 5.3   Double Tops and Bottoms; Volume

Double Tops and Bottoms   Bulls make money when the market rises. There are always a few who take profits on the way up, but new bulls come in and the rally continues. Every rally reaches a point where enough bulls look at it and say—this is very nice, and it may get even nicer, but I'd rather have cash. Rallies top out after enough wealthy bulls take their profits, while the money from new bulls is not enough to replace what was taken out.

When the market heads down from its peak, savvy bulls, the ones who've cashed out early, are the most relaxed group. Other bulls who are still long, especially if they came in late, feel trapped. Their profits are melting away and turning into losses. Should they hold or sell?

If enough moneyed bulls decide the decline is being overdone, they'll step in and buy. As the rally resumes, more bulls come in. Now prices approach the level of their old top, and that's where you can expect sell orders to hit the market. Many traders who got caught in the previous decline swear to get out if the market gives them a second chance.

As the market rises toward its previous peak, the main question is whether it will it rise to a new high or form a double top and turn down. Technical indicators can be of great help in answering this question. When they rise to a new high, they tell you to hold, and when they form bear-

Callaway Golf (ELY) reached its high of 27.18 in March, at point A, and struggled again near that level, to 26.95 in April, at point B. A few days after it recoiled from B, the double top became clearly visible. Many indicators (which we will review later) traced bearish divergences at that time.

In June the stock collapsed, as the aged founder of the company, the inventor of the famous Big Bertha golf club, became ill and died. In a fairly typical emotional reaction, people dumped their stock without stopping to think whether the demise of an individual would ruin a large, well-established company. Such declines feed on themselves, as lower prices scare more people into selling. Notice a fantastic spike of volume, which reflected mass panic. The low at point C looks like a kangaroo tail, although not in its most classical form. Prices rallied above 17 at point D in what is called "a dead cat bounce," not out of any great bullishness but simply as a reaction to the decline.

At the right edge of the chart ELY is grinding down towards its recent bottom on low volume. If it recoils from that level, it'll establish a double bottom. This is a fairly typical pattern—a crash, followed by a dead cat bounce, followed by a slow decline into the second bottom. Once prices rally from the second low, they are likely to usher in a sustainable rise.

ish divergences (see "Indicators—Five Bullets to a Clip," page 84), they tell you to take profits at the second top.

A mirror image of this situation occurs at market bottoms. The market falls to a new low at which enough smart bears start covering shorts and the market rallies. Once that rally peters out and prices start sinking again, all eyes are on the previous low—will it hold? If bears are strong and bulls skittish, prices will break below the first low, and the downtrend will continue. If bears are weak and bulls are strong, the decline will stop in the vicinity of the old low, creating a double bottom. Technical indicators help decipher which of the two is more likely to happen.

Triangles   A triangle is a congestion area, a pause when winners take profits and new trend followers get aboard, while their opponents trade against the preceding trend. It is like a train station. The train stops to let passengers off and pick up new ones, but there is always a chance this is the last stop on the line and it may turn back.

The upper boundary of a triangle shows where sellers overpower buyers and prevent the market from rising. The lower boundary shows where buyers overpower sellers and prevent the market from falling. As the two start to converge, you know a breakout is coming. As a general rule, the trend that preceded the triangle deserves the benefit of the doubt. The angles between triangle walls reflect the balance of power between bulls and bears and hint at the likely direction of a breakout.

An ascending triangle has a flat upper boundary and a rising lower boundary. The flat upper line shows that bears have drawn a line in the sand and sell whenever the market comes to it. They must be a pretty

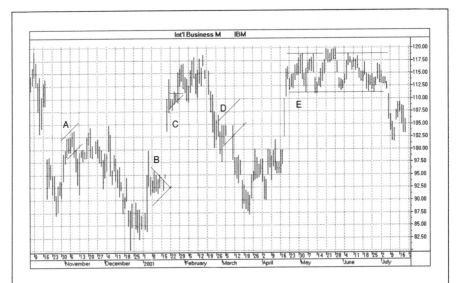

Figure 5.4   Triangles, Pennants, and Rectangles

Charts patterns are the footprints of bulls and bears. Patterns A and D are called *pennants*—a tight weave of prices that follows a sharp move up or down its flagpole. When a pennant flies in the direction of the trend (A), it is usually followed by a sharp reversal. When it flies against the preceding trend (D), it is a consolidation pattern and the trend usually continues. Place your entry orders accordingly, above or below a pennant's boundary.

Pattern B is a symmetrical triangle and pattern C is an ascending triangle. Breakouts from triangles tend to follow the trends that preceded them, especially when triangles are compact, consisting of only a few bars. Pattern E is a rectangle; notice how bulls and bears push against the rectangle walls, creating brief false breakouts—do not jump in too early. When prices decisively break out of a rectangle, the reversal is complete.

At the right edge of the chart, prices are below a rectangle that provides severe overhead resistance; the price is like a drowning man under an ice floe. The trend is down, with rallies presenting shorting opportunities.

powerful group, calmly waiting for prices to come to them before unloading. At the same time buyers are becoming more aggressive. They snap up merchandise and keep raising the floor under the market.

On what party should you bet? Nobody knows who'll win the election, but savvy traders tend to place buy orders slightly above the upper line of an ascending triangle. Since sellers are on the defensive, if the attacking bulls succeed, the breakout is likely to be steep. This is the logic of buying upside breakouts from ascending triangles.

A descending triangle has a flat lower boundary and a declining upper boundary. The horizontal lower line shows that bulls are pretty determined, calmly waiting to buy at a certain level. At the same time, sellers are becoming more aggressive. They keep selling at lower and lower levels, pushing the market closer to the line drawn by buyers.

As a trader, which way will you bet—on the bulls or the bears? Experienced traders tend to place their orders to sell short slightly below the lower line of a descending triangle. Let buyers defend that line, but if bulls collapse after a long defense, a break is likely to be sharp. This is the logic of shorting downside breakouts from descending triangles.

A symmetrical triangle shows that both bulls and bears are equally confident. Bulls keep paying up, and bears keep selling lower. Neither group is backing off, and their fight must be resolved before prices reach the tip of the triangle. The breakout is likely to go in the direction of the trend that preceded the triangle.

Volume   Each unit of volume represents the actions of two individuals—a buyer and a seller. It can be measured by several numbers: shares, contracts, or dollars that have changed hands. Volume is usually plotted as a histogram below prices. It provides important clues about the actions of bulls and bears. Rising volume tends to confirm trends, and falling volume brings them into question.

Volume reflects the level of pain among market participants. At each tick in every trade, one person is winning and the other losing. Markets can move only if enough new losers enter the game to supply profits to winners. If the market is falling, it takes a very courageous or reckless bull to step in and buy, but without him there is no increase in volume. When the trend is up, it takes a very brave or reckless bear to step in and sell. Rising volume shows that losers are continuing to come in, allowing the trend to continue. When losers start abandoning the market, volume falls, and the trend runs out of steam. Volume gives traders several useful clues.

A one-day splash of uncommonly high volume often marks the begin-ning of a trend when it accompanies a breakout from a trading range. A similar splash tends to mark the end of a trend if it occurs during a well-established move. Exceedingly high volume, three or more times above average, identifies market hysteria. That is when nervous bulls finally decide that the uptrend is for real and rush in to buy or nervous bears become convinced that the decline has no bottom and jump in to sell short.

Divergences between price and volume tend to occur at turning points. When prices rise to a new high but volume shrinks, it shows that the uptrend attracts less interest. When prices fall to a new low and volume falls, it shows that lower prices attract little interest and an upside reversal is likely. Price is more important than volume, but good traders always analyze volume to gauge the degree of crowd involvement. For a more objective rating of volume use an indicator called Force Index (see next section). Changes in volume detected by Force Index give important mes-sages to traders.

INDICATORS—FIVE BULLETS TO A CLIP

I had a friend who drove a tank in World War ll, fighting his way from Stalingrad to Vienna. He maintained his tank with only three tools—a big hammer, a big screwdriver, and the Russian version of "f... you." He won the war with a few simple tools, and we can apply his lessons to the dan-gerous environment of the markets.

An amateur tries to grab a bit of money here and there. He uses one technique today and another tomorrow. His mind is scattered and he keeps losing, enriching only his broker and floor traders. A new hunter walks into the woods with a load of fancy gear on his back but soon discovers that most of it only slows him down. An experienced woodsman travels light.

A beginner shoots at anything that moves, including his own shadow. An old hunter knows exactly what prey he is after and brings only a few bullets. Simplicity and discipline go hand in hand. To be a successful trader, choose a small number of markets, select a few tools, and learn to use them well. If you follow five stocks, your research will be deeper and results better than if you follow 50. If you use five indicators, you'll get more mileage out of them than out of 25. You can always expand later, once you make steady profits.

The indicators we are about to discuss represent the choice of one trader. I call this approach "five bullets to a clip." An old army rifle used to take five bullets, and I analyze markets using no more than five indicators.

If five do not help, 10 will not do any better because there probably is no trade. I offer you this list as a starting point for selecting your own bullets. Pay attention to the general principle of selecting indicators from different groups to focus on different aspects of crowd behavior. The key idea is to select a few core tools that fit your style of analysis and trading.

The tools we are about to review—moving averages, envelopes, MACD, MACD-Histogram, and Force Index—are the building blocks of a trading system described in the following chapter. There is no magic indicator; they all have advantages and disadvantages. It is important to be aware of both because then we can combine several indicators into a system to take advantage of their strengths, while their disadvantages cancel each other out.

Choice of Tools

Markets can confound traders. They often run in two directions at once—up on the weekly charts and down on the dailies. A market can reverse without sending you an e-mail about its change of plans. A sleepy stock can get so hot that it burns through stops, while a formerly hot stock becomes so cold it freezes your capital along with your fingers.

Trading is a complex, nontrivial game. Markets consist of huge crowds of people, and technical analysis is applied social psychology. We must select several tools to identify different aspects of market behavior. Before using any indicator, we must understand how it is constructed and what it measures. We must test it on historical data and learn how it performs under different conditions. Once you start testing an indicator, expect to adjust its settings, turning it into a personal trading tool as reliable and familiar as an old wrench.

Toolboxes vs. Black Boxes   I keep seeing ads in traders' magazines that show computers with $100 bills coming out of their disk drives. I'd love to get a hold of one of those models. The only ones I could find have the direction of money reversed. Computers can chew up cash, but pulling it out of them takes a lot of hard work. Those ads sell black boxes—computerized trading systems. Some clown has programmed a bunch of trading rules, put them on a copy-protected diskette or a CD, and now sells you a tool with a great track record. Feed it market data, and it will spit out an answer—when to buy or sell! If you believe this magic, wait until you meet Santa Claus.

A fantastic track record of a canned system is meaningless because it comes from fitting the rules to old data. Any computer can tell you which rules worked in the past. Black-box programs self-destruct as soon as the markets change, even if they include self-optimization. Black boxes appeal to beginners who derive a false sense of security from them.

A good software package is a toolbox—a collection of tools for analyzing markets and making your own decisions. A toolbox can download data, draw charts, and plot indicators, as well as any trading signals you care to program. It provides charting and analytic tools but leaves you to make your own trading decisions.

The heart of any toolbox is its collection of indicators—tools for identifying trends and reversals behind the noise of raw data. Good toolboxes allow you to modify indicators and even design your own. Indicators are objective; you may argue about the trend, but when an indicator is up, it's up, and when it is down, it's down. Keep in mind that indicators are derived from prices. The more complicated they are, the farther they are from prices and the farther away from reality. Prices are primary, indicators are secondary, and simple indicators work best.

Trend-Following Indicators and Oscillators   Learning to use indicators is like learning a foreign language. You have to immerse yourself in them, make typical beginners' mistakes, and keep practicing until you rise to the level of proficiency and competence.

Good technical indicators are simple tools that perform well when market conditions change. They are robust, that is, relatively immune to parameter changes. If an indicator gives great signals using a 17-day window but bombs when you try a 15-day window, then it's probably useless. Good indicators give useful signals at a broad range of settings.

We can divide all technical indicators into three major groups: trend-following, oscillators, and miscellaneous. Whenever we use an indicator, we must know to which group it belongs. Each group has its advantages and disadvantages.

Trend-following indicators include moving averages, MACD (moving average convergence-divergence), Directional System, and others. Big trends mean big money, and these indicators help us stay long in uptrends and short in downtrends. They have built-in inertia that allows them to lock onto a trend and ride it. That same inertia causes them to lag at turning points. Their advantages and disadvantages are the flip sides of each other, and you cannot have one without the other.

Oscillators include Force Index, Rate of Change, and Stochastic, among others. They help catch turning points by showing when markets are overbought (too high and ready to fall) or oversold (too low and ready to rise). Oscillators work great in trading ranges, where they catch upturns and downturns. Taking their signals when prices are relatively flat is like going to a cash machine—you always get something, although not very much. Their downside is that they give premature sell signals in uptrends and buy signals in downtrends.

Miscellaneous indicators, such as Bullish Consensus, Commitments of Traders, and New High–New Low Index, gauge the current mood of the market. They show whether the overall bullishness or bearishness is rising or falling.

Indicators from different groups often contradict one another. For example, when markets rise, trend-following indicators turn up, telling us to buy. At the same time, oscillators become overbought and start flashing sell signals. The opposite occurs in downtrends, when trend-following indicators turn down, giving sell signals, while oscillators become oversold, flashing buy signals. Which should we follow? The answers are easy in the middle of a chart, but much harder at the right edge, where we must make our trading decisions.

Some beginners close their eyes to complexity, choose a single indicator, and stick to it until the market whacks them from an unexpected direction. Others create a homemade opinion poll; they take a battery of indicators and average their signals. This is a meaningless exercise because its outcome depends on what indicators you include in your poll; change the selection and you'll change the outcome. The Triple Screen trading system, described below, overcomes the problem of conflicting indicators by linking them with different timeframes.

Time—The Factor of Five   A computer screen can comfortably show about 120 bars in an open-high-low-close format. What if you display a monthly chart, each of whose bars represents one month? You'll see 10 years worth of history at a glance, your stock's big picture. You can display a weekly chart and review its rallies and declines for the past two years. A daily chart will show you the action for the past few months. How about an hourly chart, each of whose bars represents one hour of trading? It will let you zoom in on the past few days and pick up short-term trends. Want to get even closer? How about a 10-minute chart, each of whose bars represents 10 minutes of market action?

Looking at all these charts, you quickly notice that markets can move in different directions at the same time. You may see an upmove on the weekly chart, while the dailies are breaking down. An hourly chart may be sagging, while a 10-minute chart is rallying. Which trend to follow?

Most beginners look at only one timeframe, usually daily. The trouble is that a new trend, erupting from another timeframe, often hurts traders who do not look beyond their noses. Another serious problem is that looking at the daily chart puts you on par with thousands of other traders who also look at it. What's your advantage, what's your edge?

Markets are so complex that we must always analyze them in more than one timeframe. The Factor of Five, first described in *Trading for a Living*, links all timeframes. Every timeframe is related to the next higher and the next lower by the factor of five. There are almost five (4.3 to be exact) weeks to a month, five days to a week, and close to five hours in many trading days. We can break an hour into 10-minute segments and those into 2-minute bars.

The key principle of Triple Screen, which we will review later, is to choose your favorite timeframe and then immediately go up to the timeframe one order of magnitude higher. There we make a strategic decision to go long or short. We return to our favorite timeframe to make tactical decisions about where to enter, exit, place a profit target and a stop. Adding the dimension of time to our analysis gives us an edge over the competition.

Use at least two, but not more than three, timeframes because adding more only clutters up the decision-making process. If you are day-trading with 30- and five-minute charts, then a weekly chart is essentially irrelevant. If you are trading market swings using a weekly and a daily, then the wiggles of a five-minute chart are no more than noise. Choose your favorite timeframe, add the timeframe one order of magnitude higher, and start your analysis at that point.

Moving Averages

Moving averages (MAs) are among the oldest, simplest, and most useful tools for traders. They help identify trends and find areas for entering trades. We plot them as lines on price charts, each of whose points reflects the latest average price.

What is the reality behind the moving averages, and what do they measure?

Each price is a momentary consensus of value among market participants, a snapshot of the market crowd at the moment of a trade. What if you show me a snapshot of your friend and ask whether he is an optimist or a pessimist, a bull or a bear? It is hard to tell from a single photo. If you take his snapshot from the same position for 10 days in a row and bring them to a lab, you can get a composite photo. When 10 pictures are superimposed upon one another, the typical features stand out, while the atypical fade away. If you start updating that composite each day, you'll have a moving average of your friend's mood. If you lay a string of composite photos side by side, it will be clear whether your friend is becoming happier or sadder.

A moving average is a composite photograph of the market. It adds new prices as they occur and drops old ones. A rising moving average shows that the crowd is becoming more optimistic—bullish. A falling moving average shows that the crowd is becoming more pessimistic—bearish.

A moving average responds not only to the data but to how we construct it. We must make several decisions to help separate the message of our moving average from the construction noise. First, we need to decide what data we'll use. We need to select the width of our time window—wider for catching longer trends, narrower for catching minor ones. Finally, we need to choose the type of moving average.

What Data to Average?   Traders who rely on daily and weekly charts usually apply moving averages to closing prices. This makes sense, because they reflect the final consensus of value, the most important price of the day.

The closing price of a five-minute or an hourly bar has no such special meaning. Day-traders are better off averaging not closing prices, but an average price of each bar. For example, they can average Open + High + Low + Close of each bar, divided by four, or High + Low + Close divided by three.

We can apply moving averages to indicators, such as Force Index (see below). A raw Force Index reflects price changes and volume for the day. Averaging produces a smoother plot and reveals a longer-term trend of Force Index.

How Long a Moving Average?   Moving averages help identify trends. A rising MA encourages you to maintain longs, whereas a falling MA tells you to hold shorts. The wider the time window, the smoother is a moving average. That benefit has a cost. The longer a moving average, the slower it responds to trend changes. The shorter a moving average, the better it tracks prices, but the more subject it is to whipsaws, temporary deviations from the main trend. If you make your moving average very long, it will miss important reversals by a wide margin. Shorter MAs are more sensitive to trend changes, but those shorter than 10 bars defeat the purpose of a trend-following tool.

At the time I wrote *Trading for a Living*, I was using 13-bar MAs, but in recent years I switched to longer moving averages to catch more important trends and avoid whipsaws. To analyze weekly charts, start with a 26-week moving average, representing half a year's worth of data. Try to shorten that number and see whether you can do it without sacrificing the smoothness of your MA. On the daily charts, start with a 22-day MA, reflecting roughly the number of trading days in a month, and see whether you can make it shorter. Whatever length you decide to use, be sure to test it on your own data. If you track just a handful of markets, you'll have enough time to try different lengths of moving averages until you get smoothly flowing lines.

The width of any indicator time window is best expressed in bars rather than days. The computer doesn't know whether you are analyzing daily, monthly, or hourly charts; it sees only bars. Whatever we say about a daily MA applies to the weekly or the monthly. It's better to call it a 22-bar MA rather than a 22-day MA.

Mathematically savvy traders can look into using adaptive moving averages whose length changes in response to market conditions, as advocated by John Ehlers, Tushar Chande, and Perry Kaufman. Ehlers' latest book, *Rocket Science for Traders,* delves into adapting all indicators to current market conditions.

What Type of Moving Average? A simple MA adds up prices in its time window and divides the sum by the width of that window. For example, for a 10-day simple MA of closing prices, add up closing prices for the past 10 days and divide the sum by 10. The trouble with a simple MA is that each price affects it twice—when it comes in and when it drops out. A high new value pushes up the moving average, giving a buy signal. This is good; we want our MAs to respond to new prices. The trouble is that 10 days later, when that high number drops from the window, the MA also drops, giving a sell signal. This is ridiculous because if we shorten a simple MA by one day, we'll get that sell signal a day sooner, and if we lengthen it by a day, we'll get it a day later. We can engineer our own signals by fiddling with the length of a simple MA!

An exponential moving average (EMA) overcomes this problem. It reacts only to incoming prices, to which it assigns more weight. It does not drop old prices from its time window, but slowly squeezes them out with the passage of time.

$$EMA = P_{today} \cdot K + EMA_{yesterday} \cdot (1 - K)$$

where K $= \dfrac{2}{N + 1}$

N = the number of days in the EMA (selected by trader)

P_{today} = today's price

$EMA_{yesterday}$ = the EMA of yesterday

Few people calculate indicators by hand these days—computers do it faster and more accurately. If we decide to look at a 22-bar EMA of closing prices, $K = 2/(22 + 1) = 2/23 = 0.087$. Multiply the latest closing price by that figure, multiply yesterday's EMA by 0.913 (i.e., $1 - 0.087$), add the two, and arrive at today's EMA. Traders sometimes ask where to get an EMA in the beginning. Begin by calculating a 22-bar simple MA and then switch to the EMA. Most indicators require you to have one or two months of data before they start giving meaningful signals.

Trading Signals   The most important message of a moving average is the direction of its slope. When the EMA rises, it shows that the crowd is becoming more optimistic and bullish, which is a good time to be long. When it falls, it shows that the crowd is becoming more pessimistic and bearish. It is a good time to be short.

When a moving average points up, trade that market from the long side. When a moving average points down, trade that market from the short side. As a trader, you have three options: go long, go short, or stand aside. A moving average takes away one of those. When it points up, it prohibits you from shorting and tells you to go long or stand aside. When it points down, it prohibits you from buying and tells you to look only for shorts or stay out. When an EMA starts jerking up and down, it indicates a vacillating, trendless market; it is better to stop using trend-following methods. Continue to monitor the EMA, but take its signals at a discount until a new trend emerges.

The only time when it is OK to override the message of a moving average is when trying to pick a bottom after a bullish divergence between MACD-Histogram (described below) and price. If you do that, be sure to use tight stops. If you succeed, bank your profits but do not think that the rules of the game have changed. A trader who thinks he is above the rules becomes careless and loses money.

Enter long positions in the vicinity of a rising MA. Enter short positions in the vicinity of a falling MA. Use MA to differentiate between "value trades" and

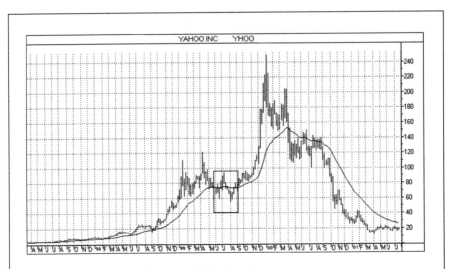

Figure 5.5   Moving Average—Major Trend

An exponential moving average is slow but steady, like a directional indicator on a steamroller. EMA works in all timeframes but shines on the weeklies, where it helps you stay with the major trend no matter how hard it tries to shake you off. Trading in the direction of a weekly moving average should help you get ahead of many traders. You can position yourself in the direction of the EMA and hold, or else trade in and out, using daily charts.

This 26-week EMA has tracked the entire glorious bull market in YHOO, from its obscure beginnings, to the breathtaking $250 peak, and back into the doghouse. If you wake up in the morning, look at the weekly EMA, and trade in its direction, you will not be in too bad a shape!

There are no perfect indicators, and an EMA has its share of difficulties when markets go flat. When the EMA starts to quiver, as it did in 1999, it is time to stand aside or trade short term, not counting on a major trend.

Notice the three tails in YHOO (and the fourth, not as pure as the first three). Every time there was a tail, the price got halved within weeks.

At the right edge of the chart prices are flat and EMA is declining. Prices are closer to the bottom than they are to the top, but there is no rush to buy. Let the EMA flatten out and tick up before positioning for a new major bull move.

"greater fool theory trades." Most uptrends are punctuated by declines, when prices return to the EMA. When we buy near the moving average, we buy value and can place a tight stop slightly below the EMA. If the rally resumes, we'll make money, but if the market turns against us, the loss will be small. Buying near the EMA helps maximize gains and minimize risks.

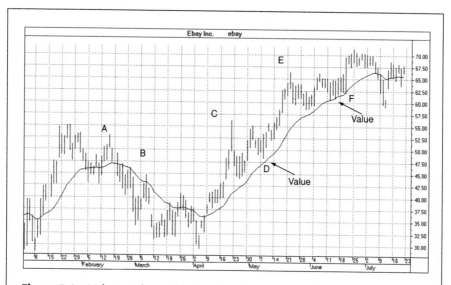

Figure 5.6   Value Trades and Greater Fool Theory Trades

When you buy near a rising moving average, you buy value (points D and F). Waiting for such opportunities requires patience, but it is infinitely safer than chasing rallies. Those who buy high above the EMA pay above value, hoping to meet a greater fool who will pay them even more. Anxious traders who buy near the tops (points C and E) get shaken out, or else they tensely wait to get out at breakeven.

Many stocks and futures have typical behavior patterns, and you should try to identify them and use them. At the time of this writing, EBAY likes to have kangaroo tails (A, B, C, and E). The C tail had the most classical shape, but others worked also. Knowing what pattern to expect helps you recognize it a little sooner when it appears.

At the right edge of the chart the EMA has stopped rising and begun to flutter. The bull move is over. If you are a trend trader, it is time to move over to other, trending stocks. Keep an eye on EBAY, waiting for a new trend to emerge.

If we buy high above the EMA, our actions say, "I am a fool, I am over-paying, but I hope to meet a greater fool down the road who'll pay me even more." Betting on the greater fool theory is a poor idea. There are very few fools in the markets. Financial markets do not attract foolish people, and counting on them is a losing proposition.

There are times when wild rallies in high-flying stocks seem to vindicate the greater fool theory. Stocks with no assets or earnings can fly on hot air. A value trader who feels he is missing those spectacular moves has a choice. He can stick to his method, soberly saying, "Can't catch them all." Or he may decide, "When living with the wolves, howl like a wolf" and start buying upside breakouts. If you do that, remember, you are now engaged in greater fool theory trading and the only asset separating you from the manic crowd is your risk control—your stops and money management.

The same rules apply to shorting in downtrends. When you go short on a rally to the EMA, you are selling value—before the market reverses and starts destroying value again. A greater fool theorist shorts far below the EMA—the farther away, the greater the fool.

Use a system of dual moving averages to identify trends and enter positions. You may select an EMA that tracks your market well, but it moves so explosively that prices never react back to that EMA, denying you a chance to put on a value trade. To solve this problem, you can add a second moving average. Use the longer EMA to indicate the trend, and the shorter to find entry points.

Suppose you find that a 22-day EMA does a good job identifying trends in your market. Plot it, but then divide its length in half and plot an 11-day EMA on the same screen in a different color. Continue to use the 22-day EMA to identify bull and bear moves, but use pullbacks to the shorter EMA to identify entry points.

Moving averages help identify trends and decide whether to trade long or short. They help mark value areas for entering trades. To find exit points, we turn to our next tool, channels on moving averages.

Channels

Markets are manic-depressive beasts. They rise in powerful rallies, only to collapse in breathtaking declines. A stock catches the public's fancy, shoots up 20 points one day, and then slides 24 points down the next. What drives those moves? Fundamental values change slowly, but waves of greed, fear, optimism, and despair drive prices up and down.

How can you tell when a market has reached an undervalued or over-valued level, a zone for buying or selling? Market technicians can use channels to find those levels. A channel, or an envelope, consists of two lines, one above and one below a moving average. There are two main types of channels: straight envelopes and standard deviation channels, also known as Bollinger bands.

In Bollinger bands the spread between the upper and lower lines keeps changing in response to volatility. When volatility rises, Bollinger bands spread wide, but when markets become sleepy, those bands start squeezing the moving average. This feature makes them useful for options traders since volatility drives options prices. In a nutshell, when Bollinger bands become narrow, volatility is low, and options should be bought. When they swing far apart, volatility is high, and options should be sold or written.

Traders of stocks and futures are better off with straight channels or envelopes. They keep a steady distance from a moving average, providing steadier price targets. Draw both lines a certain percentage above or below the EMA. If you use dual moving averages, draw channel lines parallel to the longer one.

A moving average reflects the average consensus of value, but what is the meaning of a channel? The upper channel line reflects the power of bulls to push prices above the average consensus of value. It marks the normal limit of market optimism. The lower channel line reflects the power of bears to push prices below the average consensus of value. It marks the normal limit of market pessimism. A well-drawn channel helps diagnose mania and depression. Most software programs draw channels according to this formula:

$$\text{Upper channel line} = \text{EMA} + \text{EMA} \cdot \text{Channel coefficient}$$
$$\text{Lower channel line} = \text{EMA} - \text{EMA} \cdot \text{Channel coefficient}$$

A well-drawn channel contains the bulk of prices, with only a few extremes poking out. Adjust the coefficient until the channel contains approximately 95 percent of all prices for the past several months. Mathematicians call this the *second standard deviation channel*. Most software packages make this adjustment very easy.

Find proper channel coefficients for any market by trial and error. Keep adjusting them until the channel holds approximately 95% of all data, with only the highest tops and the lowest bottoms sticking out. Drawing a channel is like trying on a shirt. Choose the size in which the entire body fits comfortably, with only the wrists and the neck poking out.

Different trading vehicles and timeframes require different channel widths. Volatile markets require wider channels and higher coefficients. The longer the timeframe, the wider the channel; weekly channels tend to be twice as wide as dailies. Stocks tend to require wider channels than futures. A good time to review and adjust channels in futures is when an old contract nears expiration and you switch to the new front month.

A channel drawn in an uptrend tends to fit the peaks. Rallies in a bull market are much stronger than declines, and bottoms seldom reach the lower channel line. In a downtrend, a channel tends to track bottoms, while the tops are too limp to rise to the upper channel line. It is unnecessary to draw two separate channels, one for the tops and the other for the bottoms; just follow the dominant crowd. In a flat market expect both tops and bottoms to touch their channel lines.

When we are bullish, we want to buy value near the rising EMA and take profits when the market becomes overvalued—at or above the upper channel line. When bearish, we want to go short near the falling EMA and cover when the market becomes undervalued—at or below the lower channel line.

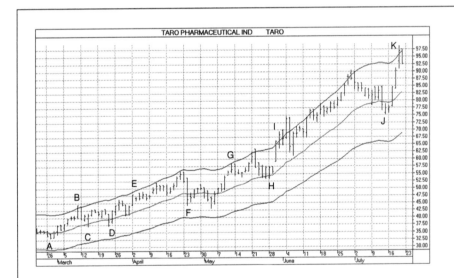

Figure 5.7   Channels for Profit Taking

When the EMA rises, it identifies an uptrend. It is a good idea to buy near that EMA or slightly higher or lower, depending on the stock's recent behavior. At point A, EMA stands at 35, while the low point of the bar reaches 33—a

If you buy near a rising moving average, take profits in the vicinity of the upper channel line. If you sell short near a falling moving average, cover in the vicinity of the lower channel line. Channels catch swings above and below value but not major trends. Those swings can be very rewarding. If you can catch a move from the EMA to the channel line in bond futures, you'll make about $2,000 in profit on a $2,000 margin. If you can do this a few times a year, you'll find yourself far ahead of many professionals.

A beginner who sells his position near the upper channel line may regret it several weeks later. In a bull market, what looks overvalued today may look like a bargain the next month. Professionals do not let such feelings bother them. They are trading, not investing. They know it's easy to be smart looking at old charts, but hard to make decisions at the right edge. They have a system, and they follow it.

When prices blow out of a channel but then return to the moving average, trade in the direction of the slope of that MA, with a profit target near the channel line. Prices break out of channels only during the strongest trends. After they pull back, they often retest the extremes of those break-

---

2-point downside penetration. At point C, the price low penetrates the EMA by 1 point, at D by 2.25, at F by 4, at point H by 0.75, and at J by 4. Those short-term bottoms keep alternating between shallow and deep—an important piece of intelligence when you try to decide where to place your buy order. If the latest penetration was shallow, expect the next one to be deep, and vice versa, and place your buy orders accordingly.

The place to sell stocks purchased near the EMA is at the upper channel line. Looking back, it is easy to see that buy-and-hold would have worked even better in TARO, but the future is not nearly as clear at the right edge of the chart. Buying value near the EMA and taking profits above value, near the upper channel line, is safer and more reliable. Stock bought at A can be sold at B, bought again at C or D and sold at E, and so on.

A trader can grade his performance, based on the percentage of the channel he takes in profits on any given trade. For example, at the right edge of the chart, the upper channel line stands at 97 and the lower at 69, making the channel 28 points high. An A trader should get the minimum of 30% or 8.4 points out of the next trade, a B trader 20% or 5.6 points, and a C trader 10% or 2.8 points.

At the right edge of the chart, prices are hitting the upper channel line. It is time to take profits on stocks purchased in area J, near the EMA, and wait for a pullback.

outs. A breakout from a channel gives us confidence to trade again in its direction.

Prices occasionally take off on wild runaway trends. They break out of a channel and stay out for a long time, without pulling back to their EMA. When you recognize such a powerful move, you have a choice: stand aside or switch to a system for trading impulse moves. Professional traders, once they find a technique that works for them, tend to stay with it. They'd rather miss a trade than change to an unfamiliar style.

If a moving average is essentially flat, go long at the lower channel line, sell short at the upper channel line, and take profits when prices return to their moving average. The upper channel line marks an overbought zone. If the market is relatively flat on long-term charts, rallies to the upper channel line then provide shorting opportunities, whereas declines to the lower channel line provide buying opportunities. Professionals tend to trade against deviations and for the return to normalcy. Amateurs think that every breakout will be followed by a massive runaway move. Once in a rare while the amateurs are right, but in the long run it pays to bet like the pros. They use channels to find when the market has outrun itself and where it is likely to reverse.

How to Grade Your Performance   Imagine two friends taking a college course. Both have similar abilities and backgrounds, but one takes a test each week, while the other waits for a final. All other factors being equal, which of them is likely to get a higher grade on the exam? The one who waited or the one who took weekly tests?

Most educational systems test students at regular intervals. Testing prompts people to fill the gaps in their knowledge. Students who take tests throughout the year tend to do better on their finals. Frequent tests help improve performance.

Markets keep testing us, only most traders don't bother to look up their grades. They gloat over profits or trash confirmation slips for losing trades. Neither bragging nor beating yourself makes you a better trader.

The market grades every trade and posts results on a wall, only most traders have no clue where to look. Some count money, but that's a very crude measure, which does not compare performance in different markets at different prices. You may take more money from a sloppy trade in a big expensive market than from an elegant entry and exit in a difficult narrow market. Which of them reveals a higher level of skill? Money is important but it doesn't always provide the best measure of success.

Channels help us grade the quality of our trades.

When you enter a trade, measure the height of the channel from the upper to the lower line. If you use daily charts to find trades, measure the daily channel; if you use a 10-minute chart, measure the channel on a 10-minute chart; and so on. When you exit that trade, calculate the number of points you've taken as a percentage of the channel. That is your performance grade.

If a stock is trading at 80 with a 10% channel, then the upper channel line is at 88 and the lower at 72. Suppose you buy that stock at 80 and sell it at 84. If you take 4 points out of the 16-point channel, then your grade is $\frac{4}{16}$ or 25%. Where does that place you on the rating curve?

Any trade where you take 30% or more out of a channel earns you an A. If you take between 20 and 30%, your grade is a solid B. If you grab between 10 and 20%, you earn a C. You get a D by taking less than 10% out of a channel or running a loss.

Good traders keep good records. Your first essential record is a spreadsheet of all your trades (we'll review this in Chapter 8, "The Organized Trader"). Add two columns to your spreadsheet. Use the first to record the height of the channel when you enter the trade. Use the second to calculate what percentage of that channel you've grabbed exiting that trade. Keep monitoring your grades to see whether your performance is improving or deteriorating, steady or erratic. Back in college, professors used to grade you. Now you can use channels to find out your grades and become a better trader.

What Markets to Trade?   Channels can help us decide which stocks or futures to trade and which to leave alone. A stock may have great fundamentals or beautiful technical signals, but measure its channel before you put on a trade. It'll show you whether the swings are wide enough to be worth trading.

You may look at a volatile stock whose channel height is 30 points. If you are an A trader, you should be able to get 30%, or 9 points, out of a trade. That will be more than enough to pay commissions, cover slippage, and leave you with profits. On the other hand, if you look at an inexpensive stock whose channel is only 5 points high, then an A trader would be shooting for a paltry 1.5-point gain. That would leave you with next to nothing after commissions and slippage—leave that stock alone, no matter how good it looks.

What if your performance slips a bit or the market throws you a curve? What if you earn only a C and take only 10% out of a channel? The first stock, with its 30-point channel, will return 3 points profit—enough to make some money after expenses. The stock with a 5-point channel will return only half a point, and commissions and slippage may push you into negative territory! Beginners are often seduced by low-priced stocks with strong technical patterns. They cannot understand why they keep losing money. When there is no room for the stock to swing, a trader can't win.

A good technical analyst who was slowly losing money called me for a consultation. When I asked him to fax me his charts, he showed $10 and $15 stocks whose channels were only $2 to $4 tall. There was simply no room for price swings, while commissions, slippage, and expenses continued to chip away at his equity. If you're going to support yourself by fishing, find a channel where the fish are big enough.

Once you become interested in a new stock, draw a channel to see whether it's wide enough to trade. We like to think of ourselves as A traders and all-around A people, but what if you pull only a C trade? If you take only 10 percent out of this channel, will it be worth trading? Beginning traders should leave alone any stock whose channel is narrower than 10 points, meaning that a C trader can take one point out of it.

A few traders said to me it was OK to trade stocks with narrrow channels, as long as one increased trading size. They think that trading 10,000 shares in a three-point channel is the same as trading 1,000 shares in a 30-point channel, but it is not, because the ratio of slippage to channel is much higher in narrow channels, raising the external barrier to victory.

Low-priced stocks with slender channels can make good investments. Think of Peter Lynch, a famous money manager, looking for his elusive 10-bagger, a stock that goes up 10-fold. A $5 stock is much more likely to rise to $50 than an $80 stock to rally to $800. But those are investments, not trades. As a trader, you are looking to take advantage of short-term swings. That is why you should not waste your energy on any stock whose channel is narrow.

The Rewards of Day-Trading Day-trading seems deceptively easy, and beginners flock to it like moths to a flame. Amateurs look at intraday charts and see strong rallies and steep declines. It looks like the money is there for the picking by any sharp-witted individual with a computer, a modem, and a live data feed. Day-trading firms make fortunes in commissions. They promote day-trading because they need to replace the great majority of customers who flame out. The firms hide customer statistics from the public, but in the year 2000 state regulators in Massachusetts subpoenaed records which showed that after 6 months only 16% of day-traders made money.

There is an old Russian saying: "your elbow is near, yet you can't bite it." Try it now—stretch your neck, bend your arm, go for it. So near, yet so far. It's the same with day-trading—the money is right in front of your face, yet you keep missing it by a few ticks. Why do so many people lose so much money day-trading? There is simply not enough height in intraday channels to make profits. Using channels to select trades sends a powerful message to day-traders.

Look at a few popular actively traded stocks—YHOO, AMZN, and AOL are in the forefront of public attention on the day I write this. The figures are likely to change by the time you read this book, but today I get the following numbers for channel heights on their daily and five-minute charts:

	Daily channel	A-level trader (30%)	C-level trader (10%)	Five-minute channel	A-level trader (30%)	C-level trader (10%)
AOL	20	6	2	3	0.9	0.3
AMZN	21	6.3	2.1	3	0.9	0.3
YHOO	54	16.2	5.4	7	2.1	0.7

A swing trader who uses daily charts to buy and hold for a few days can do very well in these active stocks. He can really clean up if he is an A-level trader, but even if he is a C trader, taking 10% out of a channel, he can stay afloat while he's learning. A person who day-trades the same stocks must be a straight-A trader in order to survive. Anything less, and he'll be eaten alive by slippage, commissions, and expenses.

I can hear a howl of protests from the crowd of vendors who make a good living from day-trading—brokers, software dealers, system sellers, etc. They can roll out their examples of successful day-traders, as if that proves anything! Brilliant day-traders do exist, and I am friends with a handful of them myself. Sadly, it's a very small handful.

The chances of becoming a successful day-trader are very low because the channels on intraday charts are not high enough. You must be a straight-A trader to make money out of those minute swings. The slightest distraction, a bit of market noise, a slight slip of performance, and another day-trader bites the dust.

Day-trading provides fantastic entertainment value. Recreational athletes expect to pay for their sport rather than make money from it.

Recreational day-traders who expect to make money are deluding themselves into believing that they will reach their elbow with their teeth. Maybe tomorrow . . . .

MACD-Histogram

MACD stands for Moving Average Convergence-Divergence. This indicator was developed by Gerald Appel, who combined three moving averages into two MACD lines. We can enhance MACD by plotting it as a histogram, reflecting the distance between those lines. It helps identify trends and rate the power of bulls and bears. It is one of the best tools in technical analysis for catching reversals.

Before we use any indicator, we must understand how it is constructed and what it measures. As noted before, each price represents a momentary consensus of value of market participants. A moving average shows us the average consensus of value during a selected period of time. A fast moving average reflects the average consensus during a short period of time, and a slow moving average during a longer period of time. MACD-Histogram measures changes in consensus by tracking the spread between fast and slow moving averages.

Appel used three exponential moving averages to create MACD:

1. Calculate a 12-day EMA of closing prices.
2. Calculate a 26-day EMA of closing prices.
3. Subtract the 26-day EMA from the 12-day EMA—this is the fast or MACD line.
4. Calculate a 9-day EMA of the fast line—this is the slow or signal line.

The values of 12, 26, and 9 have become standard numbers, used as defaults in most software packages. My testing shows that changing these values has little impact on MACD signals, unless you go way out on a limb and seriously distort their relationships by more than doubling one but not the others. If you track several markets and do not have the time to customize your indicators, you can accept the default values of MACD. If you follow only a few markets, it makes sense to experiment with higher and lower MACD values to find those that more closely track turning points in your stocks or futures. If your software doesn't include MACD, you may use two EMAs (for example, 12-day and 26-day) in lieu of the fast and slow MACD lines. Then apply the MACD-Histogram formula, on the next page, to the spread between those two averages.

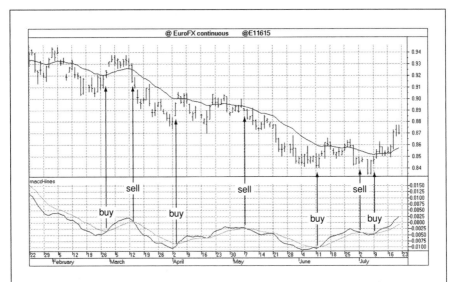

Figure 5.8   MACD Lines

Entry and exit signals are rarely symmetrical. The indicator that gives you good entry signals is usually not the best indicator for exits; some other tool will do a better job. MACD lines give entry signals when the fast line crosses the slow line. If the fast line crosses above, it gives a signal to go long. When it crosses below, it gives a signal to sell short. Waiting for a crossover in the opposite direction to close out a position is not a good idea because by that time a lion's share of profits will have evaporated.

Can you find a trading system in this chart? MACD lines tell you to enter at the crossover, but how will you decide when to exit? What tools can you use to find out when a market surge is starting to fade and hop off with profit?

At the right edge of the chart MACD lines are in a buy mode, with a fast line above the slow and both rising. Prices are hovering above the EMA—an overvalued level. Buying at the right edge would mean taking a "greater fool theory" trade. Placing a buy order in the vicinity of the rising EMA would allow us to buy value.

The fast line of MACD reflects a short-term consensus of value, while the slow signal line reflects a longer-term consensus. When the fast line rises above the slow line, it shows that market participants are becoming more bullish. When bulls are becoming stronger, it is a good time to get long. When the fast line of MACD falls below the slow line, it shows that market participants are becoming bearish. When bears become stronger, it is a good time to get short. MACD lines follow trends, and their crossovers mark trend reversals. Like all trend-following indicators, they work best when markets are moving but lead to whipsaws during choppy periods. We can make MACD more useful by converting it into MACD-Histogram.

MACD-Histogram = Fast MACD line − Slow signal line

MACD-Histogram measures the spread between short-term and long-term moving averages and plots it as a histogram. It reflects the difference between short-term and long-term consensus of value. Some software packages include MACD lines but not MACD-Histogram. In that case, run MACD lines, return to the menu and run an indicator called *spread* (or similar), which should measure the spread between the two lines and plot it as a histogram.

When you look at MACD lines, their spread may appear tiny, but MACD-Histogram rescales it to fit the screen. The slope of MACD-Histogram shows whether bulls or bears are growing stronger. That slope is defined by the

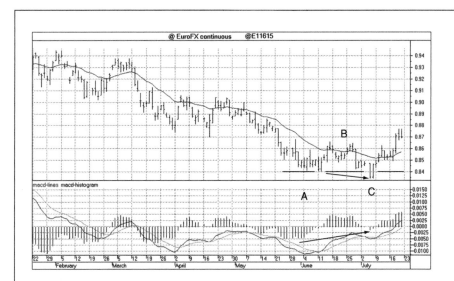

Figure 5.9 MACD-Histogram

A very powerful signal of MACD-Histogram, which occurs only once or twice per year on a daily chart, is a divergence between the indicator peaks or bottoms and price extremes. In area A the Euro grinds down to a low of

relationship between the two latest bars. When the bars of MACD-Histogram rise (like the pattern of letters g-G), they show that the crowd is becoming bullish—it is a good time to be long. When the slope of MACD-Histogram declines (like in letters Q-q), it shows that the crowd is becoming bearish—it is a good time to be short.

Markets run on a two-party system—the bulls and the bears. When MACD-Histogram rises, it shows that bulls are becoming stronger, and when it declines, it shows that bears are becoming stronger. MACD-Histogram helps you bet on the winning party and sell short the opposition.

The Strongest Signal MACD-Histogram gives two types of signals. One is ordinary, and we see it at every bar—it is the slope of MACD-Histogram. An uptick of MACD-Histogram shows that bulls are stronger than they were at the previous bar, and a downtick shows that bears are gaining. Those upticks and downticks provide minor buy and sell signals, but we shouldn't read too much into them. Markets do not move in

---

84 cents and MACD-Histogram confirms that low by tracing its own bottom, A. Prices rally into area B, and a strong rally of MACD-Histogram confirms its strength. It rises to a new multi-month high, showing that bulls are becoming stronger below the surface of the bear market. Prices trace a double top in area B. The second top of MACD-Histogram in that area is a little lower than the first, warning of the imminent resumption of the downtrend. So far, the indicator and prices are in gear, but from this point they diverge.

In area C prices crash to a new bear market low, while MACD-Histogram stops just below its centerline, creating a more shallow bottom than during its previous decline. When it ticks up from that low, it completes the bullish divergence and shows that bears have run out of steam and bulls are taking over.

When two or three diverse technical tools flash the same message, they confirm one another. Notice that prices have traced a false downside breakout in area C. That breakout has cleaned out stops placed by bulls and sucked in the most rabid bears who shorted. Premature bulls have been shaken out, late bears have been trapped, and the upside reversal is complete. Those trapped bears will have to cover shorts when they can no longer stand the pain, adding fuel to the rally.

At the right edge of the chart prices are shooting higher from a bullish divergence. This powerful pattern usually propels prices for weeks if not months.

straight lines, and it's normal for MACD-Histogram to keep ticking up and down.

The other signal occurs rarely, only a couple of times per year on the daily charts of most markets, but it's worth waiting for because it is the strongest signal in technical analysis. That signal is a divergence between the peaks and bottoms of price and MACD-Histogram. A divergence occurs when the trend of price highs and lows goes one way and the trend of tops and bottoms in MACD-Histogram goes the opposite way. Those patterns take several weeks or even more than a month to develop on the daily charts.

A bullish divergence occurs when prices trace a bottom, rally, and then sink to a new low. At the same time MACD-Histogram traces a different pattern. When it rallies from its first bottom, that rally lifts it above the zero line, "breaking the back of the bear." When prices sink to a new low, MACD-Histogram declines to a more shallow bottom. At that point, prices are lower, but the bottom of MACD-Histogram is higher, showing that bears are weaker and the downtrend is ready for a reversal. MACD-Histogram gives a buy signal when it ticks up from its second bottom.

Occasionally, the second bottom is followed by a third. This is why traders must use stops and proper money management. There are no certainties in the markets, only probabilities. Even a reliable pattern such as a divergence of MACD-Histogram fails occasionally, which is why we must exit if prices fall below their second bottom. We must preserve our trading capital and reenter when MACD-Histogram ticks up from its third bottom, as long as it is higher than the first.

A bearish divergence occurs when prices rise to a new high, decline, and then rise to a higher peak. MACD-Histogram gives the first sign of trouble when it breaks below its zero line during the decline from its first peak. When prices reach a higher high, MACD-Histogram rises to a much lower high. It shows that bulls are weaker, and prices are rising simply out of inertia and are ready to reverse.

The Hound of the Baskervilles   MACD-Histogram offers traders what x-rays offer doctors, showing the strength or weakness of the bone below the surface of the skin. Bulls or bears may appear powerful when prices reach a new extreme, but a divergence of MACD-Histogram shows that the dominant party is becoming weak and prices are ready to reverse.

Go long when MACD-Histogram traces a bullish divergence, that is, when prices fall to a new low while the indicator ticks up from a more shallow low. Get long after MACD-Histogram ticks up from its second bottom.

A bottom that is more shallow than the preceding one shows that bears have grown weaker, and the uptick tells us that bulls are taking over. Place a protective stop below the latest bottom. Rallies from bullish divergences tend to be very powerful, but you must always use protection in case a signal does not work out.

An aggressive trader can make that stop "stop-and reverse," meaning that if stopped out of a long position, he will reverse and go short. When a super-strong signal doesn't pan out, it shows that something is fundamentally changing below the surface of the market. If you buy on the strongest signal in technical analysis and then your stop gets hit, it means that bears are especially strong, making it worthwhile to sell short. Reversing positions from long to short is usually not the best idea, but the failure of a divergence of MACD-Histogram is an exception.

I call this a Hound of the Baskervilles signal, after a story by Sir Arthur Conan Doyle. Sherlock Holmes was called to investigate a murder on a country estate. His clue came from the fact that the family dog did not bark while the crime was being committed. That indicated the dog knew the criminal, and the murder was an inside job. Sherlock Holmes received his signal not from the action but from the lack of expected action. When a divergence of MACD-Histogram fails to produce a reversal, it gives a Hound of the Baskervilles signal.

Go short when the MACD-Histogram traces a bearish divergence, that is, when prices rise to a new high but the indicator ticks down from a lower peak. When the crowd gets on its hind legs and roars, it is tempting to throw caution to the wind, close our eyes, and buy. When the crowd becomes manic, it is hard to remain cool, but an intelligent trader looks for MACD-Histogram divergences. If prices rally, decline, and then rally to a higher level, but MACD-Histogram rallies, falls below its zero line, breaking the back of the bull, and rallies again, but to a lower level, it creates a bearish divergence. It shows that bulls have grown weaker, the stock is rising out of inertia, and as soon as that inertia runs out, the stock is likely to collapse.

MACD-Histogram flashes a signal to go short when it ticks down from its second peak. Once short, place a stop above the latest rally peak. Placing stops when shorting near the tops is notoriously difficult because of high volatility. Trading smaller positions allows you to place wider stops.

Divergences between MACD-Histogram and prices on the daily charts are almost always worth trading. Divergences on the weekly charts usually mark transitions between bull and bear markets.

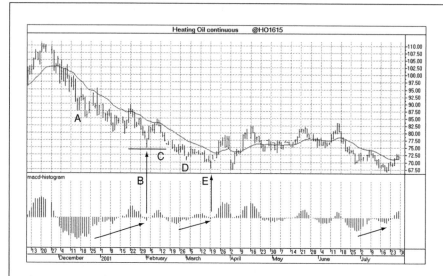

Figure 5.10   The Hound of the Baskervilles Signal

Heating oil, along with the rest of the oil complex, ran up to an historic high in November 2000. Then the demand shrunk, new supplies entered the market, bullish mania was broken, and oil began to slide. In December, it fell to 85 cents (point A), with MACD-Histogram tracing a new massive low, which

When MACD-Histogram reaches a new multi-month peak, it indicates that bulls are extremely strong, and the corresponding price peak is likely to be retested or exceeded. When MACD-Histogram falls to a new multi-month low, it shows that bears are extremely strong, and the corresponding price low is likely to be retested or exceeded.

When MACD-Histogram rises to a new record peak, it shows a terrific splash of bullish enthusiasm. Even if bulls pause to catch their breath, the upside inertia is so strong that the rally is likely to resume after a pause. When MACD-Histogram drops to a new low, it shows that bears are extremely strong. Even if bulls manage to stage a rally, the sheer downside inertia is likely to drive the market to retest or exceed its low.

MACD-Histogram works like headlights on a car—it lights up a stretch of the road ahead. It doesn't show you the entire way home, but lets you see far enough so that driving at a normal speed you can prepare for the twists and turns ahead.

indicated that bears were extremely strong. There was a brief reflex rally to the EMA, while the indicator turned positive (breaking the back of the bear) and then declined to a more shallow low (point B). At that time prices traced out a kangaroo tail, reaching down to 75 cents, and turned up. That bullish divergence, combined with a tail, gave a buy signal. Remember, no matter how strong the signal, a serious trader needs to use stops.

Heating oil resumed its decline and gave a Hound of the Baskervilles sell signal when prices violated their bottom B in area C. It paid to switch to the short side then because heating oil eventually slid below 68. A violation of a bullish divergence of MACD-Histogram is a prime example of the Hound of the Baskervilles signal. The underlying fundamentals must be extremely strong to violate a divergence, and one is well advised to trade in the direction of the break after the stop is hit.

If you have the discipline to use stops and reverse after a divergence is violated, you are not going to be afraid the next time you see a divergence. After seeing a new bullish divergence D-E you'll put on a trade again, using the same principles and rules.

At the right edge of the chart a minor bullish divergence is taking shape. Prices have briefly violated their March-April lows and rallied, completing a false downside breakout and giving a bullish signal. The EMA has stopped declining and gone flat. From here, heating oil should be traded from the long side, with a stop below the recent low.

Force Index

Force Index is an oscillator developed by this author and first described in *Trading for a Living*. The decision to reveal Force Index was one of the hardest in writing that book. I felt reluctant to disclose my private weapon but remembered how resentful I used to feel while reading books by authors who wrote, in so many words, "Now, of course, you wouldn't expect me to tell you everything," I decided I would write either everything or nothing, and describe Force Index.

The disclosure did me no harm. Force Index continues to work for me as well as it did before. Very few software companies have included it in their systems, and its behavior on my charts hasn't changed. This reminds me of a good friend with whom I served on a ship. He was the biggest smuggler I ever met, but he never hid anything far away. Sometimes he'd put the contraband right on his desk, under the noses of customs officers. Leaving a secret in the open can be the best way of hiding it.

Force Index helps identify turning points in any market by tying together three essential pieces of information—the direction of price movement, its extent, and volume. Price represents the consensus of value among market participants. Volume reflects their level of commitment, financial as well as emotional. Price reflects what people think, and volume what they feel. Force Index links mass opinion with mass emotion by asking three questions: Is the price going up or down? How big is the change? How much volume did it take to move the price?

It is very useful to measure the force of a move because strong moves are more likely to continue than weak ones. Divergences between peaks and bottoms of prices and Force Index help nail important turning points. Spikes of Force Index identify zones of mass hysteria, where trends become exhausted. Here is the Force Index formula:

$$\text{Force Index} = (\text{Close}_{\text{today}} - \text{Close}_{\text{yesterday}}) \cdot \text{Volume}_{\text{today}}$$

If the market closes higher today than yesterday, Force Index is positive, and if it closes lower, Force Index is negative. The greater the spread between today's and yesterday's closes, the greater the force. The higher the volume, the more forceful the move.

Force Index is greater when the market moves far on high volume and lesser when the market moves a short distance on thin volume. When the market closes unchanged, Force Index equals zero.

Smooth Is Better   We can plot Force Index as a histogram, with positive readings above the zero line and negative readings below. The raw Force Index looks very jagged, up one day, down the next. It works better if we smooth it with an exponential moving average and plot it as a line.

If we smooth Force Index with a long-term EMA of 13 days or longer, it will measure long-term shifts in the balance of power between bulls and bears. To help pinpoint entries and exits, we should smooth Force Index with a very short moving average, such as a two-day EMA.

When the trend of our stock or future is up and the two-day EMA of Force Index declines below zero, it gives a buy signal. When the trend is down and the two-day EMA of Force Index rallies above zero, it gives a sell signal.

The key to using a short-term Force Index is to combine it with a trend-following indicator. For example, when the 22-day EMA of price is up and the two-day EMA of Force Index becomes negative, it reveals a short-term splash of bearishness within an uptrend, a buying opportunity. Once long,

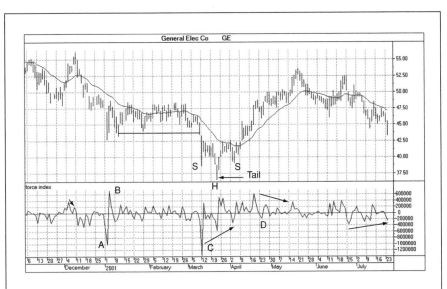

Figure 5.11   Force Index—Two-Day EMA

Spikes of a short-term, two-bar Force Index mark areas where trends exhaust themselves. The downward spike in area A showed that the move from 56 to 43 was at its end. Curiously enough, it was immediately followed by an upward spike in area B. This pattern of two adjacent spikes, pointing in opposite directions, shows a great deal of confusion in the markets and is usually followed by a period of flat prices. GE remained flat for almost two months following those two opposing spikes.

Technical patterns confirm one another when they give similar messages. The downward spike in area C showed that the downtrend was becoming exhausted. That bullish signal was followed by a bullish divergence between prices and Force Index, which traced a series of higher bottoms while prices tried to grind lower. For fans of classical charting, there was a "reverse head-and-shoulders" pattern. Finally, there was a kangaroo tail at the very low. It looks as if GE keeps ringing a bell and telling us that the decline is over, it is ready to go up! In area D, half-way through the rise from 37 to 53, Force Index starts tracing a bearish divergence, warning that bulls are losing power. When the EMA follows this up by turning down in May, the bullish game is over. It is the last good chance to take profits and position short.

At the right edge of the chart the EMA is down and prices have just fallen to a new low, but Force Index is starting to trace a bullish divergence. It tells you to tighten stops on short positions.

you have several exit strategies. If you're very short-term oriented, sell the day after Force Index turns positive, but if your time horizon is wider, hold until prices hit their channel line or the EMA turns flat.

When the 22-day EMA of prices is down, and the two-day EMA of Force Index rallies above zero, it reveals a short-term splash of bullishness within a downtrend, a shorting opportunity. If you're very short-term oriented, grab a quick profit and cover the day after Force Index turns negative. If your time horizon is wider, use the lower channel wall for the profit target.

When the two-day EMA of Force Index spikes up or down, exceeding its normal peaks or lows by several times, it identifies an exhaustion move— a signal to take profits on existing positions.

When the trend is up and the two-day EMA of Force Index traces a sharp upward spike, eight or more times above its normal height for the past two months, it marks a buying panic. The bulls are afraid of missing the train and bears feel trapped and cover shorts at any cost. Such spikes tend to occur during end-stages of bull moves. They tell you it is a good time to take profits on long positions. Prices often rally to retest the spike day's high. By then the spirit is gone from the rally and other indicators start developing bearish divergences, warning of a trend reversal.

When the two-day EMA of Force Index traces a sharp downward spike during a downtrend, four or more times deeper than normal for the past two months, it marks an hysterical stage of the downmove. It identifies a selling panic among the bulls, who are dumping their holdings at any price to get out. Such spikes tend to occur at the end-stages of bear moves. They tell you that it's a good time to take profits on short positions. Prices sometimes retest the spike day's low, but by then most indicators are developing bullish divergences and an upside reversal is coming.

Spikes are somewhat similar to the kangaroo tails we discussed earlier (see "The Reality of the Chart" on page 73). The difference between them is that tails are purely price-based, while Force Index reflects volume as well as prices. Tails and spikes identify panics among the weakest players. Once they get flushed out, the trend is ready to reverse.

A Reversal Is Coming   Trend reversals do not have to come as a surprise; divergences between Force Index and price usually precede them. If the market is trying to rally, but the peaks in Force Index are becoming lower, it is a sign of weakness among the bulls. If a stock or a future is trying to decline, but the bottoms in Force Index are becoming more shallow, it is a sign of weakness among the bears.

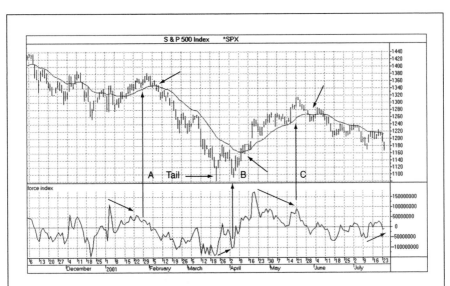

Figure 5.12 Force Index—13-Day EMA

A longer-term Force Index, smoothed with a 13-day EMA, identifies longer-term shifts of power between bulls and bears. When it is below zero, bears are in control, and when it is above that line, the bulls are in charge. Divergences between the peaks of this indicator and price peaks precede market tops, whereas divergences between their lows precede important bottoms.

In area A, Force Index traces a lower peak during the final price peak. It reveals that bulls are weak and a top is likely. A few days later, the EMA ticks down, confirming that a new downtrend has begun. A mirror image of this pattern occurs in area B, where we see a lower closing price, a higher bottom of Force Index, and a few days later an uptick of the EMA, auguring an important rally. Notice also the double bottom in that area—a kangaroo tail, followed by a retest of the lows. This is one of many examples of patterns and indicators reinforcing each other. In area C Force Index traces a bearish divergence and warns you that the bull move is over. A few days later the EMA ticks down, and it's all downhill from there. The market keeps sending you messages—all you have to do is listen.

At the right edge of the chart the market is declining, confirmed by the falling EMA. Force Index is starting to trace a bullish divergence; it is time to tighten stops on short positions.

A divergence between an EMA of Force Index and price shows that the trend is ready to reverse. Divergences between the patterns of peaks or bottoms of Force Index and prices show that the trend is becoming weaker. The power of this message depends on the length of the EMA with which we smooth our Force Index. If we use a very short EMA of Force Index, such as two days, its divergences help pinpoint the ends of short-term trends lasting a week or so. If we use a 13-day or longer EMA of Force Index, we can identify the ends of longer-term moves that last months.

If the trend is up and you are long, take profits when the two-day EMA of Force Index traces a bearish divergence—a lower peak in the indicator during a higher price in the market. If you are short, take profits when the two-day EMA of Force Index traces a bullish divergence—a higher bottom in the indicator during a lower price in the market. Take your profits and monitor the market from the sidelines. It is cheaper to exit and reenter than sit through a countertrend move.

It is essential to combine Force Index with trend-following indicators. If you use this oscillator alone, it will lead to overtrading because it is so sensitive. In that case, only your broker will make money. The signals of a short-term oscillator must be filtered using a long-term trend-following indicator. This is the key principle of the Triple Screen trading system.

The Fifth Bullet

A clip for an old army rifle held only five bullets. Going into action with such a weapon forced one to take good aim instead of shooting wildly. This is a good attitude for trading the markets.

By now, we have selected four bullets—exponential moving averages, channels, MACD-Histogram, and Force Index. A moving average and MACD are trend-following indicators. Channels, Force Index, and MACD-Histogram are oscillators. What fifth bullet shall we pick?

To help you choose your fifth bullet, we'll review several more tools. Feel free to range beyond this menu, but make sure to understand how each indicator is constructed and what it measures. Test your indicators to develop confidence in their signals.

In *Trading for a Living* I described more than a dozen technical indicators. There are dozens more in other books on technical analysis. Quality and the depth of understanding are more important than quantity. A drowning amateur, grasping at straws, keeps adding indicators. A mature trader selects a few effective tools, learns to use them well, and focuses on system development and money management.

There are no magic bullets in the markets. There is no perfect or ultimate indicator. A trader who becomes preoccupied with indicators quickly reaches the point of diminishing returns. Your choice of analytic tools depends on your trading style. The idea is to select your tools and quickly move on to where the real money is—system development and risk management.

Elder-ray Elder-ray is an indicator developed by this author and named for its similarity to x-rays. It shows the structure of bullish and bearish power below the surface of the markets. Elder-ray combines a trend-following moving average with two oscillators to show when to enter and exit long or short positions. Most software developers fail to include Elder-ray in their packages, but you can do it yourself with minimal programming.

To plot Elder-ray, divide your computer screen into three horizontal panels. Plot a chart of the stock you plan to analyze in the top panel and add an exponential moving average. The second and third panels will contain Bull Power and Bear Power, plotted as histograms. Here are the Elder-ray formulae:

$$\text{Bull Power} = \text{High} - \text{EMA}$$
$$\text{Bear Power} = \text{Low} - \text{EMA}$$

A moving average reflects the average consensus of value. The high of each bar reflects the maximum power of bulls during that bar. The low of each bar marks the maximum power of bears during that bar.

Elder-ray works by comparing the power of bulls and bears during each bar with the average consensus of value. Bull Power reflects the maximum power of bulls relative to the average consensus, and Bear Power the maximum power of bears relative to that consensus.

We plot Bull Power in the second windowpane as a histogram. Its height reflects the distance between the top of the price bar and the EMA—the maximum power of bulls. We plot Bear Power in the third windowpane. Its depth reflects the distance between the low of the price bar and the EMA—the maximum power of bears.

When the high of a bar is above the EMA, Bull Power is positive. When the entire bar sinks below the EMA, which happens during severe declines, Bull Power becomes negative. When the low of a bar is below the EMA, Bear Power is negative. When the entire bar rises above the EMA, which happens during wild rallies, Bear Power becomes positive.

The slope of a moving average identifies the current trend of the market. When it rises, it shows that the crowd is becoming more bullish; it is a good time to be long. When it falls, it shows that the crowd is becoming more bearish; it is a good time to be short. Prices keep getting away from a moving average but snap back to it, as if pulled by a rubber band. Bull Power and Bear Power show the length of that rubber band. Knowing the

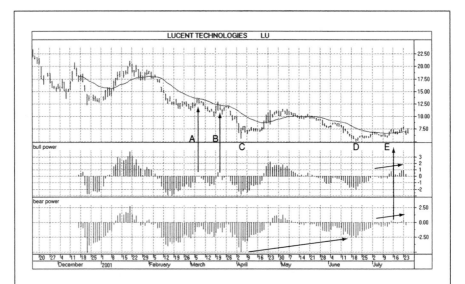

Figure 5.13   Elder-ray

"Buy low, sell high" sounds good, but traders and investors seem to have been more comfortable buying Lucent above 70 than below 7. Perhaps they are not as rational as the efficient market theorists would like us to believe? Elder-ray gives rational traders a glimpse into what is going on below the surface of the market.

When the trend, identified by the 22-day EMA, is down and bulls are under water, the rallies back to the surface mark shorting opportunities (arrows A and B). Prices draw a kangaroo tail in area C, and a sharp rally follows. A rise from 5.50 to 11.50 is nothing to sneeze at; cheaper stocks tend to have bigger percentage gains. In area D, Lucent slides to a new low, but Bear Power traces a more shallow bottom, completing a bullish divergence. That false downside breakout traps bears. As the rally accelerates, Bear power becomes positive and each dip of Bear power back to its zero line marks a buying opportunity (area E).

normal height of Bull or Bear Power reveals how far prices are likely to get away from their moving average before returning. Elder-ray offers one of the best insights into where to take profits—at a distance away from the moving average that equals the average Bull Power or Bear Power.

Elder-ray gives buy signals in uptrends when Bear Power turns negative and then ticks up. A negative Bear Power means that the bar is straddling the EMA, with its low below the average consensus of value. Waiting for Bear Power to turn negative forces you to buy value rather than chase runaway moves. The actual buy signal is given by an uptick of Bear Power, which shows that bears are starting to lose their grip and the uptrend is about to resume. Take profits at the upper channel line or when a trend-following indicator stops rising. Profits may be greater if you ride the uptrend to its conclusion, but taking profits at the upper channel line is more reliable.

Elder-ray gives shorting signals in downtrends when Bull Power turns positive and then ticks down. We can identify the downtrend by a declining daily or weekly EMA. A positive Bull Power shows that the bar is straddling the EMA, with its high above the average consensus of value. Waiting for Bull Power to turn positive before shorting forces you to sell at or above value instead of chasing waterfall declines. The actual shorting signal is given by a downtick of Bull Power, which shows that bulls are starting to slip and the downtrend is about to resume. Once short, take profits at the lower channel line or when the trend-following indicator stops falling, depending on your style. You can make more money by holding on for the duration of the downtrend, but it is easier to achieve steady results by taking profits at the lower channel line. A beginning trader is better off learning to catch short swings, while leaving long-term trend trading for a later stage of development.

Stochastic   This oscillator identifies overbought and oversold conditions, helping us buy low or sell high. Just as important, it helps avoid buying at high prices or shorting at low prices. This indicator was popularized by George Lane decades ago and is now included in most software packages.

Stochastic measures the capacity of bulls to close prices near the top of the recent trading range and the capacity of bears to close them near the bottom. It ties the high of the range, representing the maximum power of bulls, with the low, representing the maximum power of bears, and with closing prices, the final balance in the markets, representing the actions of smart money.

Bulls may push prices higher during the day, or bears may push them lower, but Stochastic measures their performance at closing time—the crucial money-counting time in the markets. If bulls lift prices during the day but cannot close them near the high of the recent range, Stochastic turns down, identifying weakness and giving a sell signal. If bears push prices down during the day but cannot close them near the lows, Stochastic turns up, identifying strength and giving a buy signal.

There are two types of Stochastic: Fast and Slow. Both consist of two lines: the fast line, called %K, and the slow line, called %D. We construct Fast Stochastic in two steps and Slow Stochastic in three steps:

1. *Obtain* %K, *the fast line.*

$$\%K = \frac{Close_{today} - Low_n}{High_n - Low_n} \cdot 100$$

where $Close_{today}$ = today's close
Low_n = the lowest low for the selected number of bars
$High_n$ = the highest high for the selected number of bars
n = the number of bars for Stochastic (selected by the trader)

We have to choose the number of days, or bars, over which to calculate Stochastic—the value of n. If we use a low number, below 10, Stochastic will focus on the recent bars and flag minor turning points. If we choose a wider window, Stochastic will look at more data and flag major turns, missing minor ones.

How wide should we make the Stochastic window? Since we use oscillators to catch reversals, short-term windows are better; we should reserve longer time windows for trend-following indicators. Five or seven days are a good starting point, but consider testing longer parameters to find the ones that work best in your market.

2. *Obtain* %D, *the slow line.* We obtain %D by smoothing the fast line %K over a number of bars that is shorter than %K. For example, if we decide to plot a five-day Stochastic, we will use the value of five for the %K formula, above, and three bars for the %D formula, below:

$$\%D = \frac{\text{Three-bar sum of} \left(Close_{today} - Low_n\right)}{\text{Three-bar sum of} \left(High_n - Low_n\right)} \cdot 100$$

Fast Stochastic is very sensitive to price changes, making its lines appear jagged. It pays to add one more step and convert it into a smoother Slow Stochastic. Of course, a computer does this all automatically.

3. *Convert Fast Stochastic into Slow Stochastic.* The slow line of Fast Stochastic becomes the fast line of Slow Stochastic. Repeat step 2, above, to obtain the slow line %D of Slow Stochastic.

Stochastic is designed to oscillate between 0 and 100. Low levels mark oversold markets, and high levels mark overbought markets. Overbought means too high, ready to turn down. Oversold means too low, ready to turn up. Draw horizontal reference lines at levels that have marked previous tops and bottoms, starting with 15 near the lows and 85 near the highs.

Look for buying opportunities when Stochastic nears its lower reference line. Look for selling opportunities when Stochastic nears its upper reference line. Buying when Stochastic is low is emotionally hard because markets usually look terrible near bottoms, which is precisely the right time to buy. When Stochastic rallies to its upper reference line, it tells you to start looking for selling opportunities. This also goes against the grain emotionally. When Stochastic rallies to a top, the market often looks fantastic, which is a good time to sell.

We should not use Stochastic alone, in a mechanical manner. When a strong uptrend takes off, Stochastic quickly becomes overbought and starts flashing sell signals. In a powerful bear market, Stochastic becomes oversold and flashes premature buy signals. This indicator works well only if you use it with a trend-following indicator and take only those Stochastic signals that point in the direction of the main trend.

Should a trader wait for Stochastic to turn up to recognize a buy signal? Should he wait for it to turn down to recognize a sell signal? Not really, because by the time Stochastic turns, a new move is usually under way. If you are looking for an opportunity to enter, the mere fact of Stochastic reaching an extreme gives you a signal.

Go long when Stochastic traces a bullish divergence, that is, when prices fall to a new low but the indicator makes a more shallow low. Go short when Stochastic traces a bearish divergence, that is, when prices rise to a new high but the indicator ticks down from a lower peak than during the previous rally. In an ideal buying situation, the first Stochastic low is below and the second above the lower reference line. The best sell signals occur when the first top of Stochastic is above and the second below the upper reference line.

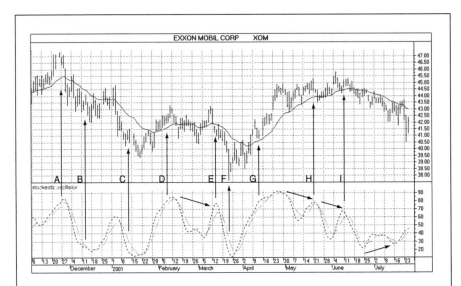

Figure 5.14   Stochastic

It may feel good to buy when prices are high and it brings relief to sell when prices fall, but Stochastic helps you do the right thing—buy low and sell high. When it declines to its lower reference line, it tells you the market is oversold and gives a signal to buy (points B, C, and F). Whether you buy or not, low Stochastic prevents you from shorting when it falls to low levels.

When Stochastic rises to its upper reference line, it gives a sell signal (points A, D, G, and H). A sell signal may be premature in a strong uptrend, but whether you take it or not, one thing is clear—it is too late to buy. Stochastic helps you avoid chasing trends.

Divergences give the strongest signals. At point E, Exxon rises to a double top, while Stochastic traces a lower top—a bearish divergence, a strong sell signal. A powerful rally begins in March, but by May there is a bearish divergence—a sign that the party is coming to an end. There is one more chance to sell and go short when a triple bearish divergence appears at point I—it is all downhill from there.

At the right edge of the chart XOM is declining, confirmed by the falling EMA. Stochastic is trying to trace a bullish divergence, but the second bottom is almost as low as the first; the bears are very strong, and the decline is likely to continue.

Do not buy when Stochastic is above its upper reference line and do not sell short when it is below its lower reference line. These "no go" rules are probably the most useful messages of Stochastic. Moving averages are better than Stochastic at identifying trends, MACD-Histogram is better at identifying reversals, channels are better at identifying profit targets, and Force Index is sharper at catching entry and exit points. The trouble with them is that they give action signals most of the time. Stochastic identifies danger zones, just like a line of red flags on a ski slope marks unsafe areas for skiers. It says "no go" just when you feel tempted to chase a trend.

Ready to Hunt?   Your choice of indicators depends on personal preferences, just like selecting a car. Be sure to combine trend-following indicators, which identify trends, with oscillators, which identify reversals.

In addition to the indicators described above, you may want to take a look at the Directional indicator, which does a good job of signaling trends. It consists of several components, one of which, ADX, helps identify new bull markets. Williams %R is an oscillator similar to Stochastic, especially useful for showing when to pyramid winning positions. Relative Strength Index (RSI) is an oscillator based entirely on closing prices. It helps track the behavior of market professionals who tend to dominate markets at closing time. All of them are described in *Trading for a Living.*

Keep in mind that no single indicator can guarantee you victory in the trading game. Trend-following indicators, such as moving averages, catch trends but produce whipsaws in trading ranges. Oscillators identify tops and bottoms during trading ranges but flash premature countertrend signals when the markets begin to run. Trading signals are easy to recognize in the middle of the chart, but hard to see at the right edge.

There is no magic indicator. All indicators are building blocks of trading systems. A good system uses several tools, combining them so that their negative features filter each other out, while their positive features remain undisturbed.

CHAPTER SIX

TRADING

Beginners become emotional when they trade, but if you want to survive and succeed, you must develop discipline. The moment you become aware of feeling fear or joy, use that as a signal to tighten your discipline and follow your system. You developed that system when the markets were closed and you felt calm. Now it gives you your only chance of survival and success in the markets.

The idea of an automatic trading system is fundamentally flawed. If those systems could work, then the smartest guy with the biggest computer would have cornered the market long ago. Automatic systems do not work because the market is not a mechanical or electronic entity that follows the laws of physics. It is a huge crowd of people acting in accordance with the imperfect laws of mass psychology. Physics and mathematics can help, but trading decisions must take psychology into account.

When you talk with a pro, one of the first questions he'll ask—or not even ask because he'll know the answer from a few of your comments—is whether you are a discretionary trader or a system trader.

A discretionary trader takes in market information and analyzes it using several technical tools. He is likely to shift and apply somewhat different tools to different markets at different times. His decision-making tree has many branches, and he follows them at different times as market conditions change. All branches are connected to the sturdy trunk of his decision-making tree, an inviolate set of rules for risk control.

A system trader develops a mechanical set of rules for entering and exiting trades. He backtests them and puts them on autopilot. At that point, an amateur and a pro go in opposite directions. An amateur, frightened by the market, feels relieved that a system, either his own or bought from someone else, will free him from worry. Market conditions always change and all systems self-destruct, which is why every amateur with a mechanical system must lose money in the end. A pro who puts his system on autopilot continues to monitor it like a hawk. He knows the difference between a normal drawdown period and a time when a system deteriorates and has to be shelved and replaced. A professional system trader can afford to use a mechanical system precisely because he is capable of discretionary trading!

In my experience, system traders tend to achieve more consistent results, but the best and most successful traders use the discretionary approach. The choice depends on your temperament rather than a cold business decision. Some people feel attracted to system trading, others to discretionary trading. Much of what you read in this book deals with discretionary trading. All of these components can be used in systematic trading. This book is written to help both types of traders.

A trading system is an action plan for the market, but no plan can anticipate everything. A degree of judgment is always required, even with the best and most reliable plans.

Think of any other plan or system in your life. For example, you probably have a system for taking your car out of the garage. You need to open the garage door, start the car, warm up the engine, and pull the car out into the street without bumping into walls, running over tricycles, or getting hit by passing trucks.

You have a system in the sense that you perform the same actions each time in the same sequence, not thinking of the routine but paying attention to what is important—watching out for dangers, such as kids on bicycles, or freshly fallen snow, or a neighbor crossing the sidewalk. When you detect an obstacle, you deviate from your system, and return to it after the situation returns to normal. You would not try to design a complete system, which would include dealing with the snow, and the bicyclists, and the neighbors because that system would be too complex and still could never be complete—a neighbor could come into your car's path from another angle. A system automates routine actions and allows you to exercise discretion when needed.

And that's what you need in the markets—a system for finding trades, setting stops, establishing profit targets—all the while paying attention to a heavy truck headed toward you in the shape of a Federal Reserve announcement or a kid on a tricycle in the form of a disappointing earnings report. Many beginners set themselves the impossible task of designing or buying a complete trading system, which is just as impossible as a complete system for pulling your car out of the garage.

I have two friends who earn a good living testing systems for traders. Both are expert programmers. One of them laughed as he told me how he gets at least one phone call a week from yet another amateur who thinks he has discovered the Holy Grail. He wants his automatic set of rules backtested to find the best parameters, and his only concern is that the programmer should not steal his secret! I asked my friend how many profitable automatic systems he found during several years of backtesting.

Not one.

Not one? Doesn't he get discouraged doing this kind of work?

Well, what keeps him going is that he has a handful of steady clients who are successful professional traders. They bring him snippets of trading methods for testing. They may test their parameters for placing stops, the length of MACD, and so on. Then they use their own judgment to bind those snippets into a decision-making tree.

An intelligent trading system includes components that have been backtested, but the trader retains control over his actions. He has several inviolate rules, mostly having to do with risk control and money management, but allows himself latitude in combining those components to reach trading decisions.

An intelligent trading system is an action plan for entering and exiting markets that spells out several specific functions, such as finding trades or protecting capital. Most actions, such as entries, exits, and adjusting stops, can be partly but not fully automated. Thinking is a hard job; a mechanical trading system tempts you by promising you won't have to think any more, but that's a false promise. To be a successful trader you need to use your judgment. A trading system is a style of trading, not an automatic turnkey operation.

SYSTEM TESTING

You must test each indicator, rule, and method before including them in your trading system. Many traders do this by dumping historical data into testing software and obtaining a printout of their system's parameters. The profit-loss ratio, the biggest and the smallest profit or loss, the average profit and loss, the longest winning and losing streaks, the average profit, and the average or the maximum drawdowns give the appearance of objectivity and solidity.

Those printouts provide a false sense of security.

You may have a very nice printout, but what if the system delivers five losses in a row, while you trade real money? Nothing in your testing has prepared you for that, but it happens all the time. You grit your teeth and put on another trade. Another loss. Your drawdown is getting deeper. Will you put on the next trade? Suddenly, an impressive printout looks like a very thin reed on which to hang your future, while your account is being whittled away.

The attraction of electronic testing is such that there is now a small cottage industry of programmers who test systems for a fee. Some traders spend months, if not years, learning to use testing software. A loser who cannot admit he's afraid to trade has a wonderful excuse that he is learning new software. He's like a swimmer who is afraid of water and keeps himself busy ironing his swimsuit.

Only one kind of system testing makes sense. It is slow, it is time-consuming, and it does not lend itself to testing a hundred markets at once, but it's the only method that prepares you for trading. It consists of going through historical data one day at a time, scrupulously writing down your trading signals for the day ahead, then clicking your chart forward and recording the trades and signals for the next day.

Begin by downloading your stock or futures data for a minimum of two years. Swing to the left side of the file, without looking at what happened next. Open your technical analysis program and a spreadsheet. The two most important keys for traders on a computer are Alt and Tab because they let you switch between two programs. Open two windows in your analytic program—one for your long-term chart with its indicators, the other for the short-term chart. Open a spreadsheet, write down your system's rules at the top of the page and create columns for the date, entry date and price, and the exit date and price.

Turn to the weekly chart and note its signal, if any. If it gives you a buy or sell signal, go to the daily chart ending on the same date to see whether it gives you a buy or a sell signal as well. If it does, record the order you have to place in your spreadsheet. Now return to the daily chart and click one day forward. See whether your buy or sell order was triggered. If so, return to the spreadsheet and record the result. Track your trade day by day, calculating stops and deciding where to take profits.

Follow this process throughout your entire data file, advancing a week at a time on the weekly chart, a day at a time on the daily chart. At every click write down your system's signals and your actions.

As you click forward, one day at a time, the market history will slowly unfold and challenge you. You click and a buy signal comes into view. Will you take it? Record your decision in a spreadsheet. Will you take profits at a set target, on a sell signal, or on the basis of price action? You are doing much more than testing a set of rigid rules. Moving ahead day by day, you develop your decision-making skills. This one-bar-at-a-time forward testing is vastly superior to what you get from backtesting software.

How will you deal with gap openings when prices open above your buy level or below your stop? What about limit moves in futures? Should the system be adjusted, changed, or scrapped? Clicking forward one day at a time gets you as close to the real experience of trading as you can ever get without putting on a trade. It puts you in touch with the raw edge of the market, which you can never experience through an orderly printout from a professional system tester.

Manual testing will improve your ability to think, recognize events, and act in the foggy environment of the market. Your trading plans must include certain absolute rules, most of them concerning money management. As long as you stay within those rules, you have much freedom in trading the markets. Your growing levels of knowledge, maturity, judgment, and skill are much more important assets than any computerized testing.

Paper Trading

Paper trading means recording your decision to trade and tracking it as if it were a real trade, only without money. Most of those who paper trade have lost their nerve after getting beat up by the markets. Some people alternate between real trades and paper trades and cannot understand why they seem to make money on paper but lose whenever they put on a real trade.

This happens for two reasons. First, people tend to be less emotional with paper. Good decisions are easier to make when your money is not on the line. Second, good trades often look murky at entry time. The easy-looking ones are more likely to lead to problems. A nervous beginner jumps into obvious-looking trades but paper trades the more promising ones. It goes without saying that hopping between real trading and paper trading is sheer nonsense. You either do one or the other.

There is only one good reason to paper trade—to test your discipline.

If you can download your data at the end of each day, do your homework, write down your orders for the day ahead, watch the opening and record your entries, and then track your market each day, adjusting your profit targets and stops—if you can do all of this for several months in a row, recording your actions, without skipping a day—then you probably have the discipline to trade that market. Someone who is in it for entertainment will not be able to paper trade this way because it requires work.

To paper trade your system, download your data at the end of each day. Apply your tools and techniques, reach trading decisions, calculate stops and profit targets, and write them down for tomorrow. Do not place your orders with a broker, but check whether they would have been triggered and write down those fills. Enter paper trades in your spreadsheet and your trading diary (see Chapter 8, "The Organized Trader"). If you have the willpower to repeat this process daily for several months, then you have the discipline for successful trading with real money.

Still, there is no substitute for trading with real money, because it engages emotions more than any paper trade. It is better to learn by putting on very small real trades than paper trades.

TRIPLE SCREEN UPDATE

One of the most pleasant encounters that occur several times each year is when a trader comes up to me at some conference and tells me how he started trading for a living after studying my book or participating in a Camp. At that point, he may be living and trading on a mountaintop, and as often as not he owns the mountaintop. I noticed long ago that half-way through our conversation these people become slightly apologetic. They tell me they use Triple Screen, but not exactly the way I taught it. They may have modified an indicator, added another screen, substituted a tool, and so forth. Whenever I hear that, I know I am talking to a winner.

First of all, I tell them they owe their success primarily to themselves. I did not teach them any differently than the dozens of others in the same class. Winners have the discipline to take what is offered and use it to succeed. Second, I see their apology for having changed some aspects of my system as an indication of their winning attitude. To benefit from a system, you must test its parameters and fine-tune them until that system becomes your own, even though originally it was developed by someone else. Winning takes discipline, discipline comes from confidence, and the only system in which you can have confidence is the one you have tested on your own data and adapted to your own style.

I developed the Triple Screen trading system in the mid-1980s and first presented it to the public in 1986 in an article in *Futures* magazine. I updated it in *Trading for a Living* and several videos. Here I will review it, focusing on recent enhancements.

What is a trading system? What's the difference between a method, a system, and a technique?

A method is a general philosophy of trading. For example; trade with the trend, buy when the trend is up, and sell after it tops out. Or—buy undervalued markets, go long near historical support levels, and sell after resistance zones have been reached.

A system is a set of rules for implementing a method. For example, if our method is to follow trends, then the system may buy when a multi-week moving average turns up and sell when a daily moving average turns down (get in slow, get out fast). Or—buy when the weekly MACD-Histogram ticks up and sell after it ticks down.

A technique is a specific rule for entering or exiting trades. For example, when a system gives a buy signal, the technique could be to buy when prices exceed the high of the previous day or if prices make a new low during the day but close near the high.

The method of Triple Screen is to analyze markets in several time-frames and use both the trend-following indicators and oscillators. We make a strategic decision to trade long or short using trend-following indicators on long-term charts. We make tactical decisions to enter or exit using oscillators on shorter-term charts. The original method has not changed, but the system—the exact choice of indicators—has evolved over the years, as have the techniques.

Triple Screen examines each potential trade using three screens or tests. Each screen uses a different timeframe and indicators. These screens filter out many trades that seem attractive at first. Triple Screen promotes a careful and cautious approach to trading.

Conflicting Indicators

Technical indicators help identify trends or turns more objectively than chart patterns. Just keep in mind that when you change indicator parameters, you influence their signals. Be careful not to fiddle with indicators until they tell you what you want to hear.

We can divide all indicators into three major groups:

Trend-following indicators help identify trends. Moving averages, MACD lines, Directional system, and others rise when the markets are rising, decline when markets fall, and go flat when markets enter trading ranges.

Oscillators help catch turning points by identifying overbought and oversold conditions. Envelopes or channels, Force Index, Stochastic, Elder-ray, and others show when rallies or declines outrun themselves and are ready to reverse.

Miscellaneous indicators help gauge the mood of the market crowd. Bullish Consensus, Commitments of Traders, New High–New Low Index, and others reflect the general levels of bullishness or bearishness in the market.

Different groups of indicators often give conflicting signals. Trend-following indicators may turn up, telling us to buy, while oscillators become overbought, telling us to sell. Trend-following indicators may turn down, giving sell signals, while oscillators become oversold, giving buy signals. It is easy to fall into the trap of wishful thinking and start following those indicators whose message you like. A trader must set up a system that takes all groups of indicators into account and handles their contradictions.

Conflicting Timeframes

An indicator can call an uptrend and a downtrend in the same stock on the same day. How can this be? A moving average may rise on a weekly chart, giving a buy signal, but fall on a daily chart, giving a sell signal. It may rally on an hourly chart, telling us to go long, but sink on a 10-minute chart, telling us to short. Which of those signals should we take?

Amateurs reach for the obvious. They grab a single timeframe, most often daily, apply their indicators and ignore other timeframes. This works only until a major move swells up from the weeklies or a sharp spike erupts from the hourly charts and flips their trade upside down. Whoever said that ignorance was bliss was not a trader.

People who have lost money with daily charts often imagine they could do better by speeding things up and using live data. If you cannot make money with dailies, a live screen will only help you lose faster. Screens hypnotize losers, but a determined one can get even closer to the market by renting a seat and going to trade on the floor. Pretty soon a margin clerk for the clearing house notices that the new trader's equity has dropped below limit. He sends a runner into the pit who taps that person on the shoulder. The loser steps out and is never seen again—he has "tapped out."

The problem with losers is not that their data is too slow, but their decision-making process is a mess. To resolve the problem of conflicting timeframes, you should not get your face closer to the market, but push yourself further away, take a broad look at what's happening, make a strategic decision to be a bull or a bear, and only then return closer to the market and look for entry and exit points. That's what Triple Screen is all about.

What is long term and what is short term? Triple Screen avoids rigid definitions by focusing instead on the relationships between timeframes. It requires you to begin by choosing your favorite timeframe, which it calls intermediate. If you like to work with daily charts, your intermediate timeframe is daily. If you are a day-trader and like five-minute charts, then your intermediate timeframe is the five-minute chart, and so on.

Triple Screen defines the long term by multiplying the intermediate timeframe by five (see "Time—The Factor of Five," page 87). If your intermediate timeframe is daily, then your long-term timeframe is weekly. If your intermediate timeframe is five minutes, then your long-term is half-hourly, and so forth. Choose your favorite timeframe, call it intermediate, and immediately move up one order of magnitude to a long-term chart. Make your strategic decision there, and return to the intermediate chart to look for entries and exits.

The key principle of Triple Screen is to begin your analysis by stepping back from the markets and looking at the big picture for strategic decisions. Use a long-term chart to decide whether you are bullish or bearish, and then return closer to the market to make tactical choices about entries and exits.

The Principles of Triple Screen

Triple Screen resolves contradictions between indicators and timeframes. It reaches strategic decisions on long-term charts, using trend-following indicators—this is the first screen. It proceeds to make tactical decisions about entries and exits on the intermediate charts, using oscillators—this is the second screen. It offers several methods for placing buy and sell orders—this is the third screen, which we may implement using either intermediate- or short-term charts.

Begin by choosing your favorite timeframe, the one with whose charts you like to work, and call it intermediate. Multiply its length by five to find your long-term timeframe. Apply trend-following indicators to long-term charts to reach a strategic decision to go long, short, or stand aside. Standing aside is a legitimate position. If the long-term chart is bullish or bearish, return to the intermediate charts and use oscillators to look for entry and exit points in the direction of the long-term trend. Set stops and profit targets before switching to short-term charts, if available, to fine-tune entries and exits.

SCREEN ONE

Choose your favorite timeframe and call it intermediate. Multiply it by five to find the long-term timeframe. Let's say you prefer to work with daily charts. In that case, move immediately one level higher, to the weekly chart. Do not permit yourself to peek at the dailies because this may color your analysis of weekly charts. If you are a day-trader, you might choose a 10-minute chart as your favorite, call it intermediate, and then immediately move up to the hourly chart, approximately five times longer. Rounding off is not a problem; technical analysis is a craft, not an exact science. If you are a long-term investor, you might choose a weekly chart as your favorite and then go up to the monthly.

Apply trend-following indicators to the long-term chart and make a strategic decision to trade long, short, or stand aside. The original version of Triple Screen used the slope of weekly MACD-Histogram as its weekly trend-following indicator. It was very sensitive and gave many buy and sell signals. I now prefer to use the slope of a weekly exponential moving average as my main trend-following indicator on long-term charts. When the weekly EMA rises, it confirms a bull move and tells us to go long or stand aside. When it falls, it identifies a bear move and tells us to go short or stand aside. I use a 26-week EMA, which represents half a year of trading. You can test several different lengths to see which tracks your market best, as you would with any indicator.

I continue to plot weekly MACD-Histogram. When both EMA and MACD-Histogram are in gear, they confirm a dynamic trend and encourage you to trade larger positions. Divergences between weekly MACD-Histogram and prices are the strongest signals in technical analysis, which override the message of the EMA.

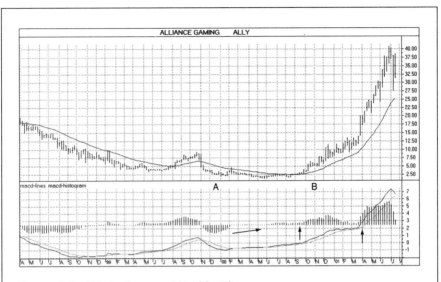

Figure 6.1 Triple Screen—Weekly Chart

Gaming stocks tend to do well in a weak economy—gambling appeals to people down on their luck. In 2000 and 2001, as the broad stock market was declining, gaming stocks put in a stellar performance. Alliance Gaming, for instance, rallied from below 2 to over 40, with very few pullbacks. How could Triple Screen help us benefit from this performance?

The pattern between points A and B is called a *saucer bottom,* a slow drawn-out minimal decline and just as minimal a rise on hardly any volume. Still, during that time ALLY had managed to put in a bullish divergence of MACD-Histogram, a hugely powerful signal that is rarely seen on weekly charts. It traced a low in area A, but could not even push below zero at the bottom of the saucer. The first vertical arrow marks the point where MACD-Histogram starts trending higher. A few weeks later the weekly EMA also turns up, and at that point, with both weekly indicators trending up, ALLY becomes a screaming buy. It is time to switch to the daily charts and look for buying opportunities. The second vertical arrow marks another period when both the EMA and MACD-Histogram are in gear to the upside, and then the stock doubles in a few weeks. The clean, steady uptrend of the weekly EMA keeps telling us to trade ALLY only from the long side.

At the right edge of the chart, the weekly EMA keeps trending higher, but wildly volatile price action shows that the easy portion of the uptrend is over. MACD-Histogram is moving opposite the EMA, warning of high volatility ahead. The relatively easy money is off the table.

SCREEN TWO

Return to the intermediate chart and use oscillators to look for trading opportunities in the direction of the long-term trend. When the weekly trend is up, wait for daily oscillators to fall, giving buy signals. Buying dips is safer than buying the crests of waves. If an oscillator gives a sell signal while the weekly trend is up, you may use it to take profits on long positions but not to sell short.

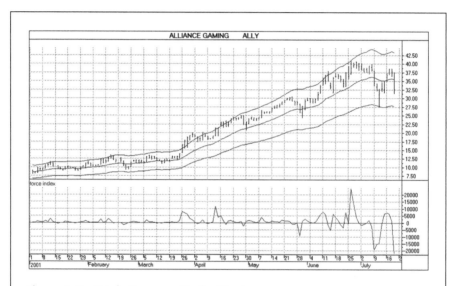

Figure 6.2   Triple Screen—Daily Chart

The uptrend on the weekly chart keeps telling us to trade ALLY from the long side or stand aside. With the daily EMA also rising, we have several options. We may buy when prices pull back to their rising daily EMA, or when short-term Force Index dips below zero. The upper channel line provides a logical profit-taking target. An experienced trader can pyramid his position, adding to it whenever a new buy signal appears and only tightening stops instead of exiting at the upper channel. That channel keeps getting wider as prices rise—from 10 points wide in April to 16 in July.

At the right edge of the chart, the alternating spikes of Force Index warn traders that the days of relatively easy money are over. The market has become hysterical, and the likelihood of trend continuation is low. Better bank your winnings and go look for another stock in another group that is rising or falling quietly, not yet discovered by the market crowd.

When the weekly trend is down, look for daily oscillators to rise, giving sell signals. Shorting during upwaves is safer than selling new lows. When daily oscillators give buy signals, you may use them to take profits on shorts but not to buy. The choice of oscillators depends on your trading style.

For conservative traders, choose a relatively slow oscillator, such as daily MACD-Histogram or Stochastic, for the second screen. When the weekly trend is up, look for daily MACD-Histogram to fall below zero and tick up, or for Stochastic to fall to its lower reference line, giving a buy signal.

Reverse these rules for shorting in bear markets. When trend-following indicators point down on the weekly charts, but daily MACD-Histogram ticks down from above its zero line, or Stochastic rallies to its upper reference line, they give sell signals.

A conservative approach works best during early stages of major moves, when markets gather speed slowly. As the trend accelerates, pullbacks become more shallow. To hop aboard a fast-running trend, you need faster oscillators.

For active traders, use the two-day EMA of Force Index (or longer, if that's what your research suggests for your market). When the weekly trend is up and daily Force Index falls below zero, it flags a buying opportunity.

Reverse these rules for shorting in bear markets. When the weekly trend is down and the two-day EMA of Force Index rallies above zero, it points to shorting opportunities.

Many other indicators can work with Triple Screen. The first screen can also use Directional System or trendlines. The second screen can use Momentum, Relative Strength Index, Elder-ray, and others.

The second screen is where we set profit targets and stops and make a go–no go decision about every trade after weighing the level of risk against the potential gain.

Set the stops. A stop is a safety net, which limits the damage from any bad trade. You have to structure your trading in such a way that no single bad loss, or a nasty series of losses, can damage your account. Stops are essential for success, but many traders shun them. Beginners complain about getting whipsawed, stopped out of trades that eventually would have made them money. Some say that putting in a stop means asking for trouble because no matter where you put it, it will be hit.

First of all, you need to place stops where they are not likely to be hit, outside of the range of market noise (see SafeZone on page 173). Second, an occasional whipsaw is the price of long-term safety. No matter how great your analytic skills, stops are always necessary.

You should move stops only one way—in the direction of the trade. When a trade starts moving in your favor, move your stop to a break-even level. As the move persists, continue to move your stop, protecting some of your paper profit. A professional trader never lets a profit turn into a loss.

A stop may never expose more than 2% of your equity to the risk of loss (see Chapter 7, "Money Management Formulas"). If Triple Screen flags a trade but you realize that a logical stop would risk more than 2% of your equity, skip that trade.

Set profit targets. Profit targets are flexible and depend on your goals and capital. If you are a well-capitalized, long-term-oriented trader, you may build up a large position at an early stage of a bull market, repeatedly taking buy signals from the daily charts, as long as the weekly trend is up. Take your profits after the weekly EMA turns flat. The reverse applies to downtrends.

Another option is to take profits whenever prices on the daily charts hit their channel line. If you go long, sell when prices hit the upper channel line and look to reposition on the next pullback to the daily moving average. If you go short, cover when prices fall to their lower channel line and look to reposition short on the next rally to the EMA.

A short-term-oriented trader can use the signals of a two-day EMA of Force Index to exit trades. If you buy in an uptrend when the two-day EMA of Force Index turns negative, sell when it turns positive. If you go short in a downtrend after the two-day EMA of Force Index turns positive, cover when it turns negative.

Beginners often approach markets like a lottery—buy a ticket and sit in front of the TV to find out whether you have won. You will know that you are becoming a professional when you start spending almost as much time thinking about exits as looking for entries.

SCREEN THREE

The third screen helps us pinpoint entry points. Live data can help savvy traders but hurt beginners who may slip into day-trading.

Use an intraday breakout or pullback to enter trades without real-time data. When the first two screens give you a buy signal (the weekly is up, but the daily is down), place a buy order at the high of the previous day or a tick higher. A tick is the smallest price fluctuation permitted in any market. We expect the major uptrend to reassert itself and catch a breakout in its direction. Place a buy order, good for one day only. If prices break out above the previous day's high, you will be stopped in automatically. You do not have to watch prices intraday, just give your order to a broker.

When the first two screens tell you to sell short (the weekly is down, but the daily is up), place a sell order at the previous day's low or a tick lower. We expect the downtrend to reassert itself, and try to catch the downside breakout. If prices break below the previous day's low, they will trigger your entry.

Daily ranges can be very wide, and placing an order to buy at the top can be expensive. Another option is to buy below the market. If you are trying to buy a pullback to the EMA, calculate where that EMA is likely to be tomorrow and place your order at that level. Alternatively, use the SafeZone indicator (see page 173) to find how far the market is likely to dip below its previous day's low and place your order at that level. Reverse these approaches for shorting in downtrends.

The advantage of buying upside breakouts is that you follow an impulse move. The disadvantage is that you buy high and your stop is far away. The advantage of bottom fishing is that you get your goods on sale and your stop is closer. The disadvantage is the risk of getting caught in a downside reversal. A "breakout entry" is more reliable, but profits are smaller; a "bottom-fishing entry" is riskier, but the profits are greater. Make sure to test both methods in your markets.

Use real-time data, if available, for entering trades. When the first two screens give you a buy signal (the weekly is up, but the daily is down), use live data to get long. You could follow a breakout from the opening range, when prices rally above the high of the first 15 to 30 minutes of trading, or apply technical analysis to intraday charts and finesse your entry. When trying to short, you may enter on a downside breakout from the opening range. You could also monitor the market intraday and use technical analysis to enter into a short trade, using live charts.

The techniques for finding buy and sell signals on real-time charts are the same as on daily charts, only their speed is much higher. If you use weeklies and dailies to get in, use them also to get out. Once a live chart gives an entry signal, avoid the temptation to exit using intraday data. Do not forget that you entered that trade on the basis of weekly and daily charts, expecting to hold for several days. Do not be distracted by the intraday chop if you are trading swings that last several days.

Day-Trading

Day-trading means entering and exiting trades on the same day. Watching money flow from the screen into your account is extremely appealing. Surely we are smart enough to use modern technology to outrun slow-moving folks who follow their stocks through the newspapers.

Every partial truth contains a dangerous lie. Day-trading can bring profits to professionals, but it is also a common last stop for losers who blow what little is left of their accounts. Day-trading offers advantages and disadvantages, while placing extreme demands on its practitioners.

Day-trading offers one of the markets' greatest challenges, but it is amazing how little literature on it exists. There are several "day-trading for dummies" types of books, a few get-rich-quick jobs, but not a single definitive volume on day-trading. Bad day-traders write bad books and good day-traders are too action-oriented to sit down to write.

A good day-trader is a street-smart person with fast reflexes. He is quick, confident, and flexible. Successful day-traders are so focused on the immediate results that they do not make good writers. I hope one of them will rise to the challenge of writing a book, but in the meantime, here are a few notes, even though each of them deserves its own chapter in a thick book on day-trading.

The late 1990s saw an explosion of interest in day-trading. Even housewives and students were pulled in by the bull market and the easy reach of the Internet. Brokers advertise for more people to come in to day-trade, knowing full well most will bust out.

The advantages of day-trading include:

Trading opportunities are more frequent. If you can trade with daily charts, you'll see similar trades more often on intraday charts.
You can cut losses very quickly.
There is no overnight risk if a major piece of news hits your market after the close.

The disadvantages of day-trading include:

You miss longer-term swings and trends.

Profits are smaller because intraday swings are shorter.

Expenses are higher because of more frequent commissions and slippage. Day-trading is a very expensive game, which is why vendors love it.

Day-trading makes several hard demands on its practitioners:

You must act instantly—if you stop to think, you're dead. With daily charts you have the luxury of time, but intraday charts demand immediate action.

Day-trading chews up a great deal of time. You have to ask yourself whether the hourly pay is better in longer-term trading.

Day-trading plays into people's gambling tendencies. If there are any gaps in your discipline, day-trading will find them fast.

There are three main groups of day-traders: floor traders, institutional traders, and private traders. They have different agendas and use different tools. Imagine three persons coming to the beach—one goes for a swim, another stretches in the sun, and the third goes jogging and runs head on into a tree. Floor traders and institutional traders tend to do better than private traders. Let us see what we can learn from them.

Lessons from Floor Traders

Floor traders stand in the pit, trading with each other, but more often against the public. They scalp, spread, and take directional trades.

Scalping is based on the fact that there are two prices for any stock or future. One is a bid—what the pros are offering to pay. The other is an ask—what the pros are willing to sell for. You may bid below the market, but as a friend said, "You can't excite the market with a flaccid bid." When in a hurry, you buy at the ask and pay what sellers demand. If you want to sell, you may place a limit order above the market or "hit the bid" and accept what buyers are willing to pay.

For example, the last trade in gold was at 308.30, but now it is quoted as 308.20 bid, 308.40 ask. This means there are willing buyers at 308.20, while sellers are asking for 308.40. When a market order to buy comes into the pit, a floor trader goes short by selling at 308.40. The outsider has paid the ask price, and the floor trader is now short and needs to buy. When a market order to sell comes to the floor, he buys at 308.20, and pockets 20 cents profit. Floor traders pay no commissions, only clearing costs, and can afford to trade even for single ticks. They stand on their feet all day, yelling to all passersby that they want to buy a tick below the market and sell a tick above. It is the highest paid form of manual labor.

This is a simplified example. The reality is less orderly, as floor traders try to widen the spread and make more than one or two ticks. They compete with one another, shouting, jumping, and getting into each other's faces. It helps to be tall and muscular and have a big voice. You get stabbed with pencils and splattered with saliva. There is a story about a floor trader who died of a heart attack on the floor but remained upright, squeezed in by the crowd.

A floor trader can get stuck if he buys a tick below the market but the market falls by two ticks, and puts him underwater. Half of all floor traders disappear in their first year. One of the Chicago exchanges puts red circular badges on the chest of new traders, making them look like shooting targets. Lest you start feeling sorry for floor traders, keep in mind that many of them make a very good living and some make a great deal of money from hitting you for a tick or more on every trade. Before electronic trading became a serious threat, seats on some exchanges sold for a million dollars.

Floor traders also get involved in spreading—buying and selling related markets when their relationships get out of line. Spread traders tend to be more cautious and better capitalized than scalpers. Finally, some of the wealthiest floor traders get involved in directional trading. They put on trades that last days or weeks, closer to the timeframe of public traders.

What lessons can we learn from the floor? If you are a position trader, you should use limit orders whenever possible. Buy and sell at specified prices, and don't let the floor scalp you. Put those fellows on a diet. Another lesson is to stay away from scalping. When a crowd of athletic young men starts fighting for ticks, jumping, salivating, and screaming, you have no business reaching into that crowd to grab a few ticks for yourself because they'll take off your fingers. If you day-trade away from the floor, forget about scalping. Look for the longer-term day-trades, where the competition tapers off a bit. Go to the middle ground between scalpers who chase ticks and position traders with their end-of-the-day charts. Try to find one or two trades a day, longer than scalping but shorter than position trades.

Lessons from Institutional Day-Traders

Institutional traders work for banks, brokerage houses, and similar firms. A company may have more than a hundred traders sitting behind rows of expensive equipment. Maintaining each seat costs several thousand dollars a month, not counting salaries and bonuses. Each institutional trader narrowly focuses on a single market. One may trade only two-year Treasury notes, another only five-year notes, and so on.

Institutional traders generate paper-thin returns on huge volumes of capital. A friend of mine who trades bonds for a leading investment bank in New York has access to essentially unlimited capital during the day, but his overnight positions are capped at $250 million. His standard deviation, the amount he usually wins or loses in a trading day, is $180,000. This is 0.072% of his overnight limit, and only about 0.010% of his intraday size.

His profits appear large until you express them as a percentage of his account and ask yourself what you would earn if you traded as well as him. Suppose your account is $250,000 or one-thousandth of his $250 million. If you could match my friend's percentage gains, you'd earn $180 on overnight trades and $25 at the end of a busy day-trading session. That would hardly cover your costs! Why do institutions do it?

The big boys benefit from economies of scale, but the main reason they stay in the game is to keep themselves visible to potential customers. Their main income comes from commissions and spreads on customer orders. Institutional traders accept paper-thin returns to maintain a presence in the market, which gives them first dibs on lucrative customer business. They work to maintain visibility, and as long as they do not lose money, they're happy.

The main thing we can learn from institutional traders is their rigid system of discipline, with managers forcing them to cut losses. A private trader has no manager, which is why he needs to design and implement a strict system of money management rules. Institutional traders benefit from focusing on a single market, unlike private traders who may jump from cocoa today to IBM tomorrow. It pays to choose just a few trading vehicles and learn them well.

Institutions are busy scalping, and a private trader is better off keeping out of this area to avoid getting trampled. If you see a trade that offers only a few ticks, it is safer to pass it up because the institutions can barge in at any moment. The longer your timeframe, the less competition you have from them.

Private traders have one enormous advantage over institutions, but most of them toss it away. Corporate traders must broadcast their bid and ask in order to maintain a presence in the markets. "How are you for 5 dollar/yen," calls a customer, wishing to trade $5 million for yen or vice versa. The bank trader must quote his bid and ask, ready to take either side of that trade. He must trade at all times, while a private trader has the luxury of waiting for the best moment.

You are under no obligation to buy or sell. You have the freedom of standing aside, but most private traders throw away this awesome advantage. People get sucked into the excitement of the game. They jump in instead of waiting for the best trades. Remember, the idea is to trade well, not to trade often.

Getting the Data

Real-time data tends to be pricey, and you must cover its cost before taking home a dime. Many exchanges make fortunes selling real-time data, forcing vendors to delay free broadcasts to the public. The 20-minute delay preserves entertainment value, but trying to use that data for day-trading is like driving a car with cardboard for a windshield, looking out through a side window. Day-trading is a very fast game, played by some very clever people. Trying to compete against them on the basis of delayed data is a joke.

Most day-traders use software to display, chart, and analyze their data. Real-time analytic software has been around for years, but the great NAS-DAQ bull market led to an upsurge in the popularity of Level 2 quotes, which show who is bidding and offering what stock. This is ballyhooed as the new road to riches. Most of those riches go to vendors and brokers who benefit from hyperactive trading. I haven't noticed any improvement in the overall performance of private traders with Level 2 quotes. The early users may have had an advantage a few years ago, when the concept was new, but once it became popular, the edge disappeared. This is a common story with new technologies—early users get an edge, the tool becomes a fad, and the edge fades away.

A day-trader needs a dedicated computer, good analytic software, and a fast connection to the Internet. This setup may cost several thousand dollars, plus a monthly bill of a few hundred dollars for live data and exchange fees. You can reduce the cost of data by following just one market, which is not a bad idea because it helps keep you focused.

Some professional futures traders dispense with computers alto-gether. They quit their day jobs and go on the floor. Some move to a city that has an exchange where they buy or lease a seat. Costs are higher on bigger exchanges that handle high volumes in popular mar-kets, and cheaper on smaller exchanges in lesser markets. The best way to learn is to get a job as a clerk on the floor and work for some-one, but this option is open only to the young—the floor generally doesn't hire people over 25. They want them young, pliable, and with-out any preconceived ideas.

Psychology

The great paradox of day-trading is that it demands the highest level of discipline, while attracting the most impulsive, addictive, and gambling-prone personalities. If trading is a thrill, then day-trading provides the best rush. It is a joy to recognize a pattern on your screen, put in an order, and watch the market explode in a stiff rise, stuffing thousands of dollars into your pockets. A former military pilot said that day-trading was more exciting than sex or flying jet aircraft.

Corporate traders are in the market because their companies gave them jobs. Private traders enter for reasons that are partly rational and partly irrational. The only rational reason is to make money, but a prof-itable day-trade delivers such a great high that it sweeps most people off their feet. Flooded with pleasure, they go looking for the next high and lose money.

The purpose of any business is to make money. A well-run business also gratifies many of its owners' and employees' psychological needs, but money is the pivot of the enterprise. Traders who become hooked on thrills take their eyes off the money and jump into impulsive trades. Vendors encourage day-traders because losers spend like drunken sailors on software, data, systems, and even coaches, most of whom have never traded or busted out. Go into any port area, and you'll see plenty of bars, brothels, and tattoo parlors. Go into day-trading, and you'll see more vendors than you can shake a stick at. There is money to be made from turkeys whose market life is measured in months or weeks.

Successful day-traders test patterns and systems, measure risks and rewards, and focus on building equity. Winners tend to be emotionally cool. If day-trading attracts you, you must answer several questions:

Are you successfully trading with end-of-day charts? If the answer is "no," stay away from day-trading. You need a minimum of one year successful trading experience before attempting to day-trade.

Do you have an addictive streak? If you have a history of drinking, drugs, overeating, or gambling, stay as far away as possible from day-trading because it will trigger your addictive tendency and destroy your account.

Do you have a written business plan? How much money will you trade? In what markets? How will you choose entries and exits? How will you manage risks, use stops, and allocate capital? Do not go near day-trading without a written plan. Be sure to keep separate records for day-trading and position trading. Find out which one is more profitable for you.

Choosing the Market

Day-trading compares to position trading like flying to driving. Comfortably seated behind the wheel of a car you can lean back, listen to music, use a cell phone, and even glance at a magazine while stopped at a red light. Do not attempt that in a jet.

Day-trading demands total concentration on a single market. It is like serial monogamy—you may trade several markets in your career, but only one at any given time. What market will you choose? The two essential features of a good day-trading market are high liquidity and volatility.

Liquidity refers to the average daily volume of your trading vehicle— the higher, the better. It is easy to join a huge crowd and just as easy to leave without drawing attention to yourself and distorting the market with your order. When you place a market order to buy or sell a thinly traded stock or a commodity, you give the pros a license to skin you alive in slippage. If you use a limit order, it may never get filled. Trading a big liquid market, such as IBM or soybeans, allows you to get in and out more easily with less slippage.

Volatility refers to the average daily range of your trading vehicle. The greater the distance between the high and the low of the day, the bigger your target. Shooting at a big target is easier than shooting at a tiny one. Remember our discussion of channels? If you know how to trade, you will get more money from a wide channel, at any level of skill. Someone who trades at C level and takes 10% from a channel will get 1 point from a 10-point channel, but 2 points from a 20-point channel. A C-level trader has no business day-trading, but even an A trader wants as big a target as possible.

You can find good liquidity and volatility in the leading stocks, futures, and currencies. Another important feature of a day-trading market is its personality. Some markets move smoothly, others like to jump. Bonds, for example, tend to spend a day or two in a very narrow range, then explode, moving more in half an hour than in several preceding days, and then fall asleep again. Trading them is like infantry fighting—90% sheer boredom and 10% sheer terror.

What markets should you day-trade? In stocks, look at those that show up on the list of the most active issues of the day. That's where the action is. These stocks' liquidity is very high, and their volatility tends to be good. Explore the list of top gainers and losers for the day. When the same name shows up on that list day in and day out, it is clearly among the most volatile issues, with great day-trading potential.

When it comes to futures, make your first steps in such relatively peaceful markets as corn, sugar, or copper. Once you've learned the ropes, consider moving up to stock index futures or the futures on the German Bund, both among the favorite vehicles of professional day-traders.

Analysis and Decision Making

If you remove price and time markings from a chart, you won't be able to tell whether it is weekly, daily, or intraday. Markets are fractal, to borrow a term from chaos theory. To recall our earlier discussion, the seashore is fractal, since the coastline looks equally jagged from any height. Since charts in different timeframes are so alike, we may analyze them using similar methods.

Coming to day-trading after a year or more of successful position trading gives you a great advantage. You can use the same methods, and only have to speed them up. You can use the principles of Triple Screen to make strategic decisions on longer-term charts and tactical choices on shorter-term charts.

SCREEN ONE

Analyze your market on a longer-term chart, using trend-following indicators, and make a strategic decision to trade long, short, or stand aside.

Choose the timeframe you prefer to trade and call it intermediate. Let us select a five-minute chart for our intermediate timeframe, with each bar representing five minutes of trading. You can choose a longer chart

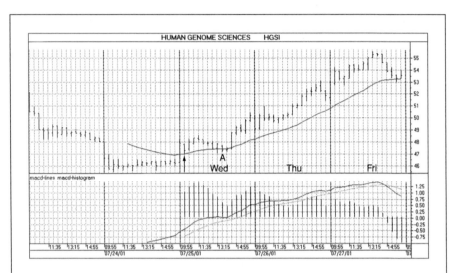

Figure 6.3 Day-Trading—25-Minute Chart

If we prefer a five-minute chart for day-trading, we should start our analysis with a timeframe that is five times longer, a 25-minute chart. Different stocks go in and of out of favor with day-traders. Human Genome Sciences (HGSI) is popular today, with strong, healthy trends and no gaps. There is a downtrend on Monday, which bottoms out on Tuesday, turns up on Wednesday, and rises into Friday, with a pullback at the end of that day as longs take profits before the weekend.

There is a strong buy signal right at the opening on Wednesday as the EMA turns up, confirmed by the uptick of MACD-Histogram. As EMA keeps rising, it tells us to trade HGSI from the long side; the first screen of Triple Screen is bullish. This signal is much more important than any uptick or downtick of MACD-Histogram. When MACD rises in gear with the EMA, it suggests trading larger size, but when it declines, it is a perfectly normal "breathing" behavior, as long as there is no bearish divergence.

At the right edge of the chart the market is closing for the weekend. The EMA is slightly rising, so bulls have to be given the benefit of doubt. Also, MACD-Histogram has declined to the level normally associated with bottoms; it is closer to a bottom than to a top. We should wait for the opening on Monday, anticipating a buy signal, while being prepared to trade from the short side if the EMA ticks down.

if you wish, but not much shorter, as that might pit you against institutional scalpers. To stand completely apart from the crowd, you may
select an unorthodox length, such as seven or nine minutes.

Some day-traders, intoxicated by the promise of technology, use
one-minute or even tick charts. These provide the illusion that you are
present on the floor, even though it can easily take half a minute or
longer for the data to be keyed in, uploaded to the satellite, and broadcast to your screen. You are not on the floor, you are behind. When
markets begin to run, time lags get even worse.

*Multiply your intermediate timeframe by five to find the long-term
timeframe.* If your intermediate timeframe is five minutes, use a 25-
minute chart. If your software does not allow plotting 25-minute charts,
round it off to half an hour. A successful trader needs to stand apart
from the crowd. This is why it pays to use uncommon parameters for
charts and indicators. There are probably thousands of people using
half-hourly charts, but only a tiny minority uses 25-minute charts and
gets its signals a little faster.

*Apply a trend-following indicator to the long-term chart and use its
direction to make a strategic decision to trade long, short, or stand aside.*
Start with a 20- or 30-bar EMA and adjust its length until it tracks your
market with a minimum of whipsaws. When the 25-minute EMA rises, it
identifies an uptrend and tells you to trade from the long side or stand
aside. When the EMA falls, it identifies a downtrend and tells you to
trade only from the short side or stand aside. Make a strategic decision on
this long-term chart before returning to your intermediate-term charts.

Successful day-traders tend to rely less on indicators and more on
chart patterns. The gaps between trading days can distort intraday indicators. Still, some indicators, such as moving averages and envelopes,
also called channels, are useful even with intraday charts.

Screen Two

Return to the intermediate (five-minute) charts to look for entries in the
direction of the trend.

*Plot a 22-bar EMA on the five-minute chart and draw a channel
that contains about 95% of price action.* Moving averages reflect the
average consensus of value, while channels show the normal limits of
bullishness and bearishness. We want to get long during uptrends, buying below the EMA on a five-minute chart, and short in downtrends,
above the EMA. Do not get long above the upper channel line, where

the market is overvalued, or sell short below the lower channel line, where it is undervalued.

Use oscillators, such as MACD-Histogram and Force Index, to identify overbought and oversold areas. Trade in the direction of the tide, entering when a wave goes against the tide. When the 25-minute trend is up, falling prices and oscillators on a five-minute chart reflect a temporary bearish imbalance—a buying opportunity. When the 25-minute trend is down, rising prices and oscillators on a five-minute chart reflect a temporary bullish imbalance—a shorting opportunity.

Day-traders sometimes ask whether they should analyze weekly and daily charts. The weekly trend is essentially meaningless for them, and even the daily is of limited value. Looking at too many timeframes can lead to "paralysis from analysis."

Place SafeZone stops. After entering a trade, place a protective stop, using the SafeZone method (see page 173). Consider making it "on close

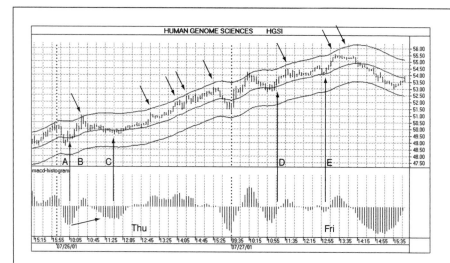

Figure 6.4 Day-Trading—Five-Minute Chart

The long-term 25-minute chart has told us to trade HGSI from the long side. The declines of the intermediate trend provide buying opportunities. On Thursday, the five-minute chart heads down from the opening, punching below its EMA. Wait for the MACD-Histogram to tick up, confirming a buy signal (point A). It shows that the decline is ending, and within half an hour HGSI rallies to its upper channel line (point B), a good place to only"; watch the screen and give an order to exit only if the five-minute bar closes beyond your stop level. This way, a brief penetration caused by market noise will not touch off a stop. Naturally, there is no bargaining or waiting for another tick. To be a day-trader, you must have iron discipline!

SCREEN THREE

This screen handles entries and exits.

Enter in the vicinity of a moving average on a five-minute chart. If the 25-minute trend is up, buy pullbacks to the EMA on a five-minute chart, especially when oscillators are oversold. Reverse the procedure in downtrends. This is better than chasing breakouts, buying at the highs, or shorting at the lows.

Take profits in the vicinity of the channel line. If you buy near the moving average, aim to sell near the upper channel line. If your five-

---

take profits. It declines back to the EMA, giving ample opportunities to position long, even if you missed the first signal. The MACD bottom in area C is more shallow, showing that bears are weaker, reinforcing the buy signal. Prices make four more attempts to reach the upper channel line. You can sell at any of them, but if you have not sold during the first three, the fourth is a must. It is getting late in the day, you already know that today prices do not seem to be able to reach their upper channel line, and as a day-trader you do not want to hold overnight. Sure enough, during the last half-hour there is a downdraft, as day-traders who overstayed the uptrend start pushing through the door, trying to get out.

On Friday, there is a buy signal right at the opening, followed by a quick rally to the upper channel line for profit taking, and then another decline to the EMA (point D). The subsequent rallies never quite reach the upper channel line, but there is another buying opportunity at point E, during a pullback to the EMA. There are two weak rallies later in the afternoon, and if you do not use them to take profits, there is one last ring for the hard of hearing when the EMA turns down. Intraday charts often have countertrend moves late in the day, as traders with paper profits start closing positions.

At the right edge of the chart, the trading day and the trading week are over. You have no overnight risk and can relax before the opening on Monday, when the 25-minute MACD-Histogram will tell you whether to trade this stock from the long or the short side.

minute oscillators, such as MACD-Histogram, are making new highs and related markets are rallying, you may wait for the channel to be hit or penetrated. If the indicators are weak, grab your profit fast without waiting for prices to touch the channel.

Measure your performance as the percentage of the channel width. You must be an A trader to make day-trading worthwhile. Even then, you have to prove to yourself that you can make more money day-trading than position trading. Try to trade only a few times a day and aim to catch at least a third of that day's range. Enter cautiously, but run fast. Do not trade during after-hours sessions when markets tend to be very thin.

Taking Day-Trades Overnight

If you enter a trade early in the day and the market keeps moving in your favor, should you hold that trade overnight? How about over the weekend? Of course, those questions only apply to profitable trades. Taking a loss overnight is strictly for losers.

A beginner must close his day-trades by the end of the day, but an experienced pro has the option of holding them overnight. When a market closes within a few ticks of its high, it usually exceeds it the next morning. A market that closes on its lows usually flirts with lower lows the next day. Those extensions are not guaranteed, as the market may close on its high, get hit with bad news overnight, and open sharply lower. This is why only experienced day-traders have the option of taking their trades overnight.

Research, knowledge, and discipline put your trades on a cooler, more rational footing. You have to research the past, calculate the odds, and make informed decisions for the future. When you day-trade, there are plenty of hours when the market goes nowhere, leaving you free to crunch the numbers. You may use a single computer or get two machines and dedicate one to trading and another to . research.

Get one year's history for the market you're day-trading. Drop it into a spreadsheet and start asking questions. Every time the market closed within 5 ticks of its high, how many times did it reach a new high the next day? How far did it go the next day? What about the days when that market closed within 5 ticks of the lows? How low did it go the next day? Once you get the answers, find out what happened when the market closed within 10 ticks of the high, and so on.

Professionals tend to trade the same market month after month, even though there is a huge turnover of amateurs. Professionals have grown used to trading in a certain way, and to trade like them you must find those patterns and express them in numbers. You must base your trades on facts and probabilities, not on gut feel and hope. You must do your own research. You cannot buy the answers, because only finding them yourself will give you the confidence to trade.

Opening Range Breakouts

People get tips at parties, from the newspapers, and on TV, that glue-box of mass culture. Investment officers at slow-moving institutions may sit in a meeting all day before getting permission to buy or sell. They tend to place orders before the open. Most overnight orders come from casual investors, gamblers chasing hot tips, and brokers who want to leave work early to play golf or make marketing calls.

The two busiest times for professional traders are the beginning and the end of each session, especially the first and last half-hour periods. The influx of overnight orders gives professionals an opportunity to perform a public service by accommodating those who are eager to get in at the opening. They unwind those positions near the close, when one loser after another throws in the towel. Many pros go out for lunch in the middle of the day, which is why many markets tend to become directionless and choppy between 12 and 1:30. The curve of intraday volume tends to be U-shaped, with peaks at the open and the close, and a low in the middle.

Serious traders watch openings because they set the tone for the balance of the day. If the total size of buy orders exceeds that of sell orders, the floor opens the market higher, forcing the crowd to pay up. Pros establish short positions at such high levels that the very first drop makes them money. If the volume of sell orders is higher, the pros open the market lower, load up on the cheap, and sell at a profit on the first bounce.

During the first 15 to 30 minutes after the open many stocks and futures swing up and down on high volume. As the bulk of overnight orders gets filled, volume starts to dry up, and the swings slow down, retreating from the high and the low of the opening range. What happens next largely depends on the width of the opening range.

When the opening range is very wide, say 80% of an average daily range for the past month, it is likely to have set both the high and the low for that day. The floor loves wide opening ranges because their

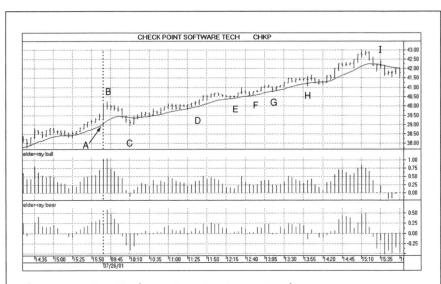

Figure 6.5   Day-Trading—Opening Range Breakout
Elder-ray, 5-minute chart

Stocks for day-trading should have heavy volume, be volatile, and be expensive rather than cheap, so that they have decent intraday ranges. At the time of this writing, Checkpoint is definitely on the list, along with NVDA, TARO, and a few other swingers. By the time you read this, other stocks will be in the forefront of day-traders' attention.

CHKP has been rallying, coming off the market's recent lows and closing at 39.44. Today it opens at 39.26 at 9:30 (point A) and within 10 minutes runs up to 40.25 (point B), establishing the high of the opening range. It then drifts lower, hitting the low of 38.93 at 10:10 A.M.—the low of the opening range (point C). For the next hour and a half CHKP meanders within its fairly narrow opening range of only 1.32, but by 11:35 it runs up to its upper edge and penetrates it by 3 ticks (point D). The next bar is 7 ticks higher—this is no false breakout, this is a real opening range breakout, the trend is up, and we have to get long. The 13-bar EMA is steadily rising. Whenever Bear Power returns to the zero line and turns negative, it shows that bears have regained their footing—a good time to add to longs within an uptrend (points E, F, G, and H). At 15:25 (point I) the EMA turns down, giving a sell signal—time to take profits on long positions.

At the right edge of the chart, the day is over, and we may count profits before going home. If you bought on the first buy signal following the opening range breakout and sold when the EMA turned down, your profit is 42.15 – 40.40 = 1.75. Multiply this by the number of shares you traded, and add other positions if you pyramided.

extremes provide two good levels of support and resistance. The pros keep buying near the lows, shorting near the highs, and spending the rest of the day unwinding their positions at a profit. A narrow opening range makes it more likely that the market will break out of it and start a new trend for the day.

The high and the low of an opening range are like the feet of a boxer. When they are wide apart, the boxer is stable and in control, but when they are close, it is easy to knock him off balance and force him to move.

Outsiders love trends and chase breakouts, but the floor operates in a reactive mode, selling the highs and buying the lows. It prefers flat trading ranges to runaway trends. The floor usually wins, but once in a while outsiders overwhelm the pros and push the market into a trend. When that happens, smart floor traders cut their losses and run, while the dumb and the stubborn contribute to the mortality rate.

The opening range has several implications for day-traders:

> The opening and closing prices, like two poles of a magnet, tend to be at the opposite extremes of a day's bar. If the market opens near the low of a wide opening range, expect it to close near the upper edge and look for buying opportunities. If it opens near the high of a wide opening range, expect it to close lower and look for shorting opportunities.
>
> Breakouts from wide opening ranges tend to be false. When prices take out the high or the low of a wide opening range, be alert to the possibility of the breakout petering out and be ready to trade its return into the range.
>
> When the opening range is narrow, expect a breakout and be ready to trade in its direction.

Successful traders test everything. There are hours in most days when the market is undecided, neither a buy nor a sell. Use that time to research its opening ranges—how many minutes they take to form in your stock or future, how wide they tend to be, and so on. Create a graph linking the height of the opening range with the likelihood of a breakout, and you'll acquire a private tool, a real edge in the markets.

Currencies—Trading the 24-hour Markets   The United States is the only country in the world where most people don't think much about currencies. We live in the dollar universe, but the moment an American sets foot abroad, he realizes that everyone, from executives to taxi drivers, watches exchange rates. When the people outside the United States, and even recent immigrants to the United States, get a bit of trading capital, their first idea is to trade currencies. The bulk of currency trading takes place in the interbank market, directly between dealers. Beginners turn to unscrupulous currency trading shops that bucket their orders (hold their money without executing trades) and kill them with commissions, spreads, and interest charges. Survivors discover currency futures, where spreads are more narrow, commissions more reasonable, and no interest is charged for the privilege of holding a position.

Aside from the horrors of forex shops, the biggest challenge of currencies is that they trade around the clock. You may enter a trade, analyze it in the evening, and decide to take profits the next day. When you wake up, there is no profit to be taken. The turning point you saw coming has already come and gone, not in the United States, but in Asia or Europe. Someone has picked your pocket while you slept! Markets are tough enough without exposing yourself to 24-hour risk.

Big financial institutions deal with this problem by implementing a system of "passing the book." A bank may open a position in Tokyo, manage it intraday, and then transfer it to its London branch before closing for the night. London continues to trade that position and in the evening passes the book to New York, which trades it until it passes it back to Tokyo. Currencies follow the sun, and small traders can't keep up with it. I once visited a wealthy Thai gentleman who was planning to install his two sons and himself in three different cities around the globe to trade currencies, but the boys balked.

If you trade currencies, you should either take a very long-term view and ignore daily fluctuations, or else day-trade, avoiding overnight positions. If you trade currency futures, use two sets of data. Use cash or interbank data for your weekly charts and futures data for the dailies to pinpoint entries and exits. The daily charts of currency futures are full of overnight gaps because those markets are open for only a few hours a day, but the charts of cash are smooth.

S&P 500—*False Breakouts*   S&P futures are notoriously hard to trade, but newcomers are drawn to them like moths to a flame. "Are you man enough to trade the S&P?!" is the battle cry of those overgrown boys. Most traders are woefully undercapitalized for this expensive contract. It is hard to see how anyone with less than a quarter million in his account could trade a single contract of this volatile market, which often jumps several points of $250 each within minutes.

The floor takes full advantage of the fact that most gamblers do not have enough money to carry overnight positions, place sensible stops, or ride out small adverse moves. The floor has got the art of shaking out inexperienced day-traders down to a science. They use false breakouts to make losers jump like Pavlov's dogs, buying high and selling low.

The floor tries to push prices through several well-known levels on most days, flushing out weak holders. There is always a mass of sell stops below the low of the opening range and the low of the day. Shoving the market through those lows leads to selling by weak holders, and the pros then buy their merchandise on sale. There is always a mass of buy stops at the high of the opening range, the high of the day, and the high of the previous day, placed by weak shorts. Pushing the S&P through those levels sets off panicky buying. That's when the floor sells short, positioning itself for the next downswing. There is nothing uniquely devious about this game, only it works especially well in the S&P because there are so many amateurs and this market is so expensive that they have no staying power.

A day-trader who recognizes the special challenges of the S&P can reach several conclusions:

This is not a good market for beginners; it is too expensive and too fast. Learn to drive an old Chevy before a turbocharged Ferrari.

Have a good-sized account if you plan to trade this market. A quarter of a million dollars for each contract gives you staying power and allows you to place sensible stops.

Fade false breakouts in the S&P—trade against them. Use oscillators to detect when a false breakout starts running out of steam, and trade for the return into the middle of the day's range.

The Daily Plan

A day in front of a live screen includes many dead hours when nothing seems to happen. People grow bored and restless, and the next thing you know, a day-trader turns his screen into an entertainment center. Professionals tend to follow a timetable to reinforce their discipline.

Your trading day should start before the opening. Give yourself at least half an hour to assemble and analyze overnight data. Watch the first half hour of trading with no interruptions, not even phone calls. If you put on a trade, then manage it. Otherwise dedicate two hours to research, database maintenance, reading a trading magazine or a book, or trolling the net for fresh ideas, all the while in front of the screen. Suspend everything if the market looks close to giving a buy or sell signal. Have lunch at your desk if you are managing a trade. Review trading-related posts on the net and put more time into research. Consider keeping exercise equipment in your trading room, such as a stationary bicycle or a rowing machine. A healthy mind in a healthy body. As the closing approaches, the market again demands your undivided attention, especially if you are exiting a trade.

There are two reasons to have a daily plan. You need to make sure that all the necessary work gets done, trades found, placed, exited, recorded, and research conducted. The other reason is to remind yourself that you are day-trading as a business and not for amusement and that you are serious about success.

Remember that your feelings, desires, and anxieties are part and parcel of the game. When feelings are unsettled, trading becomes a problem. I had a client in the late 1990s who had achieved phenomenal success day-trading just one stock, AOL. He looked at yesterday's closing price, checked the levels at which AOL traded in Europe, and reviewed any overnight news. When AOL shot out of the gate after the open, he traded its first swing, and sometimes two or three more during the first 30 minutes or an hour. He grossed $5,000 almost daily within the first hour of trading, buying and selling 1,000 shares at a clip. Then he spent the rest of day pissing that money away and losing!

When he came to consult me, it was obvious that his system worked well only during the first hour. It tracked an overnight buildup of pressure, and once that pressure equalized, he had no edge. His system was fantastically effective—as long as he stopped trading an hour after the opening. But he could not stop!

It turned out that his self-esteem was largely based on trying to win his old father's respect. The father was an immigrant who built a successful business by the dint of hard work, and he only respected men who worked hard and put in long hours. My client felt that he had to keep on "working" in the markets all day rather than turn off his computer and go outside to play golf, drive his boat, or putter in the garden. He did not want psychotherapy. I tried calling him at 10:30 to remind him to stop trading, but then he got caller ID to avoid my calls. A great system is only half the game; the other is trading psychology. The only goal of successful traders is to grow equity. Everything else, including love, respect, and so forth, has to be gained outside the markets.

THE IMPULSE SYSTEM

High volatility during the bull market of the 1990s made momentum trading very popular. The idea is to jump aboard a fast-moving stock as it begins to run and hop off after it slows down. Momentum traders do not care about company fundamentals; they may not even know what that company does. All they care about is direction and speed. They buy when a stock rallies (they rarely go short) and hope to cash out before the impulse runs out.

The game of momentum trading appears deceptively easy. The owners of trading rooms make fortunes in commissions, while legions of traders lose even bigger fortunes trying to grab money from fast-moving stocks. Impulse trading tends to degenerate into impulsive trading, and the game is over.

Momentum trading has a built-in psychological contradiction that's deadly to most people. On the one hand, this fast game, like infantry fighting or video game playing, is best suited for young people with strong hunting instincts, capable of abandoning themselves to the game. On the other hand, momentum trading requires the cold detached discipline of a professional card counter in a casino. Successful momentum trading, like professional gambling, is a boring business. The ability to accept small steady gains—essential for momentum trading—is very rare. Few people can walk away from the table just as the party gets going.

One of my favorite clients is a professional trader in London who sometimes, for entertainment, goes to a casino at night. He plays blackjack for a minimum stake of £5 and quits when he is either £200 ahead or £400 behind. He has worked out a card-counting method and a money management system that have him going home with £200 13 times out of 14. He has proven to himself that he can steadily win at the casino, and now he rarely goes there because he must spend 6 or 7 hours counting and betting before reaching his winning or losing limit. It is hard work, counting all the time. The crowd of amateurs around him is having a lot of fun losing. My client prefers to stay home and trade stocks where the odds are much more to his liking.

Successful momentum trading requires great discipline. You must identify a price move, hop aboard without waiting for a better confirmation, and jump off as soon as that move slows down. The longer you wait to identify the momentum, the less money is left for you. Taking profits is stressful because of a normal human tendency to hold out for a little more and then beat yourself up for having left too early. A momentum trader needs a set of technical rules, a money management system, and iron discipline to enter when the time is right and exit without regrets after hitting his profit target or a loss limit.

Entries

I designed this system to identify the inflection points where a trend speeds up or slows down. The Impulse System works in any timeframe, including intraday. It provides buy and sell signals, but leaves it up to you to select good markets, tweak parameters, and supply the discipline.

Choose an active market whose prices swing in a broad channel. What happens if you make a C trade and grab only 10% of a channel width? This result is not too bad if the channel is 20 points wide, but a C trade is an exercise in futility if the channel is only 5 points wide. Chase fat rabbits, don't waste your time on skinny ones.

The Impulse System combines two simple but powerful indicators. One measures market inertia, the other its momentum. When both point in the same direction, they identify an impulse worth following. We get an entry signal when both indicators get in gear, but as soon as they stop confirming one another, we take that as an exit signal.

The Impulse System uses an exponential moving average to find uptrends and downtrends. When the EMA rises, it shows that inertia favors the bulls. When EMA falls, inertia works for the bears. The second component is MACD-Histogram, an oscillator whose slope reflects changes of power among bulls or bears. When MACD-Histogram rises, it shows that bulls are becoming stronger. When it falls, it shows that bears are growing stronger.

The Impulse System flags those bars where both the inertia and the momentum point in the same direction. When both the EMA and MACD-Histogram rise, they show that bulls are roaring and the uptrend is accelerating. When both indicators fall together, they show that bears are crushing the market. Those indicators may stay in gear with each other for only a few bars, but that's when the market travels fast—the impulse is on!

Before you rush to apply the Impulse System to your favorite market, remember how Triple Screen analyzes markets in more than one timeframe. Select your favorite timeframe and call it intermediate. Multiply it by five to define your long-term timeframe. If your favorite chart is daily, analyze the weekly chart to make a strategic decision to be a bull or a bear. Use a 26-week EMA, the slope of weekly MACD-Histogram, or both, on the weekly chart.

Once you've defined the long-term trend, return to your daily chart and look for trades only in the direction of the weekly. The Impulse System uses a 13-day EMA and a 12-26-9 MACD-Histogram. The EMA, tracking market inertia, is a little shorter than our usual 22 bars, making the system more sensitive.

When the weekly trend is up, turn to the daily charts and wait for both the 13-day EMA and MACD-Histogram to turn up. When both inertia and momentum rise, you have a strong buy signal, telling you to get long and stay long until the buy signal disappears.

When the weekly trend is down, turn to the daily charts and wait for both the 13-day EMA and MACD-Histogram to turn down. They give you a signal to go short, but be ready to cover when that signal disappears.

Some technical programs allow you to mark price bars with different colors. Make them green when both the EMA and MACD-Histogram rise, and red when both indicators fall. Don't mark the bars where the indicators point in the opposite directions. This lets you easily see signals at a glance.

Programming differs for different software packages, but here's how I programmed buy signals into Internet Trader Pro:

AlertMarker (mov (c,13,e) > ref (mov (c,13,e), −1) and fml ("MACD-Histogram") > ref (fml ("MACD-Histogram"), −1), Below)

Here is the code for sell signals:

AlertMarker (mov (c,13,e) < ref (mov (c,13,e), −1) and fml ("MACD-Histogram") < ref (fml ("MACD-Histogram"), −1), Above)

If you know how to program, you can add more features to the system. You can make its EMA length variable and test different lengths, looking for those that work best in your market. You can program sound alarms for buy and sell signals and monitor a number of markets without being glued to the screen. There is a fisherman on the esplanade near where I live who has several fishing poles, each with a little bell. Whenever a fish bites, a bells rings, the man puts his newspaper down and starts reeling it in.

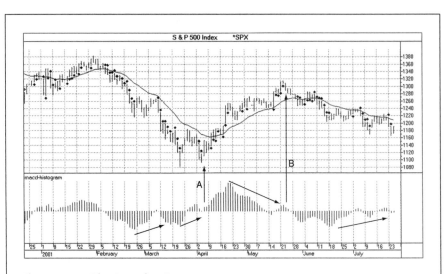

Figure 6.6   The Impulse System

When both EMA and MACD-Histogram point in the same direction, they identify an accelerating market move. The best way to see Impulse signals is to program buys and sells in different colors. Trade in the direction of an impulse to catch the sharpest, most dynamic moves. Also, never, ever trade against the Impulse. For example, a bullish divergence, a double bottom, and a kangaroo tail in March and April all point to an important bottom, but you may not buy as long as Impulse is down. The sell signal disappears at point A, and that's when you may go long.

The Impulse System beautifully tracks the bear move in January-March and the bull move in April–May. In May, bearish divergence B is followed by the disappearance of an Impulse buy signal, which permits shorting. The resulting downtrend is not as dynamic as the two preceding moves, with alternating Impulse buy and sell signals. It is a sign of an indecisive market, which is hard to trade. If in doubt, stay out.

At the right edge of the chart, a triple bullish divergence of MACD-Histogram gives a buy signal. The Impulse System has just gone off its sell signal. The stock market appears poised for a rally. If you buy, with a stop below the latest low, make sure that order is stop-and-reverse. If this bullish divergence gets aborted, the market will give a Hound of the Baskervilles signal and fall out of bed.

Exits

When a cowboy at a rodeo hops on the back of a wild bronco, how long does he ride it? Twenty seconds, 35 maybe, 50 if he is good and lucky. Wild momentum trades don't last long either. Try to hop off while you're still in the money.

The time to buy into a momentum trade is when all your ducks are in a row, that is, when the weekly trend is up and the daily EMA and MACD-Histogram are rising. Hop off as soon as a single indicator turns down. Usually, daily MACD-Histogram turns first as the upside momentum starts weakening. When the buy signal disappears, sell without waiting for a sell signal.

Reverse the procedure in downtrends. A momentum trade on the short side starts when the weekly trend turns down and the daily EMA and MACD-Histogram also fall, showing that the downward momentum is accelerating. Cover shorts as soon as one of those indicators stops giving a sell signal. The most dynamic part of the decline is over, and your momentum trade has fulfilled its goal.

The Impulse System encourages you to enter cautiously but exit fast. This is the professional approach to trading, the total opposite of the amateurs' style. Beginners jump into trades without thinking too much and take forever to get out, hoping and waiting for the market to turn their way.

The Impulse System, like Triple Screen, is a method of trading rather than a mechanical system. It identifies islands of order in the ocean of market chaos by showing when the crowd, usually so aimless and disorganized, becomes emotional and starts to run. You get in when its pattern emerges and hop off when it starts to sink back into chaos.

Test the Impulse System on your own market data to answer several important questions. Should you enter and exit at the open, after seeing the signal in the evening, or should you try to anticipate those signals? What if you do your homework 15 minutes before the close and buy or sell without waiting for tomorrow? Experiment with several different parameters of the EMA and MACD-Histogram.

You must be very disciplined to trade this system because it is hard to place an order when the market is already flying, but even harder to quit while you're ahead without waiting for a reversal. You are not allowed to kick yourself if the trend continues after you get out. Do not touch this system if you have the slightest problem with discipline.

The Impulse System can help you trade other systems. Check its message when Triple Screen gives you a signal to buy. If the Impulse System flashes a sell signal, hold off buying; do not trade against it. You want to buy a dip, not a waterfall decline. Reverse the procedure in downtrends. Hold off shorting if the Impulse System flashes a buy signal. Such "negative rules," designed to keep you out of trouble, are among the most useful for serious traders.

MARKET THERMOMETER

A beginner needs to learn a battery of standard technical indicators and start tweaking their parameters. Some traders create their own indicators to gauge different aspects of crowd behavior and identify market moves. Let us walk through the process of creating a new technical indicator and see how to go about building your own private indicators.

All good indicators reflect some aspect of market reality. Market Thermometer helps differentiate between sleepy, quiet periods and hot episodes when market crowds become excited. It can help you adapt your trading to the current environment.

Quiet markets typically have narrow bars that tend to overlap one another. Hot, boiling markets tend to have wide bars whose highs and lows extend far outside the previous day's range. Beginners jump into trades during those wide bars, afraid to miss a runaway move. If you enter when the markets are quiet, your slippage is likely to be lower. Hot markets are good for taking profits because then slippage may work in your favor.

When gold recently ran up $40 in one week, a journalist asked a famous investor whether it was a good buy. Gold was good, he said, but the time to get on this bus was when it stood in front of the station, and not rolling down the highway at 40 miles an hour. Market Thermometer helps you recognize when the bus slows down in front of the station, picks up speed, or roars down the highway.

Market Thermometer measures how far the most extreme point of today, either high or low, protrudes outside of yesterday's range. The greater the extension of today's bar outside of yesterday's, the higher the market temperature. Here's the formula of Market Thermometer:

$$\text{Temperature} = \text{the greater of either } (\text{High}_{\text{today}} - \text{High}_{\text{yesterday}})$$
$$\text{or } (\text{Low}_{\text{yesterday}} - \text{Low}_{\text{today}})$$

To program Market Thermometer into Windows on WallStreet software, use the following formula:

if (hi<ref(hi,–1) and lo>ref(lo,–1), 0, if ((hi – ref(hi,–1)) > (ref(lo,–1) – lo), hi – ref(hi,–1), ref(lo,–1) – lo)).

It is easy to adapt this formula to other software packages.

Market temperature is always a positive number, reflecting the absolute value of either the upward or the downward extension of yesterday's range, whichever is greater. Plot temperature as a histogram above zero. Calculate a moving average of market temperature, and plot it as a line on the same chart. I use a 22-day EMA because there are 22 trading days in a month, but feel free to experiment with shorter EMA values if you want to make this indicator more sensitive to short-term swings.

When markets are quiet, the adjacent bars tend to overlap. The consensus of value is well established, and the crowd does little buying or selling outside of yesterday's range. When highs and lows exceed their previous day's values, they do so only by small margins. Market Thermometer falls and its EMA slants down, indicating a sleepy market.

When a market begins to run, either up or down, its daily bars start pushing outside of the previous ranges. The histogram of Market Thermometer grows taller and crosses above its EMA, which soon turns up, confirming the new trend.

Market Thermometer gives four trading signals, based on the relationship between its histogram and its moving average:

The best time to enter new positions is when Market Thermometer falls below its moving average. When Market Thermometer falls below its EMA, it indicates that the market is quiet. If your system flashes an entry signal, try to enter when the market is cooler than usual. When Market Thermometer rises above its moving average, it warns that the market is hot and slippage more likely.

Exit positions when Market Thermometer rises to triple the height of its moving average. A spike of Market Thermometer indicates a runaway move. When the crowd feels jarred by a sudden piece of news and surges, it is a good time to take profits. Panics tend to be short-lived, offering a brief opportunity to cash in. If the EMA of Market Thermometer stands at 5 cents, but the Thermometer itself shoots up to 15 cents, take profits. Test these values for the market you are trading.

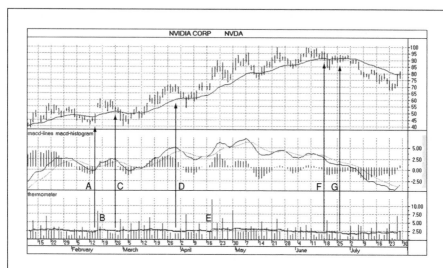

Figure 6.7 Market Thermometer

Nvidia Corp (NVDA) is one of the current favorites among active traders. Just look at its many tradable features—a powerful rally to 100, its triple top, a MACD bearish divergence, and a subsequent downtrend. Markets oscillate between quiet and active periods, and the Thermometer helps you identify them.

Get ready for an explosive move if the Thermometer stays below its moving average for five to seven trading days. Quiet markets put amateurs to sleep. They become careless and stop watching prices. Volatility and volume fall, and professionals get a chance to run away with the market. Explosive moves often erupt from periods of inactivity.

Market Thermometer can help you set a profit target for the next trading day. If you are a short-term trader and are long, add the value of today's Thermometer EMA to yesterday's high and place a sell order there. If you are short, subtract the value of the Thermometer's EMA from yesterday's low and place an order to cover at that level.

I had two purposes in presenting the Market Thermometer. I wanted to give you a new indicator, but even more I wanted to show you how to use your understanding of the markets to design your own analytic tools. Once you understand the principles of market analysis, you can create your own indicators. Use your knowledge, understanding, and discipline to get on the right side of the markets.

At point A, the stock is in an uptrend, while the Thermometer has been below its 22-day EMA for five days. This is a quiet before the storm. An explosive move in the direction of the trend (point B) rewards buyers. At the same time a very high Thermometer reading, three times above the average, warns that the fun and games are over; the move is exhausted, and it is time to take profits. At point C the Thermometer shrinks again, spending five days below its EMA and warning that a sharp move is coming. Since prices are above their EMA, expect a decline. A similar message emerges at point D. After the next rally (point E), an extremely high reading of the Thermometer, more than four times the average, warns that it is a good time to take short-term profits. Prices make a triple top near 100, MACD-Histogram traces a severe bearish divergence, and at points F and G prices hang flat. This is another quiet before the storm as bears swing the stock down.

The EMA of the Thermometer tells you how far today's high or low is likely to be above or below yesterday's extreme. This is a useful piece of intelligence for those who like to buy low or sell high; you can place your order for the day near the projected extreme.

At the right edge of the chart, prices have just shot up to their declining EMA. They deserved a rally after sliding from 100 to below 70, but a very high reading of the Thermometer, three times above average, indicates that the excitement is overdone, a pause is coming, and the downtrend is about to resume.

EXITING TRADES

Whenever you enter a trade, three factors must be crystal clear in your mind—where to get in, where to take profits, and where to bail out in case of an emergency. Daydreaming about profits will not make you rich. You must decide in advance where you'll take your winnings off the table or cut and run if the market turns against you.

Beginners keep looking for promising trades and assume that finding them will make them money. They search for entries, while professionals spend a lot of time and energy planning their exits. They always ask themselves where to take profits or cut losses. Survivors know the essential truth—you don't get paid for entering trades, you get paid for exiting them.

Why think about an exit before you enter a trade? Isn't it better to get in, monitor the trade, and exit in response to price action? There are two main arguments for deciding on an exit before you enter a trade.

First, knowing your targets and stops allows you to weigh rewards and risks. If you have a clear signal to buy, with a price target of $2 above and a stop $4 below, is that trade worth taking? Do you want to risk $4 to gain $2? Price targets and stops prompt you to focus only on trades whose potential rewards far outweigh the risks. The ability to walk away from a potential trade is as important as the ability to decline a drink when you want.

Second, setting profit targets and stops before entering trades helps sidestep the pernicious "ownership effect." We get attached to things we own and lose objectivity. That old ratty jacket hanging in your closet should have been given to the Salvation Army years ago. That trade you entered last week is starting to come apart at the seams. Why don't you chuck it? You own both the jacket and the trade; they feel comfortable, familiar. That's why you need to decide on exits before you enter, before a trade becomes yours.

A friend who is a top-notch technical analyst temporarily took a job as a broker after falling on hard times when his hedge fund closed. Naturally, I moved one of my accounts to him. Whenever I called to place an order, he would not let me hang up unless I gave him a stop. Sometimes I'd plead for a little more time and he'd take my order, on the condition that I call back within five minutes to give him a stop, or else he would call me. Six months later he found work as a technical analyst, and I have never seen another broker like him since. He really stressed the need to know your safety parameters before you took on market risk.

Before entering a trade, you should set two specific price levels, a target and a stop, one above and the other below current prices. This is all you need for a short-term trade, where you shoot at a clearly visible target. You may find a broker who accepts OCO (one cancels other) orders. Then, if your profit target is hit, the stop is automatically cancelled, and vice versa. If your broker does not accept OCO orders, give him your stop and keep an eye on your profit target.

What if you're planning a fairly long-term trade that may last for several days or even weeks? Profit targets shift with the passage of time, and protective stops need to be tightened as the trade moves in your favor. You must write down your rules for exiting trades and follow them from that piece of paper without arguing, haggling, or hoping for a better price. For example, you may decide to exit if the upper channel line gets hit or if the market makes lower lows for two days in a row. Whatever rules you use, write them down and execute immediately once the market hits a profit target or a stop-loss level in accordance with your rules.

Very experienced traders know how to recognize unusually forceful trends, during which they shift exit strategies, take partial profits, and carry the balance of their positions with a modified exit strategy for runaway trends. As you become more experienced, you can become a little more relaxed with your plans, but a beginning or an intermediate trader must be very strict. Entries are easy because any clown can buy a lottery ticket, but exits separate winners from losers.

Channel Targets

Traders all over the world squint at their charts, trying to recognize patterns, and let their imaginations run wild. Statistical studies, however, consistently confirm only one pattern—the tendency of prices to fluctuate above and below value. Markets may be chaotic most of the time, but their overbought and oversold conditions create islands of order that provide some of the best trading opportunities. Markets swing between elation and despair, and we can make money from those moods.

Channels are technical tools that help us take advantage of market swings. We draw them parallel to the moving average in the intermediate timeframe, usually daily. A well-drawn channel contains approximately 95% of recent prices. Its upper line represents the manic and the lower line the depressive moods of the market.

If we buy value near a rising moving average, we can sell mania in the vicinity of the upper channel line. If we go short near a falling moving average, we can cover at the depressed level near the lower channel line. Channels provide attractive targets for profit taking.

People say that a neurotic is a person who builds castles in the clouds, a psychotic lives in them, and a psychiatrist is the fellow who collects the rent. Channels help us collect rent from what drives most investors crazy—the relentless swings of the markets. The idea is to buy normalcy and sell mania or go short normalcy and cover depression.

Straight channels or envelopes work better for profit taking than standard deviation channels, or Bollinger bands. Those bands grow wide when volatility rises and narrow when it declines. They help options traders, who depend heavily on volatility, but those of us who trade stocks or futures are better off with straight channels.

Channels are for traders, not investors. If you want to invest in a $10 stock and ride it to $50, channels are not for you. Exits from investments or very long-term trades are based on the fundamentals or such long-term technical signals as the reversals of a 26-week moving average. Envelopes or channels work best when you trade relatively short-term swings between undervalued and overvalued levels.

If you buy near a rising EMA, place a sell order where you expect the upper channel line to be tomorrow. If the upper channel line has been rising a half a point a day for the past few days and closed at 88 today, then you can place a sell order at 88.50 for tomorrow. Adjust this number every day as the channel moves higher or lower.

Whenever I teach a group how to use channels for profit taking, someone raises a hand and points to an area where prices overshot their channel. Taking profits at that channel line would have caused us to miss a large part of a rally. What can I say? This system is good but not perfect. No method, except for hindsight, nails down all tops and bottoms. Robert Prechter, who used to be a famous market analyst, put it well when he said, "Traders take a good system and destroy it by trying to make it into a perfect system."

If a trend is very strong, you may want to ride swings a little farther. Sell half of your position when prices hit the upper channel line, but use your judgment to dance out of the second half. You may monitor intraday prices and sell on the first day when they do not make a new high. Use your judgment and skills, but do yourself a favor—give up the idea of nailing tops. Greed is a very expensive emotion.

If a rally is weak, prices may begin to sink without reaching their upper channel line. There is no law that says the market must become manic before returning to value. Force Index can help measure the strength of a rally. When the two-day Force Index rises to a new high, it confirms the power of bulls and encourages you to hold until prices hit the upper channel line. If the two-day Force Index traces a bearish divergence, it shows that the rally is weak and you better grab profits fast.

An A trader is someone who takes 30% or more out of a channel. That is a little more than half the distance from the moving average to the channel line. Even if you buy slightly above the moving average and sell below its upper channel line, you can be an A trader and profit handsomely. Channels help catch normal tops and bottoms, and you can become very rich by steadily raking in normal profits. Channels help set up realistic profit targets.

Protective Stops

Amateurs swing between fantasy and reality, making most decisions in the realm of fantasy. They dream of profits and avoid unpleasant thoughts about possible losses. Since stops force us to focus on losses, most traders resist using them.

A friend told me she needed no stops because she was an investor. "At what price did you buy that stock?" I asked. She had gotten in at 80 and now it was at 85. "Would you still hold it if it fell back to 80?" She said she would. "What about 75?" She said she would probably buy more. "What about 70?" She winced. "What about 55? Would you still want to own it?" No, no, she vigorously shook her head. "Well, then you need a stop somewhere above 55!"

I recently had dinner with a lawyer who obtained inside information that a certain penny-stock company was about to announce a strategic partnership with a telecom giant. Questions of legality and morality aside, he put most of his money into that stock at an average price of 16.5 cents a share. Once the announcement came out, his stock ran up to $8, but by the time he told me his secret over a tray of sushi, it was down to $1.50. He had no stop. I asked him whether he would continue to hold if his stock slid to 8 cents, half of what he paid. He was shocked and promised to put in a stop at $1. Did he do it? Probably not. It is easier to dream and close one's eyes to reality.

You must put in a stop immediately after entering a trade and start moving it in the direction of that trade as soon as it starts moving in your favor. Stops are a one-way street. When long, you may raise, but never lower them. When short, you may lower but never raise them. Only losers say, "I'll give this trade a little more room." You already gave it all the room it needed when you placed your stop! If a stock starts moving against you, leave your stop alone! You were more rational at the time you placed it than you are today, with prices hovering and threatening to hit it.

Investors must reevaluate their stops once every few weeks, but traders have a harder job. We must recalculate our stops every day and move them often.

A Deadly Delusion   Many traders think they can stay out of trouble without using stops, thanks to their superior market analysis. Trading is a high-wire act. You may walk that wire a hundred times without a safety net, but the very first fall can cripple you. You cannot afford to take that chance. No amount of brains will help you if you abandon stops.

Several years ago I got a call from a world-famous developer of trading software. He invited me on a camping trip, and mentioned in passing that he had developed a fantastic system for trading futures. It was based on computerized pattern recognition, backtested on 20 years of data with breathtaking results. He had no money to trade that system, having lost his capital on an earlier venture, but showed his discovery to a group of money managers. They were so impressed they began to set up a hedge fund for him, and in the meantime gave him what they called a small account—$100,000.

I flew across the country and spent the first evening admiring my friend's system. "Are you trading anything now?" The system had given him six signals: in soybeans, Swiss francs, pork bellies, and three other markets. He had entered trades in all six. "How much did you allocate to each?" He had divided his account into six parts, one for each market. No reserves. Fully margined. "Where did you put your stops?" He told me in so many words that real men didn't use stops.

He had mathematical proof that stops lowered profitability. Safety lay in trading unrelated markets. If one or two went against him, others would move in his favor. "What about a catastrophic event, with all markets moving against you?" He assured me that was impossible because he traded unrelated markets, and there was no correlation between Swiss francs and pork bellies. Furthermore, his system had not a single wipeout in 20 years of backtesting.

I suggested we forget about camping and stay closer to the screen, since his entire capital was at risk. My friend insisted he had total confidence in his system, and so we drove to the Sierra Nevada, some of the most breathtaking scenery in America. We had a grand time, and on the last day my son, who was about 8 at the time, hauled in a plastic pail full of gold nuggets. It was fool's gold, of course, but to this day I keep one of them on my desk as a paperweight, engraved "All that glitters is gold."

By the time we returned to civilization the impossible had happened. All six markets went against my friend, nearly wiping out his equity. The next morning we watched in horror as the markets opened one after another, continuing to go against him in huge gobs. I talked him into closing two out of six positions, but then it was time to drive to the airport.

A few days later I called to thank my friend for the trip. His account was wiped out, and he bitterly complained that his money men weren't gentlemen; they weren't returning his phone calls. I resisted the temptation to say that if he lost $100,000 for me, I would not return his phone calls either.

A trader who doesn't use stops will eventually take the mother of all losses. Spectacular disasters hit brilliant individuals who believe that their general sharpness and great systems override the need for stops. A careless trader can get away with no stops for a while, but if he trades long enough the market will kill him.

No amount of brains will save a trader who doesn't use stops. A Nobel Prize for research in the financial markets will not help him. Look at Long-Term Capital Management, a hedge fund owned and operated by a clutch of certified geniuses, including a former Salomon director, a former Fed governor, and two Nobel Prize winners. Those people were too bright to use stops. They came to the brink of failure in 1998 and didn't bust out only because the US Federal Reserve stepped in to arrange a bailout to avoid disrupting world markets.

No amount of intelligence, knowledge, or computer power will save you from a disaster if you trade without stops. Stops are essential for your survival and success.

What about mental stops—deciding on your exit point and then watching the market? If it violates that level, you exit your position, trying to get the best price. This is a common strategy among pros who have a lot of experience and iron discipline. A beginner, on the other hand, watches the market the way a rabbit watches a snake—frozen in fear, unable to move. He must place actual stops.

Stops do not provide total protection because prices are not continuous and can gap across the stop level. You can buy a stock at 40 and place a protective stop at 37, but a bad earnings report or an announcement can force that stock to open at 34 tomorrow, filling your order at a much worse level than expected. This is not an argument against stops. An umbrella with holes is better than no umbrella at all. Also, money management rules provide an extra level of protection.

Stops in Two Dimensions Placing stops is one of the hardest challenges in trading, more so than finding good trades. You want to place them close enough to protect your capital but far enough to avoid being stopped out by meaningless noise. It is a delicate balancing act.

Most trading books repeat the same advice: place a stop below the latest low when long or above the latest high when short. This method is so simple and common that tons of stops become bunched up at the same obvious levels. Professionals are not blind; they look at charts and know where those stops are. They gun for them, trying to trigger stops with false breakouts.

When a stock hangs just above support, the inflow of fresh buy orders dries up, and those with stops below support just suck air and wait. The pros sell short, giving that stock a bit of a push. It stumbles below support, setting off a flurry of sell stop orders. The pros who shorted at a higher level begin to cover, buying on the cheap from amateurs whose stops they hit. As soon as the decline slows down they redouble their buying, and go long. The market rallies, and the pros who bought below support now sell into the rally. Most breakouts from trading ranges are false breakouts—fishing expeditions by the pros gunning for stops at common levels. Once those stops are cleaned out, the market is ready to reverse. Most traders become so disgusted after getting hit by several false breakouts that they give up using stops. That's when a real reversal catches them. They end up losing money, with and without stops, and wash out of the markets.

Placing stops at obvious levels is not a good idea. You are better off placing them a bit closer to protect capital or a bit farther to reduce the risk of getting hit. Try not to do what everybody else does. Be sure to place your stop where you do not expect the market to go. If you expect prices to fall to a certain level, why place a stop there? You're better off closing your trade without waiting.

There are two inputs into placing stops: technical analysis and money management. You can combine them to find the right size for your trade as well as the right place for your stop. The first step is to decide how many dollars you should risk on the trade you're about to take. Later, in the section on money management, you'll learn to limit your risk on any trade to a tiny percentage of your account. If you're not fully confident, risk an even smaller percentage. Once you have the dollar figure for your maximum risk, turn to technical analysis to find where to place your stop. A stop based on technical analysis is almost always tighter, that is, closer to the market, than the money management stop. Your account is now starting to look like a submarine with a double hull—softer on the outside and harder on the inside.

Your money management stops belong in the market. They represent your maximum allowable risk level, which you may not violate under any circumstances. If your technical analysis stops are closer to the market, you may hold them in your mind as you monitor prices and are prepared to exit if those levels gets hit.

Here, I want to share with you two advanced methods for placing stops. Try to program them into your software and test them on your market data. Until now, I have never disclosed SafeZone to traders, except to small groups in Traders' Camps, where I like to share my latest research. It is my principle not to withhold information from my books. I write as I trade and maintain my edge not by secrecy but by developing new methods.

The SafeZone Stop

Once in a trade, where should you put your stop? This is one of the hardest questions in technical analysis. After answering it, you'll face an even harder one—when and where to move that stop with the passage of time. Put a stop too close and it'll get whacked by some meaningless intraday swing. Put it too far, and you'll have very skimpy protection.

The Parabolic System, described in *Trading for a Living*, tried to tackle this problem by moving stops closer to the market each day, accelerating whenever a stock or a commodity reached a new extreme. The trouble with Parabolic was that it kept moving even if the market stayed flat and often got hit by meaningless noise.

The concept of signal and noise states that the trend is the signal and the nontrending motion is the noise. A stock or a future may be in an uptrend or a downtrend, but the noise of its random chop can obscure its signal. Trading at the right edge is hard because the noise level is high. I developed SafeZone to trail prices with stops tight enough to protect capital but remote enough to keep clear of most random fluctuations.

Engineers design filters to suppress noise and allow the signal to come through. If the trend is the signal, then the countertrend motion is the noise. When the trend is up, we can define noise as that part of each day's range that protrudes below the previous day's low. When the trend is down, we can define noise as that part of each day's range that protrudes above the previous day's high. SafeZone measures market noise and places stops at a multiple of noise level away from the market.

We may use the slope of a 22-day EMA to define the trend. You need to choose the length of the lookback period for measuring noise level. It has to be long enough to track recent behavior but short enough to be relevant for current trading. A period of 10 to 20 days works well, or we can make our lookback period 100 days or so if we want to average long-term market behavior.

If the trend is up, mark all downside penetrations during the lookback period, add their depths, and divide the sum by the number of penetrations. This gives you the Average Downside Penetration for the selected lookback period. It reflects the average level of noise in the current uptrend. Placing your stop any closer would be self-defeating. We want to place our stops farther away from the market than the average level of noise. Multiply the Average Downside Penetration by a coefficient, starting with two, but experiment with higher numbers. Subtract the result from yesterday's low, and place your stop there. If today's low is lower than yesterday's, do not move your stop lower since we are only allowed to raise stops on long positions, not lower them.

Reverse these rules in downtrends. When a 22-day EMA identifies a downtrend, count all the upside penetrations during the lookback period and find the Average Upside Penetration. Multiply it by a coefficient, starting with two. When you go short, place a stop twice the Average Upside Penetration above the previous day's high. Lower your stop whenever the market makes a lower high, but never raise it.

I anticipate that SafeZone will be programmed into many software packages, allowing traders to control both the lookback period and the multiplication factor. Until then, you will have to do your own programming or else track SafeZone manually (see Table 6.1). Be sure to calculate it separately for uptrends and downtrends.

Here are the rules for calculating SafeZone using an Excel spreadsheet. Once you understand how it works, try to program SafeZone into your technical analysis software and superimpose its signals on the chart. Compare the numbers from the spreadsheet and the trading software. They should be identical; otherwise, you have a programming error. Comparing results from two software packages helps overcome pesky programming problems.

Rules for Longs in Uptrends   When the trend is up, we calculate SafeZone on the basis of the lows because their pattern determines stop placement.

Table 6.1 SafeZone Stops—Spreadsheet

	A	B	C	D	E	F	G	H	I	J	K	L	M	N	O	P	Q	R
1	IBM				For uptrends							For downtrends						
2	Date	High	Low	Close	Dn Pen	Sum	Pen Y/N	Dn numb	Dn Avg	Short Stop	Protected	Up Pen	Sum	Pen Y/N	Up numb	Up avg	Long Stop	Protected
3	04/19	115.90	110.30	114.47														
4	04/20	116.40	113.75	114.83	0		0					0.5		1				
5	04/23	114.05	111.68	112.00	2.07		1					0		0				
6	04/24	114.75	112.28	112.67	0		0					0.7		1				
7	04/25	114.85	111.99	114.85	0.29		1					0.1		1				
8	04/26	116.70	113.68	113.74	0		0					1.85		1				
9	04/27	116.90	114.55	116.20	0		0					0.2		1				
10	04/30	118.05	114.72	115.14	0		0					1.15		1				
11	05/01	118.65	114.90	118.51	0		0					0.6		1				
12	05/02	118.95	113.74	115.40	1.16		1					0.3		1				
13	05/03	115.10	112.35	113.70	1.39	4.91	1	4	1.23			0	5.4	0	8	0.68		
14	05/04	115.86	111.20	115.86	1.15	6.06	1	5	1.21	109.90		0.76	5.66	1	8	0.71	116.45	
15	05/07	117.25	115.00	115.90	0	3.99	0	4	1.00	108.78		1.39	7.05	1	9	0.78	117.28	
16	05/08	117.75	115.50	117.70	0	3.99	0	4	1.00	113.01	113.01	0.5	6.85	1	9	0.76	118.82	116.45
17	05/09	118.18	115.30	116.98	0.2	3.9	1	4	0.98	113.51	113.51	0.43	7.18	1	9	0.80	119.27	117.28
18	05/10	118.90	115.20	115.20	0.1	4	1	5	0.80	113.35	113.51	0.72	6.05	1	9	0.67	119.78	118.82
19	05/11	114.15	110.96	111.81	4.24	8.24	1	6	1.37	113.60	113.60	0	5.85	0	8	0.73	120.24	119.27
20	05/14	113.18	111.00	112.56	0	8.24	0	6	1.37	108.21	113.60	0	4.7	0	7	0.67	115.61	115.61
21	05/15	114.15	112.50	113.58	0	8.24	0	6	1.37	108.25	113.60	0.97	5.07	1	7	0.72	114.52	114.52
22	05/16	115.80	112.20	115.80	0.3	7.38	1	6	1.23	109.75	109.75	1.65	6.42	1	7	0.92	115.60	114.52
23	05/17	117.09	113.36	115.07	0	5.99	0	5	1.20	109.74	109.75	1.29	7.71	1	8	0.96	117.63	114.52
24	05/18	117.68	114.90	117.44	0	4.84	0	4	1.21	110.96	110.96	0.59	7.54	1	8	0.94	119.02	115.60
25	05/21	119.90	117.55	119.04	0	4.84	0	4	1.21	112.48	112.48	2.22	8.37	1	8	1.05	119.57	117.63
26	05/22	119.70	117.05	118.01	0.5	5.34	1	5	1.07	115.13	115.13	0	7.87	0	7	1.12	121.99	119.02
27	05/23	118.95	117.10	117.40	0	5.14	0	4	1.29	114.91	115.13	0	7.44	0	6	1.24	121.95	119.57

1. Obtain at least a month of data for your stock or future in high-low-close format, as shown in Table 6.1 (lows are in column C with the first record in row 3).

2. Test whether today's low is lower than yesterday's. Go to cell E4, enter the formula =IF(C3>C4,C3–C4,0) and copy it down the length of that column. It measures the depth of the downside penetration below the previous day's range, and if there is none, it shows zero.

3. Choose the lookback period and summarize all downside penetrations during that time. Begin with 10 days and later experiment with other values. Go to cell F13, enter the formula =SUM(E4:E13), and copy it down the length of that column. It will summarize the extent of all downside penetrations for the past 10 days.

4. Mark each bar that penetrates below the previous bar. Go to cell G4, enter the formula =IF(C4<C3,1,0) and copy it down the length of that column. It will mark each downside penetration with 1 and no penetration with 0.

5. Count the number of downside penetrations during the lookback period, in this case 10 days. Go to cell H13, enter the formula =SUM(G4:G13), and copy it down the length of that column. It will show how many times in the past 10 days the lows have been violated.

6. Find the Average Downside Penetration by dividing the sum of all downside penetrations during the lookback period by their number. Go to cell I13, enter the formula =F13/H13, and copy it down the length of that column. It will show the Average Downside Penetration for each day, that is, the normal level of downside noise in that market.

7. Place your stop for today at a multiple of yesterday's Average Downside Penetration below yesterday's low. Multiply yesterday's Average Downside Penetration by a selected coefficient, starting at 2 but testing as high as 3, and subtract the result from yesterday's low to obtain today's stop. Go to cell J14, enter the formula =C13–2•I13, and copy it down the length of that column. It will place a stop two Average Downside Penetrations below the latest low. If today's low penetrates yesterday's low by twice the normal range of noise, we bail out.

8. Refine the formula to prevent it from lowering stops in uptrends. If the above formula tells us to lower our stop, we simply leave it at the previous day's level. Go to cell K16, enter the formula

=MAX(J14:J16), and copy it down the length of that column. It will prevent the stop from declining for three days, by which time either the uptrend resumes or the stop is hit.

Rules for Shorts in Downtrends   When the trend is down, we calculate SafeZone on the basis of the highs because their pattern determines stop placement.

1. Obtain at least a month of data for your stock or future in high-low-close format, as shown in Table 6.1 (highs are in column B with the first record in row 3).
2. Test whether today's high is higher than yesterday's. Go to cell L4, enter the formula =IF(B4>B3,B4–B3,0), and copy it down the length of that column. It measures the height of the upside penetration above the previous day's range, and if there is none, it shows zero.
3. Choose the lookback period for summarizing upside penetrations. Begin with 10 days and experiment with higher values. Go to cell M13, enter the formula =SUM(L4:L13), and copy it down the length of that column. It will summarize the extent of all upside penetrations for the past 10 days.
4. Mark each bar that penetrates above the previous bar. Go to cell N4, enter the formula =IF(B4>B3,1,0), and copy it down the length of that column. It will mark each upside penetration with 1 and no penetration with 0.
5. Count the number of upside penetrations during the lookback period, in this case 10 days. Go to cell O13, enter the formula =SUM(N4:N13), and copy it down the length of that column. It will show how many times in the past 10 days the highs have been violated.
6. Find the Average Upside Penetration by dividing the sum of all upside penetrations during the lookback period by their number. Go to cell P13, enter the formula =M13/O13, and copy it down the length of that column. It shows the Average Upside Penetration, the normal level of upside noise in that market.
7. Place the stop for your short position today at a multiple of yesterday's Average Upside Penetration above yesterday's high. Multiply yesterday's Average Upside Penetration by a selected coefficient, starting at 2 but testing as high as 3, and add the result to yesterday's high to obtain today's stop. Go to cell Q14, enter

the formula =B13+2•P13, and copy it down the length of that column. It will place a stop two Average Upside Penetrations above yesterday's high. If today's high shoots above yesterday's high by twice the normal amount, it hits our stop and we bail out.

8. Refine the formula to prevent it from raising the stop during a downtrend. If the above formula tells us to raise our stop, we simply leave it at the previous day's level. Go to cell R16, enter the formula =MIN(Q14:Q16), and copy it down the length of that column. It will prevent the stop from rising for three days, by which time either the downtrend resumes or the stop is hit.

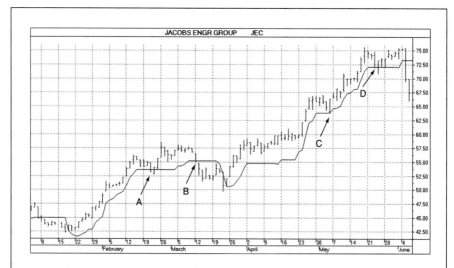

Figure 6.8 SafeZone Stops—Uptrend

To use SafeZone with your favorite stock or future during an uptrend, begin by multiplying the average downside penetration by the factor of three, and subtracting that from the low of the latest bar. Putting your stop closer than the average level of noise means asking for trouble, and even twice the average level is often too close. Once your system identifies an uptrend, SafeZone starts following prices, getting you out before the trend reverses. You can see that SafeZone stop was hit at points A, B, C, and D, catching the bulk of the uptrend and avoiding downdrafts.

The right edge of the chart illustrates why it is a good idea never to hold a stock below its SafeZone level. JEC is in a free fall, wiping out the profits of a month in just two days—a trader using SafeZone cashed out early in the decline.

SafeZone offers an original approach to placing stops. It monitors changes in prices and adapts stops to the current levels of activity. It places stops at individually tailored distances rather than at obvious support and resistance levels.

SafeZone works on the way down just as well as on the way up. Here we count each upside penetration of the previous day's range during a selected time window and average that data to find the Average Upside Penetration. We multiply it by a coefficient, starting with 3, and add that to the high of each bar.

Like all systems and indicators in this book, SafeZone is not a mechanical gadget to replace independent thought. You have to establish the lookback period, the window of time during which SafeZone is calculated. Do not go back beyond the last important turning point. If the market has reversed from down to up two weeks ago, then SafeZone for the current long trades should not look back more than 10 trading days.

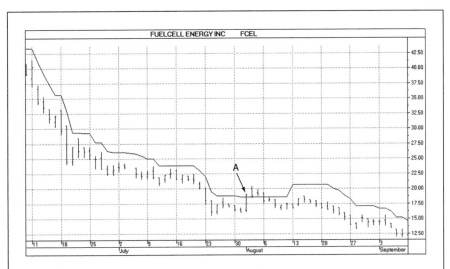

Figure 6.9   SafeZone Stops—Downtrend

Once your system identifies a downtrend, SafeZone helps you ride your short position all the way down, covering before a rally starts eating into your profits. Notice how SafeZone rode the decline in FCEL, constantly lowering its stop, until taken out by a rally at point A.

At the right edge of the chart, the downtrend continues, with SafeZone protecting a short position. It is safe to hold shorts with a close stop.

Another important decision is choosing the coefficient for the SafeZone stop. Usually, a coefficient between two and three provides a margin of safety, but you must research it on your own market data. Once you have done your homework and tweaked this indicator, it will become your own private tool in the battle for survival and success in the markets. You can add it to almost any trading system, including Triple Screen.

The Chandelier Exit

When a trend speeds up, you may want to shift gears and ride it instead of trading swings. Catching swings calls for tight stops, but a longer-term position demands more breathing room. The Chandelier Exit is designed to protect such positions.

When buyers place stops, they usually count back from the lows and put stops below recent important bottoms. When traders go short, they usually count back from the highs and place stops above the recent peaks. The Chandelier Exit takes a different approach. When traders are long, it hangs their stops from the highest peak reached by that trend, like a chandelier hangs from the tallest point in the room. As prices move up, the Chandelier Exit, suspended from the highest point of that trend, also rises. It tracks volatility as well as prices, as its distance from the peak grows with the rise in volatility. We will review Chandelier Exits for up-trends, but you may reverse these rules and apply them to downtrends.

There is no telling how high a trend may go, and a Chandelier will rise until prices peel off from the ceiling and hit that stop. This method, along with several others, was presented by Chuck LeBeau in our Traders' Camp in January 2000 in the Caribbean and again in March 2001 in the Pacific.

The Chandelier Exit draws on the concept of Average True Range, described by Welles Wilder in 1966. The True Range is the greatest of the three figures—the distance between today's high and low, or today's high and yesterday's close, or today's low and yesterday's close. The True Range reflects overnight volatility by comparing today's and yesterday's prices.

The True Range is included in many software packages. The Average True Range (ATR) is obtained by averaging True Range over a period of time. How long a period? You can begin by looking back a month, but a modern computerized trader can easily test different lookback periods for Average True Range.

The Chandelier Exit subtracts the Average True Range, multiplied by a coefficient, from the highest point reached by the trend. Its formula is:

$$\text{Chandelier} = \text{HP} - \text{coef} \cdot \text{ATR}$$

where
Chandelier = the Chandelier Exit
HP   = the highest point for a selected number of days
coef   = the coefficient, selected by the trader
ATR   = Average True Range for a selected number of days

If an uptrend is boiling and daily ranges are wide, then stops fall a little farther away. If the uptrend is quiet and calm with more narrow ranges, the stops inch a little closer.

In Windows on Wallstreet software, the formula for the Chandelier Exit is:

$$\text{Hhv(hi, 22)} - 3 \cdot \text{ATR(22)}$$

Hhv(hi, 22) is the highest high reached in the past 22 days and ATR(22) is the Average True Range for the past 22 days. Try to test other parameters in the markets you like to trade.

This formula multiplies the Average True Range by three before subtracting it from the high of the past 22 trading days. A serious trader is passionate about his research. Such a person will immediately notice that this formula contains three variables—the length of the lookback period for the highest high, the length of the lookback period for the True Range, and the coefficient for multiplying Average True Range. It probably doesn't pay to fiddle with the first variable, as the highest high in a runaway uptrend is likely to be close to the right edge and most lookback periods catch it. The Average True Range is only slightly more sensitive to the length of its lookback period. A more fertile ground for experimenting is the ATR coefficient. If everyone has their stops at 3 ATRs below the peak, wouldn't you like to see what happens if you set your stop at 3.5 or 2.5?

The Chandelier Exit can be used to trail profits on short positions in runaway downtrends. There the formula becomes:

$$\text{Llv(lo, 22)} + 3 \cdot \text{ATR(22)}$$

Llv(lo, 22) is the lowest low reached in the past 22 days and ATR(22) is the True Range for the past 22 days.

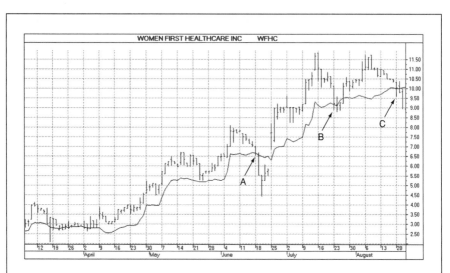

Figure 6.10   The Chandelier Exit

In an uptrend, the Chandelier Exit hangs from its uppermost point, 3 Average True Ranges below the extreme. It does a good job of helping catch the bulk of the uptrend, stopping traders out and protecting profits at points A, B, and C. Notice that as volatility increases the Chandelier gives a stock a little wider stop, receding from prices.

At the right edge of the chart, the Chandelier Exit has taken profits just as the decline got under way. Wait until your system gives you a new buy signal, and when it does, hang a new Chandelier on that trend.

Experienced traders sometimes joke that bear markets have no support and bull markets no resistance. A runaway trend can overshoot all rational expectations. The Chandelier deals with that by tying its stops to the price extreme as well as volatility.

The negative side of Chandelier Exits is that they give up a great deal of profit. Three Average True Ranges can amount to a lot of money in a volatile market. A beginning trader is better off taking his profits at the channel wall. A more advanced trader whose market is hitting its channel wall while showing great strength is more likely to switch to a Chandelier Exit. If he holds a large position, he may take partial profits at the channel wall and carry the rest using the Chandelier. The Chandelier Exit may act a backup exit strategy for experienced traders.

Gamblers lose fortunes trying to nail tops and bottoms. A good trader is a realist who wants to grab a chunk from the body of a trend, leaving top- and bottom-fishing to people on an ego trip. The Chandelier Exit helps take care of that chunk.

CHOOSING WHAT TO TRADE

Open a newspaper, and thousands of listings leap at you from the pages—stocks, mutual funds, futures, options, bonds, currencies. Your data provider may offer a menu of 20,000 items or more. Were you to download and review all of them, spending just two seconds on each, that process would take 11 hours.

Beginners worry about missing opportunities and try to look at as many markets as possible. They often ask for advice on scanning software. They want to sift through thousands of stocks for something like a bullish divergence in MACD-Histogram. First of all, divergences, so visible to the naked eye, are notoriously hard to program. The best programmer I know tells me he's done it—it is the pinnacle of his success—using the most expensive software. Even if a beginner could get hold of his program, that expense would be wasted because he wouldn't know what to do with the stocks he found in that search. He wouldn't know how to trade them correctly. A beginner is better off focusing on a handful of markets, learning all about them, and trading them with care and attention.

You are better off limiting yourself to as many markets as you can realistically follow each day. Professionals study their markets daily to detect transitions from sleepy trading ranges to new trends. The best time to profit from a trend is before it becomes overpriced and volatile.

Markets that make headlines tend to be overpriced and volatile. If you read an article on the front page of a financial newspaper about a bull market in biotech stocks or see a report on the evening news about the high price of coffee, those trends are probably nearer the end than the beginning, and buying biotech stocks or coffee futures is probably very dangerous.

To understand a person or a group, it pays to know what they want and what they fear. Journalists and editors most fear making a mistake that will make them look foolish. They report trends only after anyone can see them because that way there is no mistake. Even if they knew how to catch trends early, which they don't, they wouldn't dare print their findings for fear of being wrong and appearing ignorant. Traders aren't afraid of mistakes as long as they use money management, but journalists cannot afford such risks. By the time they write up a trend, it has been going on for a while, volatility is high, risk management is difficult, and a major reversal is probably in the cards.

Should you trade stocks or futures, currencies or options? Options are rough for beginners, who should learn to trade the underlying securities first, whether stocks or futures. People outside the United States are often drawn to currencies, forgetting that those are truly global markets, and when you trade them, you go against banks that have traders in all time zones. The choice between stocks or futures is seldom made on a rational basis. Trading stocks seems more respectable, while futures have more of a swashbuckling reputation. Futures get their wild image from their enormous leverage. If you scrupulously observe money management rules, they become much safer and less nerve-racking.

Stocks

Stocks tend to move more slowly than futures, thus reducing risks for beginners, especially those who avoid margin. It is one of the mysteries of markets that cash traders are more likely to win, and margin traders to lose. Why? Interest rates on margin loans are a serious expense, raising a barrier to winning, but there's more. People who buy stocks for cash tend to feel more relaxed, buying as much or as little as they want. Margin traders are more likely to feel stressed. An anxious trader is a troubled trader. It is better to buy only what you can afford, polish your skills, and the money will follow.

The sheer number of stocks drives people to distraction. Beginners throw their arms in the air and beg for a list of stocks to follow. A disciplined trader makes several choices that help him concentrate. He begins by selecting an industry group or groups and then zeros in on individual stocks.

A beginner should start with one or two groups, an intermediate trader can go up to four or five, and an expert knows how many he can handle. Chances are, he sticks to the few groups he knows well. Begin by choosing a group that you think has a great future or one in which you have a personal interest. For example, you may decide to concentrate on biotechnology because of its promise or the hospitality industry because that's where you work.

Select a broad rather than a narrow group. For example, if you decide to track autos, look not just at car manufacturers, but also at companies that make auto parts, tires, etc. The disadvantage of focusing on a single group is that you miss spectacular moves in others, but there are several advantages. You learn which stocks tend to lead or follow. When leaders start to move, they give you an advance signal to trade the laggards. You can use relative strength, that is, buy the strongest stocks when the group moves up and short the weakest on the way down. You can create an index that includes all the stocks you follow in your industry group, and then analyze that index. This analytic tool is not available to any other trader. If you use fundamental analysis, then having your finger on the pulse of a single industry, such as software, puts you miles ahead of competitors who trade Microsoft today and McDonald's tomorrow.

A broadly defined industry group may include over a hundred stocks, but an intelligent beginner should not follow more than a dozen. We can divide all stocks into blue chips and speculative "cats and dogs." Blue chips are the stocks of large, well-established companies, held by many institutions and followed by many researchers. They have a fairly well-established consensus of value around which they more or less gently oscillate. If you design a system for catching their swings several times each year, the potential gains can be very attractive. Don't ignore the big Dow-type stocks. Their orderly swings from the moving average to the channel wall create good trading opportunities.

The so-called cats and dogs may spend months, if not years, flat at the bottom, in a speculative doghouse, until a fundamental change, or even a rumor of change, propels them to a breakout and a new uptrend. Other cats and dogs may go nowhere or expire. Those stocks offer much higher percentage gains than blue chips, but the risks are greater and you must spend a great deal of time waiting for them to move. It makes sense to trade a large portion of your account in blue chips, while keeping a smaller portion in longer-term speculative positions.

What if you've paid your dues, learned to trade a few stocks in a few groups, and now want to forage in wider pastures? After all, technical patterns and signals are not all that different in various markets. What if you want to scan a larger number of stocks for MACD divergences, Impulse breakouts, or other patterns that you learned to recognize, trust, and trade?

Go on the Internet and find a website that gives you the 100 most active stocks on the NASDAQ (and if you do not know how to find such a website, you haven't got what it takes to trade them). Keep an eye on any stock that floats by you. A newspaper article mentions several companies—look up their stocks. People at a party talk about stocks—jot them down, drop them into your system, and see how they look on your screen. Many tips call for an exercise of contrary thinking. In summer 2001, Lucent (LU) was in the news with another earnings disappointment, having slid from 80 to 6. The journalists were aghast, but that stock has completed its bear market, traced an attractive bullish divergence, and was poised for a rally. A rise from 6 to 9 is a 50% increase. Stocks that people tout at parties are often good candidates for shorting. By the time outsiders become interested, the rise tends to be over. The idea is to maintain your curiosity and use tips not on their face value but only as invitations to look at this or that stock. I find that my yield, the percentage of tips that I end up trading in either direction, is about 5%—I end up trading one out of 20. I have a friend, a brilliant trader, who often calls me asking to take a look at this or that stock. My yield on her tips is 10%—she is the best.

The Turnover Ratio   The Turnover Ratio (TRO) predicts expected volatility of any stock by comparing its average daily volume with the available float. This formula was brought to my attention by Roger Perry of *The RightLine Report* (www.rightline.net):

TRO = monthly volume divided by the available float

Volume for the past month is easy to calculate. The available float refers to the total float, or number of shares issued, minus the holdings of institutions and insiders. Those groups tend to hold positions more tightly than private traders, who are more likely to sell if the price is right. All of the above figures are widely available from financial databases.

You can calculate the average monthly volume by multiplying the daily volume by 22, the number of trading days in a month. Using the daily volume makes the TRO more responsive to changes in volume as a stock rolls into or out of favor with traders.

TRO shows how many times the float trades in a month. For example, if a stock's monthly volume is 200 million shares and its available float 100 million, its TRO is 2%. If monthly volume of another stock is also 200 million, but its available float is 50 million, its TRO is 4.

If the average volume is much lower than the float, that stock has a low turnover rate and an onrush of buyers is unlikely to move the price much. However, if the volume is high relative to the float, then a lot of people compete for few available shares, and a sudden rush of buyers can move the price dramatically.

High-TRO stocks tend to be more volatile. Whoever wants to buy them has to pay a premium to pry them out of the hands of relatively few holders. When a selling wave hits the markets, the stocks with high TROs tend to go down harder because they do not have a large pool of institutional holders looking to pick up extra shares at a discount. All other factors being equal, the stock with a higher TRO will make a bigger percentage move.

For example, at the time of this writing, the monthly volume in GE was 355.9 million, with the available float of 9,809 million, resulting in a turnover ratio of 4%. The figures for JNPR were 387.2 million, 155.6 million, and 249%. No wonder; GE is a slow-moving blue chip, whereas JNPR is a high-flyer. Check these numbers once a month, as they keep changing. Stock splits reduce TROs by increasing the float. One split too many in DELL has oversaturated the market to the point where the stock has become unattractive for day-traders.

Blue chips, such as General Electric and IBM, are widely held by institutions and individuals. Their daily volume, no matter how high, is but a tiny percentage of their float. New unseasoned stocks often have very small floats, but when they catch the public's eye, their daily volumes go sky-high, lifting the TRO.

You can keep close tabs on the TROs of stocks you track. Whenever the market is active and running, switch into high-TRO stocks. Whenever the market goes into a choppy stage, switch to low-TRO stocks and trade their swings. TRO can help you switch between aggressive and defensive positions.

Trading Swings or Trends   Whenever you glance at a chart, your eye is immediately drawn to major rallies and declines. Big moves attract us with their promise of a killing. Exactly who gets killed is a question that seldom crosses beginners' minds. The trouble with major rallies and declines is that they are clearly visible in the middle of the chart, but the closer you get to the right edge, the murkier they become.

Big uptrends are punctuated by drops, while downtrends are interrupted by rallies. Emotionally, it is extremely hard to hold a position through a countertrend move. As profits melt away, we begin to wonder whether this is a temporary interruption or a full-blown reversal. There is a strong temptation to grab what little money is left and run. Shorter swings are easier to catch because price targets are closer and stops are tighter.

Should you trade long-term trends or short-term swings? Be sure to decide before you put on a trade; it is easier to be objective when no money is at risk. Different stocks have different personalities, which is why trend traders and swing traders tend to follow different stocks.

Traders have three choices. Trend traders identify major trends which run for months. Swing traders catch short-term swings between optimism and pessimism, which last from a few days to a few weeks. Day-traders enter and exit during the same trading session, with trades lasting only minutes or hours.

Successful trend trades that catch large moves bring in more money per trade. Other advantages include having more time to decide when to enter or exit, not being tied to the screen, and having the emotional satisfaction of calling major moves. Trend trading does, however, have its drawbacks. The stops are farther from the market—when they get hit, you lose more. Also, you have to sit through long periods of inactivity, which many people find hard to tolerate, and you miss many short-term trading opportunities.

Swing traders have more opportunities than trend traders, gaining more experience from frequent trades. The dollar risk is lower thanks to closer stops, and quick rewards provide emotional satisfaction. Swing trading also has its drawbacks. Expenses for commissions and slippage are higher, due to more frequent trading. You must work every day, actively managing trades. Also, you are likely to miss major moves—you can't catch big fish on a small hook.

Trend trading—buying and holding in a major bull market—works best with the type of stocks that Peter Lynch calls 10-baggers, those that go up by a factor of 10. They are usually newer, cheaper, less seasoned issues. An Internet or a biotech company with a hot new invention, a new patent, or a new idea is more likely to go up by a huge percentage than the stock of an old established firm. A small company may bet its future on a single idea or product, and its stock will soar if the public buys that bet or stay in the doghouse if it doesn't. Had a large multinational company come up with the same invention, its stock would have barely budged because one more product makes little difference for a huge firm.

The lure of big trends makes stocks of small companies in promising new industries attractive to trend traders. Swing traders should select their candidates from among the most actively traded stocks on major exchanges. Look for large-cap stocks which swing within broad, well-defined channels.

Once you choose a stock, don't assume it will continue to behave the same way forever. Companies change, and you must stay on top of your picks. For example, DELL, started by Michael Dell in his college dorm room, used to be a tiny public company, but grew into one of the largest computer firms in the world. A friend of mine bought $50,000 worth of Dell in the early 1990s and cashed out three years later at $2.3 million, but DELL's days of spiking through the roof and doubling twice a year are gone. Instead, this widely held stock has become a vehicle for swing traders, and not a very active one at that.

A beginning trader is better off learning to catch swings, because profit targets and stops are clearer, feedback comes faster, and money management is easier. The choice between trend trading and swing trading is partly objective and partly subjective. Should you trade trends or swings? My impression, after meeting thousands of traders and investors, is that the elite tend to trade the big moves and ride major trends, but people who can do it successfully are few and far between. There are many more traders who make money—sometimes very serious money—by trading swings. The principles of Triple Screen work for both, even though the entries and especially the exits are different.

TREND TRADING   Trend trading means holding your positions for a long time, sometimes for months. It requires holding while your stocks react against the main trend. Bull and bear markets are driven by shifts in the fundamentals, such as new technologies and discoveries in the case of stocks, weather patterns in the case of agricultural markets, political shifts in the case of currencies, and so on. Fundamental factors are behind bull and bear markets, but prices move only in response to actions by traders and investors. When your fundamental information forecasts a major move, you need to analyze the charts to see whether the technicals confirm the fundamentals.

A market doesn't send you an invitation before it takes off. When a trend first climbs out of the cellar, few people pay attention. Amateurs are fast asleep, while professionals monitor their markets and scan for breakouts and divergences. Active markets get into the news because the lows and especially the highs attract journalists. One of the key differences between the pros and the outsiders is that the pros always track their markets, while amateurs wake up and look at charts only after a market hits the news. By that time the train has already left the station. The ABC Rating System, described on page 255, can help you handle the challenge of tracking stocks through inactive periods.

A new breakout is easy to recognize but hard to trade and even harder to hold. As a trend speeds up, more and more people pray for a pullback. The stronger the trend, the less likely it is to accommodate bargain hunters. It takes a lot of patience and confidence to hold a position in a trend. Traders tend to be active men with the attitude of "don't just sit there, do something." Learning to be passive comes hard to them. One reason women tend to trade better is that they are more likely to be patient.

How can you teach yourself to trade trends? You may begin by studying historical charts, but remember, there is no substitute for experience. The idea is to learn by doing. Start by putting on positions so small that you can be relaxed and not tie your mind into a knot. Trade only a few hundred shares or a single futures contract while you're learning.

To apply Triple Screen to trend trading, monitor long-term charts for breakouts or look for well-established moves, identified by a weekly EMA. When the weeklies tell you to be bullish or bearish, return to the dailies and use oscillators to find entry points. Put on long positions in uptrends when prices touch their rising daily EMA and keep adding on pullbacks. You can also add when daily oscillators, such as MACD-Histogram or Force Index, give buy signals, especially when they coincide with pullbacks. Reverse the procedure in downtrends. When the weekly trend is down and daily oscillators rally and reach overbought levels, they signal to sell short, especially when they coincide with rallies to the EMA.

The idea is to position yourself in the direction of the market tide and use the waves that go against that tide to build up your initial position. As a beginner, learn to trade a single small position, but once you start making money, the size of your positions and the number of additions become a function of money management.

Once you recognize a new trend, get in! New trends, springing out of trading ranges, are notoriously fast, with few or no pullbacks. If you think you have identified a new trend, hop aboard. You can reduce your risk by trading a smaller size, but do not wait for a deep pullback. Those may come later, and you will be able to add to your position. Jumping aboard a new trend feels counterintuitive, but being in the market makes you more alert to its behavior. The great George Soros was only half-joking when he said, "Buy first, investigate later."

Place your initial stop at the breakout level, where the new trend erupted from the range. A rocket that takes off from its launching pad has no business sinking back to the ground. Do not hurry to move your initial stop. Wait for a reaction and then a new move before moving your stop to the bottom of that reaction. The SafeZone stops, which work so well for swings, are much too tight for big trends. While riding a tide, you must expect the waves to swing against you and still hold your position.

Trend trading means retaining your initial position through thick and thin. You are fishing for very big fish, and you need plenty of room. One of the reasons so few people make big money from big trends is that they become anxious and hyperactive and forget to hang on. Trends are unlike swings, where you must take profits and run fast. Stay with the trend unless weekly trend-following indicators go flat or reverse.

Amateurs often outsmart themselves by trying to pick the end of a trend—a notoriously hard task. As Peter Lynch aptly put it, trying to catch a bottom is like trying to catch a falling knife—you invariably grab it in the wrong spot. Trends tend to overshoot rational expectations. News, daily chart patterns, and other distractions try to throw you off the saddle. Hang on! Consider trading a core position and supplementary positions. You may put on a core position with a wide stop and no definite profit target, while swinging in and out of additional positions—buying on declines to the EMA or selling on rallies to the upper channel line. Consider using two different accounts for easier record keeping.

SWING TRADING Markets spend most of their time going nowhere. They rally a few days, pause, decline a few days, and rally again. Small swings—weekly, daily, or hourly—are more common than big trends. By the end of the month the market may be higher or lower, but it has traveled up and down several times. Newcomers get shaken out, while professionals enjoy the short rides.

Markets' tendency to swing above and below value has been statistically confirmed by several researchers. Swing trading means buying normalcy and selling mania (buy near the rising moving average, sell near the upper channel line) or shorting normalcy and covering depression (sell short near the falling moving average and cover at the lower channel line). The best swing-trading candidates are among the most active stocks and blue chips that tend to rock, more or less regularly, within their channels. Cats and dogs are best left for trend trading. To draw a list of candidates, start with the 20 most active stocks and a handful of famous blue chips, and choose the ones with the widest channels and the most regular swings.

Be sure to select only those candidates whose daily channels are wide enough for a C-level trader to take at least a point out of a trade. A C trader is someone who normally takes 10% or more out of a channel. The only way you can prove you are a B or even an A trader is by trading at that level for at least six months. Even A traders are better off with broad channels because profits are fatter. Beginners have no choice but to use the "1 point for a C trader" rule. This translates into 10-point channels. Technical signals may look delicious, but if a channel is narrower than 10 points, click on to the next stock.

Some stocks give better technical signals than others. Look for a handful of regular performers; you need six or seven, certainly no more than 10. Tracking just a handful of issues allows you to keep up your daily homework without running ragged or falling behind. Learn the personalities of your stocks, rate yourself on every trade, and once you become a steady B trader, increase your trading size.

When the weekly trend is up, wait for daily oscillators to become oversold while prices decline toward the EMA. When the weekly trend is down, look for sell signals from daily oscillators while prices rally toward the EMA. If an oscillator falls to a new multi-month low while prices are moving toward the EMA, it shows that bears are extra strong and it is better to put off buying until the following bottom. The reverse applies to shorting.

In a weekly uptrend, the bottoms of daily charts tend to be very sharp affairs. The best time to buy is when the market stabs below its daily EMA. The best time to short is when the market stabs above it. To place an order near the EMA, estimate its level for tomorrow. The math is simple. You know where the EMA was yesterday and where it closed today. If it has risen, say, by half a point, expect tomorrow's rise also to be half a point and add that to today's EMA.

Take a look at how your stock has behaved since the latest trend began. If the trend is up, look at the previous declines. If the stock has returned to the EMA three times and penetrated it by an average of a point and a half, place a buy order approximately a point below the moving average, a little more shallow than the previous declines. Estimate the EMA for tomorrow and adjust your buy orders daily. Electronic brokers do not become irritated when you change orders each day!

Swing trading, like fishing, demands a great deal of attention and patience. You need to do your homework daily, calculate the estimated EMA for tomorrow, and place orders. You also must calculate your profit targets and stops.

After entering a swing trade, place a protective stop, using the SafeZone method. Swing trading is a high-wire act, requiring a safety net. Stops and money management are essential for your survival and success.

Take profits near the channel line. The exact level depends on the strength of the swing. If MACD-Histogram and Force Index are making new highs, the market is strong, and you can wait for the channel line to be hit. If they act weak, grab your first profit while it's still there. What if a strong swing overshoots the channel line? An experienced trader may shift his tactics and hold a little longer, perhaps until the day when the market fails to reach a new extreme. A beginner must train himself to take profits near the channel wall because he does not have the skills to switch on the fly. Being able to take a limited profit without kicking yourself for missing a big part of a move is a sign of emotional maturity. It is liberating to accept what you asked for and not worry about the rest. Profit targets help you create a structure in an unstructured environment. Measure your performance as the percentage of the channel width. You must grade yourself to know where you stand.

Early in your trading career, it is safer to concentrate on swings. As your level of expertise rises, allocate a portion of your capital to trading trends. Major trends offer spectacular profit opportunities—the big money is in big moves. You owe it to yourself to learn to trade them. Concentrate on quality, and money will follow.

Options

The number of shares in any company is fixed, but options are created out of thin air by writers responding to buyers' demand. An option buyer hopes that the price will get to his target fast enough, and the writer sells him that hope. Most hopes never get fulfilled, but people keep hoping and buying options. Fund managers, floor traders, and exchange members sell hope by the truckload to amateurs who buy calls in bull markets and puts in bear markets.

A call gives its holder a right, but not an obligation, to buy a certain quantity of a specified security at a specified price at a specified time.

It is a bet on a price increase. A put is a right, but not an obligation, to sell a certain quantity of a specified security at a specified price at a specified time. It is a bet on a price drop.

Each option has an exercise price (also called *strike price*). If a stock fails to reach that price before the exercise date, the option expires worthless and the buyer loses what he paid; meanwhile, the writer keeps his loot, the polite name of which is *option premium*. To profit from buying or shorting stocks, you must pick the right stock and the right direction. An option buyer's job is much harder because in addition to that he must bet on how fast the stock will get to his level.

An option is at-the-money when the current price of the underlying security equals the exercise price.

A call is out-of-the-money when the current price of the underlying security is below the exercise price. A put is out-of-the-money when the current price of the underlying is above the exercise price. The farther out-of-the-money, the cheaper the option.

A call is in-the-money when the current price of the underlying security is above the exercise price. A put is in-the-money when the current price of the underlying is below the exercise price.

An option can be at-the-money, out-of-the-money, or in-the-money at different times in its life, as the price of the underlying security changes. The price of every option has two components: intrinsic value and time value.

An option's intrinsic value is above zero only when it's in-the-money. If the exercise price of a call is $80, and the underlying security rises to $83, the intrinsic value is $3. If the security is at or below $80, the intrinsic value of that call is zero.

The other component of each option's price is time value. If the stock trades at $74 and people pay $2 for an $80 call, the entire $2 represents time value. If the stock rises to $83, and the price of the call jumps to $4, $3 of that is intrinsic value ($83 − $80), while $1 is time value (the hope that this stock will rise even higher during the life of that option).

Option price depends on several factors:

The farther out-of-the-money, the cheaper the option—the underlying security must travel a longer distance to make it worth anything before it expires.

The closer the expiration day, the cheaper the option—it has less time to
  fulfill the hope. The speed with which an option loses value is called
  time decay, which becomes steeper as the expiration nears.
The less volatile the underlying security, the cheaper the option, because
  the chance of that security making a large move is lower.
Other factors influencing the price of an option include the current level
  of interest rates and the dividend rate of the underlying stock.

When a stock trades at 100, a 110 call is worth more that a 120 call
because that stock is more likely to rise to 110 than to 120. A stock is
more likely to rise to 110 in five months than in two, making a longer
call more valuable. Finally, if two stocks are selling for 100, but one
has moved 50 so far this year while the other has moved only 30, then
a 110 call for the more volatile stock is likely to be priced higher.

Different factors of option pricing may clash and partially cancel
each other out. For example, if a market drops sharply, reducing the
value of calls, the increase in volatility will lift option values, and the
calls may lose less value than expected. There are several mathematical models, such as Black-Scholes, widely described in options literature, to determine what is called a *fair value* of an option.

The simplest option strategy is to buy them. That's what beginners
do, especially buying calls when they cannot afford to buy stocks.
They miss the fact that options are more complex than stocks and
someone who can't make money in stocks is doomed in options. A more
sophisticated strategy involves writing, or selling, options. A writer may
be either covered or naked.

Covered writers own the underlying securities. For example, a fund
may hold IBM stock and sell calls against them, figuring that if the
stock does not reach its exercise price and the options expire worthless, they'll pocket the extra income. If IBM rises to the exercise price
and their option is called, they'll sell their stock at a profit, use the
money to buy another, and sell calls against it. Covered writing was
very profitable in the early years of exchange-traded options. By now
the field is very crowded, and the returns have shrunk. Naked writing,
to be reviewed later involves selling options without owning the
underlying securities, with writers backing up what they sell only with
cash in their accounts.

The above was a brief summary of option terms. To learn more, please
turn to the literature on options, listed at the end of this chapter. Just

watch out for the books that promise a "simple strategy for tripling your money in a year, working 15 minutes a day, with no math." People who make money in options tend to be mathematically savvy and highly capitalized, the exact opposite of an average wide-eyed gambler who hopes to make a quick buck from his $5,000 stake. Let us now review options strategies for buying and writing.

Buying Options—The Major Reversal Tactic   It is harder to make money buying options than stocks. You face all the usual problems, such as choosing the right stock, identifying its trend, and selecting entry and exit points. In addition, you must worry how fast your stock will get where you expect it to go. If you buy a rising stock and it takes five months instead of three to reach its target, you still have a winning trade. Do the same with options, and they'll expire worthless. If you decide to buy more time by getting longer-term options, you'll lose money in a different way, because those options are more expensive and move more slowly. All options keep losing time value. Poor beginners who buy them as a substitute for stocks rush in where the pros fear to tread!

Professionals tend to buy options only on special occasions, when they expect a major reversal, especially to the downside. If you expect not a little downtrend in a stock but a massive crash, buying a put may be a good idea. When a long-term trend begins to turn, especially near the top, it creates massive turbulence, like an ocean liner changing its course. A stock may collapse today and soar tomorrow, only to collapse again. When volatility goes through the roof, even well-heeled traders have trouble placing stops. A stop belongs outside the zone of market noise, but where do you put it when the noise level rises to a roar? Options allow you to sidestep this problem, at a price which can only be covered by a major move.

Prices tend to fall twice as fast as they rise. Greed, the dominant emotion of uptrends, is a happy and lasting feeling. Fear, the dominant emotion of downtrends, is sharper and more violent. Professionals are more likely to buy puts because of shorter exposure to time decay. When you expect a major downside reversal, buying a put can be a sensible trade. The same principles apply to calls, but uptrends are better traded with stocks.

A trader who expects a downswing must decide which put to buy. The best choice is counterintuitive and different from what most people get.

Estimate how low you expect a stock to collapse. A put is worth buying only if you expect a waterfall decline.

Avoid puts with more than two months of life. Buying puts makes sense only when you expect a sharp decline. If you anticipate a drawn-out downtrend, it is better to sell short the underlying security.

Look for cheap puts whose price reflects no hope. Move your finger down the column of put strikes. The lower you go, the cheaper the puts. At first, each time you drop to the next strike price, a put is 25% or even 35% cheaper than the previous level. Eventually you come to the strike level at which you would only save a tiny fraction of price. This shows that all hope has been squeezed out of that put, and it is priced like a cheap lottery ticket. That is the one you want!

Buying a very cheap, far-out-of-the-money put is counterintuitive. It is so far-out-of-the-money and has so little life left in it that it seems likely to expire worthless. You can't place a stop on it, so if you're wrong, the entire premium will go up in smoke. Why not buy a put closer to the money?

The only time to buy a put is when you're shooting for an exceptional gain from a major reversal. In an ordinary downtrend it's better to short stocks. Cheap far-out-of-the-money puts provide the most bang for the buck. Aim for a 10-fold gain or better, rather than the usual 2:1 or 3:1 ratio. Returns like these allow you to be wrong on a string of trades, yet come out ahead in the end. Catching one major reversal will make up for a string of losses and leave you very profitable.

The best options trade I ever made was during the October 1989 minicrash in the stock market. On Thursday the market closed weak, with new lows exceeding the new highs for the first time in over a year, which gave me a long-awaited sell signal. On Friday morning, while at a trade show in Chicago, I bought OEX puts at ⅜. On Friday afternoon the bottom fell out of the market. On Monday the market opened sharply lower and my puts, purchased just a few trading hours ago at less than half a point, were bid at 17.

Why don't more people use this tactic? First, it requires a great deal of patience, as opportunities are very infrequent. It offers very little entertainment value. Most people cannot stomach the idea of being wrong three, four, or five times in a row, even if they are likely to make money in the end. This is why so few traders play one of the greatest games in the options market.

Writing Options   Beginners, gamblers, and undercapitalized traders make up the majority of option buyers. Just think of all the money lost by those hapless folks in their eagerness to get rich quick. Have you sent a few dollars down the options hole? Who got all that money? Brokers, of course, but mostly options writers. Well-capitalized professionals tend to write options rather than buy them. Covered writers sell options against securities they own. Naked writers sell options without owning the underlying securities.

A stock or a future can do one of three things: rise, fall, or stay flat. When you buy a call, you can profit only if the market rises, but lose if it goes down or stays flat, and sometimes even if it rises but not fast enough. When you buy a put, you win only if the market falls fast enough. An options buyer makes money only if the market goes his way, but loses if it goes against him or stays flat. A buyer has one chance to win out of three, but the odds are two out of three for an option writer. No wonder the pros prefer writing options.

Large funds tend to use computerized models to buy stocks and write covered calls against them. If a stock stays below the strike price, they pocket the premium and write a new call with a new expiration date. If a stock rises high enough to be called, they deliver it, collect the money, invest in another stock, and write calls against it. Covered writing is a mathematically demanding, capital-intensive business. Most serious players spread their costs, including staff and equipment, across a large capital base. A small trader doesn't have much of an edge in this expensive enterprise.

Naked writers sell options without owning the underlying securities, similar to shorting. A naked writer collects his premium at the outset of the trade but his risk is unlimited if the position goes against him and he fails to get out. If you own a stock, sell a call, and that stock gets called, you have something to deliver. If you sell a naked call and the stock rises to its exercise price, the option buyer can demand delivery, whether you own that stock or not. Imagine selling calls on a stock that becomes a takeover play and opens $50 higher the next morning—you still have to deliver. It can hurt.

Limited reward with unlimited risk scares most traders away from naked writing, but the reality and perception are usually quite different in the markets. Writing naked options seems very dangerous, but most of the time a far-out-of-the-money option with a short time to the expiration is very likely to expire worthless, to the benefit of the writer. Its chance of reaching the exercise price and causing a loss to a writer is very low. The risk/reward ratio in naked writing is a lot better than it looks, and there are techniques for reducing the impact of a rare adverse move.

Savvy naked writers tend to sell out-of-the-money calls and puts at levels that a stock or a commodity is unlikely to reach during the option's life. They sell distant hopes. Good writers track market volatility to find how far a stock is likely to move, based on its recent conduct, and sell options outside that range. If a stock took a year to rise from 60 to 130, the pros are going to fall all over themselves trying to serve some greenhorn who wants to buy 170 calls that will expire in a few weeks. The chance of that stock rising 40 points before the option expiration is exceedingly low. A gullible amateur wants to buy hope, and the pros are delighted to sell it to him. This game goes into high gear during the week or two prior to option expiration, when the floor mints money out of thin air, selling naked puts and calls that have almost no chance of reaching their exercise price.

Cautious writers may close their positions without waiting for the expiration date. If you write a call at 90 cents and it goes down to 10, it may make sense to buy it back and unwind your position. You've already earned the bulk of profit, so why expose yourself to continued risk? It is cheaper to pay another commission, book your profits, and look for another writing opportunity.

Becoming a naked writer requires absolute iron discipline. The size of your writes and the number of positions must be strictly determined by money management rules. If you sell a naked call and the stock rallies above its exercise price, it exposes you to the risk of ruin. You must decide in advance at what level you will cut and run, taking a relatively small loss. A naked seller cannot afford to sit when a stock moves against him. Amateurs hang on and wait for the underlying security to turn around. They wait for the wasting time value to get them off the hook. The longer you wait for a miracle, the deeper the steel hook of the market lodges in your intestines. Stay away from naked writing if you have the slightest problem with discipline!

WRITER'S CHOICE   All options buyers know this sad sequence: you're right on the direction of the market, right on the stock, but still lose money on the option. Time is the enemy of options buyers. Buyers lose when the underlying security takes longer than expected to get to the level at which they can collect on their bet. As the expiration date nears, an option becomes worth less, and less, and less.

What if we reverse this process and write rather than buy options? Now time will work in our favor because each passing day will reduce the likelihood of that option having any value before it expires.

The first time you write an option, and do it right, you'll experience the delicious sensation of time working in your favor. The option loses some of its time value each day, making the premium you've collected safer and safer. When the market goes nowhere, you still make money, as time value evaporates with each passing day.

If living well is the best revenge, then taking a factor that kills most options buyers—time—and making it work for you is a gratifying experience.

We must not forget that an option is a hope, and it is better to sell empty hopes which are unlikely to be fulfilled. Take three steps before writing a call or a put. First, analyze the underlying security, decide which way it's moving, and estimate its price target. Second, decide whether to write a put or a call. Third, choose the strike price and the expiration date for the option you'll write. If any one of these steps seems unclear, stand aside, do not force a decision, and look for another opportunity.

One of the key factors in pricing options is the volatility of the underlying security. A tool included in most trading software, called Bollinger bands, can help you rate volatility. Those standard deviation bands are centered around a moving average but unlike envelopes, whose walls are parallel, they expand and contract as volatility changes. Bollinger bands become narrow when markets are sleepy and wide when they grow wild. Flat, narrow bands indicate a sleepy market where options are cheap and it is better to buy them rather than sell. When Bollinger bands go to a wide spread, they mark an overheated market where options tend to be overpriced, creating an opportunity for writers. Here are the steps to follow:

Analyze a security against which you want to write options. Use Triple Screen to decide whether a stock, future, or an index is trending or nontrending. Use weekly and daily charts, trend-following indicators, and oscillators to identify trends, detect reversals, and set up price targets.

Select the type of option to write. If your analysis is bearish, consider writing calls. If bullish, consider writing puts. When the trend is up, sell the hope that it will turn down, and when it's down, sell the hope it'll turn up. Do not write options when markets are flat and Bollinger bands are tight because premiums are low, and a breakout from a trading range can hurt you.

Estimate how far, with a generous safety margin, the market would have to move in order to change its trend, and write an option beyond that zone. Write an option with a strike price the market is unlikely to reach before the expiration. Suppose a stock is at 80, having risen from 50 in the past year and is now rising half a point per week, with 8 weeks left to option expiration. The trend is up, and selling a 70 put under those circumstances means selling an option that is likely to expire worthless.

The temptation to sell naked options close to the money and get fatter premiums is dangerous, because a slight countertrend move can push your position underwater. Look at the number of weeks remaining to the expiration, calculate the distance the market is likely to travel based on its recent behavior, and write an option outside that range.

Write options with no more than two months to the expiration. The shorter the time, the fewer surprises. The erosion of time value accelerates in the last few weeks of option life. When you write options close to the expiration, you benefit from faster time decay. You can get more money for options with longer life, but do not get greedy. The goal of a writer is not to make a killing on any single trade but to grind out a steady income.

LIMITING RISK   A trader can keep writing naked calls or puts, but do it long enough, and some day he will get caught on the wrong side of a powerful move. Profits of several years can be wiped out in a single day.

For example, whenever there is a great bull market, the pros look at selling puts like a license to print money. The contrarians, the alarmists, and "the end is nigh" crowd keep buying puts for years and losing money, but suddenly there is a crash and buyers have their day in the sun. The pros who have been feeding off them for years face their day of reckoning—the quick ones survive, while the slow ones are carried out feet first.

A trader can grow fat and greedy writing naked options, selling useless contracts created out of thin air and pocketing profits. A smug feeling of self-satisfaction blinds people to reality. Naked positions in options need to be protected by stops and money management rules.

Use a mental stop-loss on the underlying security. Set a stop on the underlying stock, future, or index and not on the price of your option. Buy back that option if the underlying security reaches your stop level. For example, if you sell a naked 80 call on a stock trading at 70, place your stop at 77. Get out of your naked option position before it gets into the money by crossing its exercise price.

Your stop is like an ejection seat on an aircraft. If you write an out-of-the-money option and the market starts moving into the money, there is no point in sticking around, waiting to see what happens next. You are wrong, and you're losing—push the eject button before the damage turns deadly. If you sold an option for 1.50, by the time it hits your at-the-money stop level it may double in price to 3. If you use stops, you'll be nowhere near the "unlimited loss" that makes people afraid to write options.

Set your profit-taking zone—consider buying back your naked option. When you write a call or a put, you sell a wasting asset. When the underlying security moves far from the exercise price but there is still time left to the expiration, the price of that option may reach its rock bottom. It loses value only in tiny dribs and drabs. The loser who bought that option still has a bit of a chance that the market may reverse in his favor. He continues to hold that call or put like a lottery ticket, and once in a rare while his ticket may win.

Why hold an open position in an option that has already given you most of its value? You have little to gain, while remaining exposed to the risk of an adverse move. Consider buying back that option to close out your profitable trade.

Open an insurance account. A naked seller needs insurance against a catastrophic reversal. You may write a put and the market crashes the next day, or you write a call and suddenly there is a takeover. You hope this never happens, but trade long enough and eventually everything will happen! That's why you need insurance. Nobody will write it for you, so you'll have to self-insure.

Open a money market account, and every time you close out a naked writing position, throw a percentage of your profit, 10 percent or more, into that account. Do not use it for trading. Have it sit there, in a money market fund, for as long as you write options. Your insurance account grows with each new profit, ready to cover a catastrophic loss or to be taken out in cash when you stop writing options!

Option writers get hurt in one of three ways. Beginners overtrade and write too many options, breaking money management rules. Intermediate-level traders get hurt when they fail to run fast enough when their options move against them. Experienced traders can get blown out if they do not have a reserve against a major adverse move. The longer you trade, the greater your risk of a catastrophic event. Having an insurance account confirms your position as a professional option writer.

WHERE DO I GO FROM HERE? Every options trader should own Lawrence McMillan's *Options as a Strategic Investment* and use it as a handbook. Most professional traders read Sheldon Natenberg's *Option Volatility and Pricing Strategies*. Harvey Friedentag's *Options: Investing without Fear* has a nice angle on covered writing.

Futures

Futures used to have such a bad reputation that several states tried to outlaw them a century ago. They used to have Sunday sermons against futures in parts of the agricultural belt. None of that prevented futures from evolving into a potent economic force.

Futures markets have prospered because they serve two groups that have a great deal of money. On the one hand, futures permit major commercial producers and consumers to hedge price risks, giving them a fantastic competitive advantage. On the other hand, futures offer speculators a gambling palace with more choices than all the casinos in Nevada. Between the hedgers and the speculators, on a ground richly soaked with blood and money, are professional futures traders. They help move the wheels of commerce and take a fee for their services. A sign of their profitability is the fact that many of those public servants pass their craft to their sons and now occasionally even to their daughters.

Hedging means opening a futures position that is the opposite of one's position in the actual commodity. It removes the price risk from holding a cash commodity or planning to buy such a commodity in the future. Hedgers transfer price risks to commodity speculators. This allows them to concentrate on their core businesses, offer better consumer pricing, and obtain a long-term competitive advantage over their unhedged competitors.

For example, I have two friends, brokers in Moscow, who teach sugar importers how to hedge (Russia has become the world's biggest importer of sugar since the breakup of the Soviet Union). Their clients are big players in the food industry, who know up to a year in advance how much sugar they're going to need. Now they can buy sugar futures in London or New York when prices are low enough. They are going to need their trainloads of sugar many months from now, but meanwhile they hold sugar futures, which they plan to sell when they buy their cash position. In effect, they are short cash, long futures. If sugar prices go up and they have to pay more than expected, they will offset that loss by making roughly the same profit on their futures positions. Their unhedged competitors are in effect flipping a coin. If sugar prices fall, they'll buy on the cheap and reap a windfall, but if they rise, they'll be hung out to dry. The importers who are hedged can concentrate on running their core business instead of watching the price ticker.

Producers of commodities also benefit from hedging. An agribusiness can presell its wheat, coffee, or cotton when prices are high enough to guarantee profits. They sell short as many futures contracts as it takes to cover their prospective crop. From that point on, they have no price risk. If prices go down, they'll make up their losses on cash commodities by profits on futures. If prices go up, they'll lose money on their short positions in futures but make it back selling the actual commodities. Producers give up a chance of a windfall but insulate themselves from the risk of lower prices. Survivors thrive on stability. That why the Exxons, the Coca-Colas, and the Nabiscos are among the major players in the commodity markets. Hedgers are the ultimate insiders, and a good hedging department not only buys price insurance, but serves as a profit center.

Speculators step in to assume market risks, lured by the glitter of profits. Hedgers, with their inside information, are not fully confident about future prices, while crowds of cheerful outsiders plunk down money to bet on price direction. It reminds me how, years ago, I walked into a liquor store with a scientist friend to buy some wine for dinner. This was soon after the state of New Jersey introduced a lottery to pay for education. There was a huge line at the counter, as lottery tickets in those days were sold only in liquor stores. When my friend, who owned a house in New Jersey, saw what was happening, he doubled up laughing, "You mean these people are lining up to keep my taxes down?!" That's pretty much what most speculators do in futures.

The two largest groups of speculators are farmers and engineers. Farmers produce commodities, while engineers love to apply scientific methods to the market game. Many small farmers enter futures markets as hedgers but catch the bug and start speculating. There's nothing wrong with that, as long as they know what they are doing. It never ceases to amaze me how many farmers end up trading stock index futures. As long as they trade corn, cattle, or soybeans, their feel for the fundamentals gives them an edge over city slickers. But what's their edge in the S&P 500? Faster reflexes than the rest of us? Gimme a break!

There is one profound difference between futures and stocks, making the futures game extremely fast, furious, exciting, and deadly. The futures markets are turbocharged by a simple but potent device of low margin requirements.

United States securities law demands that in the stock market you pay at least half the cash value of your position. Your broker can give you a margin loan for the other half. If you have $30,000 in your account, you may buy $60,000 worth of stocks, and no more. The law was passed after the Crash of 1929 when people realized that low margins led to excessive speculation, which contributed to the viciousness of declines. Prior to 1929, speculators could buy stocks on a 10% margin, which worked great in bull markets but wiped them out in bear markets.

Margins of only three to five percent are common in the futures markets. Here you can bet big with little money. If you have $30,000, you can control $1,000,000 worth of merchandise, be it pork bellies or gold. If you catch a 1% move in your market, you'll make $10,000, or over 30% profit on your account. A few trades like that, and you've made it. A small trader looks at these numbers and thinks he's found the secret to getting rich quick. There is only one problem. Before that market rises 1% it may dip 2%. It may be a meaningless blip, but at the bottom the amateur's equity will be nearly wiped out, and his broker will sell him out on a margin call. He'll go bust even though his price forecast was correct.

The mortality rate among futures traders is over 90 percent, even though brokerage houses try to hide statistics. Easy margins attract gamblers and adrenaline addicts who quickly go up in smoke. There is nothing wrong with trading futures that money management won't cure. Futures are very tradable, as long as you observe money management rules and do not go crazy with an easy margin. You have to be more than disciplined—to trade commodities you must be colder than a freezer. If you cannot follow money management rules, better go to Las Vegas. The entertainment value is just as high and the outcome is the same, but the drinks are free and the floor show more glitzy.

Precisely because they require a high degree of discipline and excellent money management skills, futures markets are hard for beginners. A new trader is better off learning to trade slower-moving stocks, but later on, futures definitely deserve a look.

If you know how to trade and want to make a quick fortune, futures are the place to be. You may put on small initial positions, fenced in by strict money management rules, but then you can pyramid them to the hilt as a trade moves in your favor and you keep moving stops beyond breakeven and adding new contracts.

There are only a few dozen futures, making the choice of which to trade much easier than among the thousands of stocks. Be sure to focus on markets in your own time zone. It is shocking how many beginners, especially outside the United States, want to trade currencies. Few of them stop to think that this is a 24-hour market, operating around the clock, in which an individual trader has many disadvantages. You may brilliantly analyze a currency and forecast a move, but that move is just as likely to take place in another time zone while you are sleeping. Try to select markets that trade in your time zone that are open when you are awake and closed when you're asleep.

It is a good idea to make your first steps in those markets where you know something about the fundamentals. If you are a cattle rancher, a house builder, or a loan officer, then cattle, lumber, or interest rate futures are logical starting points, if you can afford to trade them. If you have no particular interests, your choice is limited only by your account size. It is important to make your first steps in relatively inexpensive markets. All markets have a certain amount of random noise, or quick countertrend moves. The high dollar value of random moves in expensive markets can be deadly.

Take yourself through a simple exercise. Create a spreadsheet on your computer and write down the names of several futures markets that interest you in column A. Write the value of their price units in column B. Corn trades in cents, and the value of a cent is $50; S&P trades in points, and the value of a point is $250, so those values go into column B. Write the latest closing price in column C. Now complete the exercise by creating column D which multiplies B by C and shows how much each contract is worth. How much more expensive is the richest contract compared to the cheapest contract? Five times? Ten? Twenty? Thirty? Do the exercise and find out.

Beginners are drawn to the S&P 500 futures, but few have accounts large enough for proper money management in this expensive market. In North America, corn, sugar, and, in a slow year, copper are good markets for beginners, allowing you to learn in your own time zone. They are liquid, reasonably volatile, and not too expensive.

Some very good books, listed on page 213, have been written about futures. Most technical analysis tools were originally developed for futures and only later migrated to the stock market. Let us review a few aspects of futures that make them different from stocks.

CONTANGO AND INVERSION   All futures markets offer contracts for several delivery months at the same time. For example, you can buy or sell wheat for delivery in September or December of this year, March of next year, and so on. Normally, the nearby months are less expensive than the faraway months, and that relationship is called a *contango market.*

Higher prices for longer-term contracts reflect the so-called *cost of carry,* that is, the cost of financing, storing, and insuring a commodity. A futures buyer plunks down his 3% margin and controls a contract without having to bring the rest of the money until the settlement date. Meanwhile the seller has to store, finance, and insure the merchandise.

The differences between delivery months are called *premiums.* Hedgers and floor traders closely watch premiums because they reflect the degree of tightness in the market. When the supply shrinks or the demand rises, people start paying up for the nearby months. The premium for the faraway months begins to shrink. As the demand grows, the front months become pricier than faraway months—the market becomes inverted! This is one of the strongest fundamental signs of a bull market. There is a real shortage out there, and people are paying extra to get their stuff sooner rather than later.

Whenever you look at the commodity page of a financial newspaper, move your finger down the column of closing prices and look for inversions. They signal bull markets, and that's when you want to use technical analysis to look for buying opportunities.

Serious hedgers do not wait for inversions. They monitor premiums and get their signals from their narrowing or widening. A good speculator can rattle off the latest prices, but a good hedger will quote you the latest premiums of faraway contracts over the nearby ones.

As you scan futures markets for inversions, keep in mind that there is one area in which inversion is the norm. Interest rate futures are always inverted because those who hold cash positions keep collecting interest instead of paying finance and storage charges.

SPREADS   Hedgers tend to dominate the short side of the markets and most speculators are perpetual bulls, but floor traders love to trade spreads. Spreading means buying one delivery month and selling another in the same market, or going long one market and short a related one.

Futures are the basic building blocks of the economy, essential for society's daily functioning. Economic necessities tightly link commodity markets and delivery months. If the price of corn, a major animal feed, starts to rise faster than the price of wheat, at some point ranchers will start using wheat rather than corn. They'll reduce their purchases of corn while buying more wheat, pushing their spread back towards the norm. A savvy commodity trader knows his normal spreads by heart. Spread traders bet against deviations and for a return to normalcy. In this situation, a spreader will short corn and buy wheat, instead of taking a directional trade in either market.

Spread trades are much safer than directional trades, with even lower margin requirements. Amateurs do not understand spreads and have little interest in these reliable but slow-moving trades. There are several books on spreads but not a single good one at the time of this writing, a sign of how well professionals have sewn up this area of knowledge and kept the amateurs out. There is a handful of niches in the markets where professionals are making fortunes without the benefit of a single good how-to book. It looks almost as if the insiders have posted a sign for the outsiders to keep out.

COMMITMENTS OF TRADERS   The Commodity Futures Trading Commission collects reports from brokers on the positions of traders and releases their summaries to the public. Those COT (commitments of traders) reports are among the best sources of information on what the smart money is doing in the futures markets. COT reports reveal positions of three groups: hedgers, big traders, and small traders. How do they know who is who? Hedgers identify themselves to brokers because that entitles them to several advantages, such as lower margin rates. Big traders are identified by holding the number of contracts above "reporting requirements," set by the government. Whoever is not a hedger or a big trader is a small trader.

In the old days, big traders used to be the smart money. Today, the markets are bigger, the reporting requirements much higher, and big traders are likely to be commodity funds, most of them not much smarter than the run-of-the-mill trader. Hedgers are today's smart money but understanding their positions isn't as easy as it seems.

For example, a COT report may show that in a certain market, hedgers hold 70% of shorts. A beginner who thinks this is bearish may be completely off the mark without knowing that normally hedgers hold 90% of shorts in that market, making the 70% stance wildly bullish. Savvy COT analysts compare current positions to historical norms and look for situations where hedgers, or the smart money, and small traders, many of whom are gamblers and losers, are dead set against each other. If one group is heavily short while the other is just as heavily long, which one would you like to join? If you find that in a certain market the smart money is overwhelmingly on one side, while the small specs are mobbing the other, it is time to use technical analysis to look for entries on the side of hedgers.

SUPPLY AND DEMAND MARKETS   In futures, there are two types of bull and bear markets: supply-driven and demand-driven. Supply-driven markets tend to be fast and furious, whereas demand-driven markets tend to be quiet and slow. Why? Think of any commodity, say coffee, which grows in Africa and South America.

Changes in demand come slowly, thanks to the conservatism of human nature. The demand for coffee can go up only if drinking becomes more popular, with a second espresso machine in every little bar. The demand can fall only if coffee drinking becomes less popular, which may happen in a deteriorating economy or in response to a health fad. Demand-driven markets move at a leisurely pace.

Now imagine that a major coffee growing area is hit by a hurricane or a freeze. Suddenly the world supply of coffee is rumored to be reduced by 10% and prices shoot through the roof, cutting off marginal consumers and rising to the point where supply and demand are in balance. Supply-driven markets are very volatile. Imagine torrential rains in the cocoa-producing areas of Africa, or a new OPEC policy sharply curtailing oil supply, or a general strike in a leading copper-mining country. When the supply of a commodity is reduced and rumors of further damage swirl, the trend shoots up, reallocating tight supplies to those best able to afford them.

Every futures trader must be aware of key supply factors in his market and keep an eye on them, such as the weather during the critical growing and harvesting months in agricultural commodities. Trend traders in the futures markets tend to look for supply-driven markets, while swing traders do better in demand-driven markets.

The United States grain markets often have price spikes during the spring and summer planting and growing seasons as dry spells, floods, and pests threaten supplies. Traders say that a farmer loses his crop three times before harvesting it. Once the harvest is in and the supply is known, demand drives the markets. Demand-driven markets have narrower channels, making profit targets smaller. Channels have to be redrawn and trading tactics adjusted as seasons change. A lazy trader wonders why his tools stopped working. A smart trader gets out a new set of tools for the season and puts old ones in storage until the next year.

FLOOR AND CEILING   The fundamental analysis of futures is more straight-forward than that of stocks. Most analysts monitor supplies since demand changes very slowly. What is the planted acreage? What are the warehouse stocks? What is the weather forecast for the growing areas? Fundamentals put a floor underneath most, though not all, commodities. They also have a natural ceiling above which they almost never rise.

The floor depends on the cost of production. When the market price of a commodity, be it gold or sugar, falls below that level, miners stop digging and farmers stop planting. Some third-world governments, desperate for dollars and trying to avoid social unrest, may subsidize production, paying locals in worthless currency and dumping the product on the world market. Still, if enough producers go broke and quit, the supply will shrink and prices will rise to draw in new suppliers. If you take 20-year charts of most commodities, you'll see that the same price areas have served as a floor year after year. Curiously enough, those levels have held without being adjusted for inflation.

The ceiling depends on the cost of substitution. If the price of a commodity rises, major industrial consumers will start switching away from it. If soybean meal, a major animal feed, becomes too expensive, the demand will switch to fishmeal; if sugar becomes too costly, the demand will switch to other sweeteners.

Why don't more people trade against those levels? Why don't they buy near the floor and short near the ceiling, profiting from what is similar to shooting fish in a barrel? First of all, the floor and the ceiling are not set in stone, and markets may briefly violate them. Even more importantly, human psychology works against those trades. Most speculators find it impossible to sell short a market that is boiling near the high or go long a market after it has crashed.

SEASONALS   Most commodities fluctuate through the seasons. For example, grains tend to be cheapest soon after the harvest, when the supply is plentiful and the demand pretty well known. The spring planting season, when the coming weather is uncertain, is the most likely time for price spikes. Freezing spells in the northern parts of the United States are bullish for heating oil futures. Orange juice futures used to have wild runups during the frosts in Florida, but have become much more sedate with the growth of orange production in Brazil in the Southern Hemisphere.

For some, seasonal trading degenerates into calendar trading. Spinning past data to find that a certain market should be bought during the first week of March and sold on the last week of August is a misuse of technology. It is easy to find what worked in the past, but any pattern that has no justification in the fundamentals or mass psychology probably is due to market noise. Seasonal trades take advantage of annual swings, but you have to be careful. They shift from year to year, and seasonal trades must be put through the filter of technical analysis.

OPEN INTEREST All exchanges report trading volumes, but futures exchanges also report open interest, that is, the number of contracts outstanding on any given day, reported a day later. In the stock market the number of outstanding shares doesn't change, unless a company issues more or repurchases existing ones. In the futures markets, a new contract is created whenever a new buyer and a new seller come together. If both of them get out of their positions, a contract disappears. Open interest goes up and down each day, and its changes provide important clues to the commitments of bulls and bears.

Every futures contract has a buyer and a seller, a winner and a loser. Rising open interest shows more winners are coming into that market. Just as important, it shows more losers are coming in, because without their money there would be nothing for winners to win. An uptrend in open interest reflects a rising level of commitment on all sides and indicates that a trend is likely to continue. A downtrend in the open interest shows that winners are taking away their chips, while losers are accepting losses and quitting the game. Falling open interest shows that the trend is becoming weaker, which is a valuable piece of information when you need to decide whether to stay or take profits.

SHORTING Few traders active today were in stocks in 1929, but the aftershocks of that year's crash still impact us. The government responded to the hue and cry of the hurt and angry public. Among its many acts was an attempt to root out evil short sellers, accused of driving stocks down. It promulgated the *uptick rule,* which allows shorting a stock only after it has ticked up. The bad bears can no longer hammer down innocent stocks with their sell orders. They may only sell short stocks that are rising. How about a parallel law to outlaw buying stocks that have ticked up and permitting people to buy only after a downtick, to prevent excessive bullishness?

The uptick rule is an example of a bad law passed in response to mass hysteria. It is short-sighted because during bear moves it is the short sellers who break declines with their profit taking. There is no uptick rule in the futures markets. A futures trader is much more likely to be comfortable shorting than a stock trader.

In stocks, most people are long and very few are short. Exchanges report short interest each month, which almost never rises into double digits. In futures, short interest is always 100%—there is a short contract for every long because if someone is buying a contract for future delivery, someone else has to sell them a contract for future delivery, that is, go short. You have to feel comfortable shorting if you want to trade futures.

LIMIT MOVES   Now that the stock market has its own "circuit breakers," fewer newcomers to futures are shocked to discover that most have daily limits beyond which prices are not allowed to go. Limits are designed to prevent hysterical moves and give people time to rethink their positions, but they have a downside. Just like a pedestrian can get crushed against a traffic barricade put up to protect him, a trader can get crushed in a limit move. A string of limit days is especially terrifying, as a loser is stuck, unable to get out, while his account is being destroyed.

Fears of limit moves are greatly overdone. Their heyday was during the inflationary 1970s, and the markets have become much more peaceful since then. If you trade with the trend, a limit move is much more likely to go in your favor, not against. With the globalization of the futures markets, many more emergency exits appeared, allowing you to unwind a trade elsewhere. A good trader learns to find those exits before he needs them. Last but not least, a futures trader may consider opening an "insurance account," as recommended above for naked options writers, albeit on a much smaller scale.

MINICONTRACTS Futures traders with tiny accounts sometimes ask whether they should trade regular contracts or minicontracts. For example, a regular contract of S&P represents $250 times the index, but a minicontract is only one-fifth its size, representing $50 times the index. In British pounds a regular contract represents £62,500, but a minicontract only one-fifth its size represents only £12,500. Minicontracts trade during the same hours as regular contracts and closely track them in price.

The only advantage of minis is the reduction of risk, but their commissions take a bigger percentage from each trade. Beginners may use them for practice, but full-size contracts are much better trading vehicles.

WHERE DO I GO FROM HERE? *The Futures Game* by Teweles and Jones has educated several generations of futures traders. Make sure to get the latest edition; the book is updated every 12 years or so. *Economics of Futures Trading* by Thomas A. Hieronymus is probably the wisest book on futures. It has long been out of print; try to find a copy in the library. *Charting Commodity Market Price Behavior* by L. Dee Belveal has some of the sharpest analysis of volume and open interest. *The Inside Track to Winning* by Steve Briese is a video on the commitments of traders, produced by my firm.

MONEY MANAGEMENT FORMULAS

Do you trade for the money or for the thrill? Don't tell me, just show your trading records. Don't have good records? Well, that's an answer in itself. If you keep records, then the slope of your equity curve will show how serious you are about trading.

Most people enter the markets for the money, but soon loose track of that goal and start chasing some private version of fun. The trading game is a lot more interesting than solitaire and feeds dreams of wealth and power. People trade to escape boredom or show off their smarts. There are as many neurotic reasons to trade as there are traders, but only one realistic one—to make more money than from riskless investments, such as Treasury bills.

Successful trading is based on 3 M's: Mind, Method, and Money. Mind is trading psychology, Method is market analysis, and Money refers to risk management. This last M is your ultimate key to success. The slope of your equity curve, which you must draw as a part of your money management process, reflects the state of your mind as well as the quality of your method.

Anyone can make money on a single trade or even several trades. Even in the casinos of Las Vegas you continuously hear the music of the jackpots. Coins pour from the slot machines, making a happy noise, but how many players go back to their rooms with more money than they came with? In the markets, almost anyone can make a good trade, but few can grow equity.

Money management is the craft of managing your trading capital. Some call it an art, others a science, but really it is a combination of both, with science predominating. The goal of money management is to accumulate equity by reducing losses on losing trades and maxi-

215

mizing gains on winning trades. When you cross the street after the "Walk" sign lights up, you still glance right and left because some crazed driver may be barreling toward the crosswalk, sign or no sign. Whenever your trading system gives you a signal, money management becomes the equivalent of glancing right and left. Even the most beautiful trading system requires money management to make consistent profits.

I once met a father and son team of successful money managers. The father began grooming his son for the business while the boy was still a teenager. On weekends he used to take him to the track and give his son $10 for the day. That was his lunch money and betting money. The father spent the day with his cronies, while the kid could come up and ask questions but never got another dollar. He had to make his money betting horses and manage his resources if he wanted to eat lunch that day. Learning to handicap horses (technical analysis), manage his stake (money management), and wait for the best odds (psychology) paid off a million-fold after the son joined his father in managing a hedge fund.

A good trading system gives you an edge in the market. To use a technical term, it provides a positive expectation over a long series of trials. A good system ensures that winning is more likely than losing over a long series of trades. If your system can do that, you need money management, but if you have no positive expectation, no amount of money management will save you from losing.

For example, a roulette player has a negative expectation. A roulette wheel has 38 slots in the United States and 37 in Europe, but only 36 are in play, as the house "owns" the remaining one or two. Since a slot represents roughly 2.7% of a wheel, over a period of time the house skims that much from each game, slowly bleeding players dry. There is a primitive money management system called a *martingale* that has players start with a minimum bet, usually $1, and double up after each loss, so that in theory, when they eventually win, they get back all they lost plus $1, and start with $1 again. Martingale does not work in real life because casinos limit maximum bets. Once your loss runs up to that limit, a martingale just hits its head on the ceiling and dies. In blackjack, on the other hand, a very disciplined trader who follows a tested strategy and counts cards has a slight edge over the casino, on the order of 1 or 2 percent, sometimes higher. Here a good card counter needs money management to keep bets small on iffy hands and double up on strong hands.

Once you have a trading system with a positive expectation, you must establish money management rules. Follow them as if your life depended on them, because it does. When we lose money, we die as traders.

Whatever percentage of capital you lose, you must make a greater percentage to come back. I used to carry a receipt from a car rental agency to illustrate this point. The receipt showed a charge of $70, followed by a 10% discount, and 10% tax. What was the bottom line? If you said $70, go back to the books! $70 − 10% = $63. $63 + 10% = $69.30. If 10% is taken away and 10% added, you end up below the starting point. Losing equity is like falling into an ice cave—it's easy to slide in but hard to claw your way out because the edges are slippery. What happens when a trader knocks his $10,000 account down to $6,600? He's down 34% and must make 50% just to come back to even. How likely is it that a trader who just dropped a third of his equity will earn 50%? He's at the bottom of an ice hole. He'll either die or get a new lease on life from an outside source. The key question is whether he learns from his experience.

Markets are about as soft as a gladiator fight. Life on the battlefield is measured in money. Everybody's fighting to take it away from you—competitors, vendors, and brokers. Losing money is easy; making it is hard.

Money management has two goals: survival and prosperity. The first priority is to survive, then to grind out steady gains, and finally, to make spectacular gains. Beginners tend to have those priorities reversed. They shoot for spectacular gains but never think about long-term survival. Putting survival first makes you focus on money management. Serious traders are always focused on minimizing losses and growing equity.

The most successful money manager I know keeps saying he's afraid of ending up as a taxi driver. His engineering degree is out of date, he has no work experience outside the markets, and if he fails as a trader, all he can do is drive a cab. He's made millions, but still does everything in his power to avoid losing money. He is one of the most disciplined people I know.

No Math Illiterates

Modern society makes it easy to live without counting. Most of us rarely count, having grown accustomed to calculators and digital screens on appliances. If you can add up the number of guests at a dinner party or figure out how many beers are left in a six-pack after you have drunk two, you're in good shape. It's easy to go through life with hardly any arithmetic. Not so in the markets.

Trading is a numbers game. If you cannot count, you cannot trade. You do not need calculus or algebra, but you must be on easy terms with basic math—adding, subtracting, multiplying, and dividing. In addition, you need to calculate percentages and fractions and round off numbers in order to count fast. Also, you must be at ease with the concept of probability. This may sound simple, but it never ceases to amaze me how poorly and slowly most beginners count. All good traders are on easy terms with math. They are practical and sharp people who quickly calculate risks, results, and odds.

What if you're a product of modern education and need a calculator to subtract 26.75 from 183.5 or figure out 15% of 320? You need to educate yourself. You have to drill yourself in arithmetic. One of the easiest ways to do so is by counting change when you go shopping. Estimate the total price. Once you give money to a cashier, calculate how much change you'll need. Figure out sales tax in your head. Keep practicing, keep stepping out of the comfortable shell of modern consumer society where counting isn't necessary. Read a couple of popular books on the theory of probability.

Troublesome? Yes. Time consuming? For sure. Learning to count on your feet is not entertaining, but it'll help you succeed in trading.

How wide is the channel? What is the ratio of the distances to your stop-loss and the profit target? If you want to risk no more than 1% of your account and the stop is 1.25 points away, how many shares may you buy? These and similar questions go to the heart of successful trading. Being able to answer them on the fly gives you a real advantage over the crowd of innumerate amateurs.

BUSINESSMAN'S RISK VS. LOSS

Remember our example of a small businessman who ran a fruit and vegetable stand, selling several crates each day? What if his wholesaler offered him a crate of some new exotic fruit? He could make money on it, but if locals did not like the fruit and it rotted, a single crate would not hurt his business. It is a normal businessman's risk.

Now imagine he bought a tractor-trailer of that fruit at a super low price. If it sold, he could make a quick killing, but if that load rotted on him, it would hurt his business and could endanger his survival. A crate presented an acceptable risk, but a truckload was a rotten risk.

The difference between a businessman's risk and a loss is its size relative to the size of your account.

A businessman's risk exposes you to normal equity fluctuation, but a loss threatens your prosperity and survival. You must draw a line between them and never cross it. Drawing that line is a key task of money management.

Whenever you buy a stock and place a stop under it, you limit your dollar risk per share. Money management rules limit your total risk on any trade as a whole, allowing you to risk only a small percentage of your account. If you know your maximum permitted risk per trade as well as your risk per share or contract, it is a matter of simple arithmetic to calculate how many shares or contracts you may trade.

Money management rules are essential for your survival and success. Few traders have the discipline to follow them. Promises are easy to make while reading a book, but wait until you are in front of the screen. "This time is different, it's free money, I'll give this trade a little extra room." The market seduces traders into breaking their rules. Will you follow yours?

I was recently invited to chair a panel on market psychology at a gathering of money managers. One of my panelists had nearly a billion dollars under management. A middle aged man, he started in business in his 20s, while working for a naval consulting firm after graduate school. Bored with his job, he designed a trading system but did not have enough money to trade it because it required a minimum of $200,000. "I had to go to other people," he said, "and ask them for money. Once I explained to them what I was going to do and they gave me money, I had to stick to my system. It would have been unconscionable to deviate from it. My poverty worked for me." Poverty and integrity.

If you want to trade, you have to accept risks. A nitpicker, obsessing over dimes, is too stiff to place orders. While you accept risks, you may not accept losses. What is the definition of a loss?

A loss is a violation of the percentage rules—the 2% and the 6% Rules. Markets kill traders in one of two ways. If your equity is your life, a market can snap it with a single shark bite, a disastrous loss that effectively takes you out of the game. It can also kill like a pack of piranhas, with a series of bites, none of which is lethal alone but which together strip an account to the bone. These two money management rules are designed to protect you from the sharks and the piranhas.

THE 2% SOLUTION—PROTECTION FROM SHARKS

Ugly losses stick like sore thumbs out of most accounts. Traders who review their records usually find that a single terrible loss or a short string of bad losses did most of the damage. Had they cut their losses sooner, their bottom line would have been much higher. Traders dream of profits but often freeze like deer in the headlights when a losing trade hits them. They need rules that tell them when to jump out of harm's way instead of waiting and praying for the market to turn.

Good market analysis alone will not make you a winner. The ability to find good trades will not guarantee success. No amount of research will do you any good unless you protect yourself from the sharks. I've seen traders make 20, 30, and once even 50 profitable trades in a row, and still end up losing money. When you're on a winning streak, it's easy to feel you've figured out the game. Then a disastrous loss wipes out all profits and tears into your equity. You need the shark repellent of good money management.

A good system gives you an edge in the long run, but there is a great deal of randomness in the markets, and any single trade is close to a toss-up. A good trader expects to be profitable by the end of the year, but ask him whether he'll make money on his next trade and he'll honestly say he doesn't know. He uses stops to prevent losing trades from hurting his account.

Technical analysis helps you decide where to place a stop, limiting your loss per share. Money management rules help you protect your account as a whole. The single most important rule is to limit your loss on any trade to a small fraction of your account.

Limit your loss on any trade to 2% of equity in your trading account.
The 2% Rule refers only to your trading account. It doesn't include your savings, equity in your house, retirement account, or money in the Christmas club. Your trading capital is the money you have dedicated to trading. This is your true risk capital, your equity in the trading enterprise. It includes cash and cash equivalents in the account, plus today's market value of all open positions. Your system should make you money, while the 2% Rule lets you survive the inevitable drawdowns.

Suppose you're trading a $50,000 account. You want to buy XYZ stock, currently trading at $20. Your profit target is $26, with a stop at $18. How many shares of XYZ you are allowed to buy? Two percent of $50,000 is $1,000, the maximum risk you may accept. Buying at $20 and putting a stop at $18 means you'll risk $2 per share. Divide the maximum acceptable risk by the risk per share to find how many shares you may buy. Dividing $1,000 by $2 gives you 500 shares. This is the maximum number, in theory. In practice, it has to be lower because you must pay commissions and be prepared to be hit by slippage, all of which must fit under the 2% limit. So, 400 rather than 500 shares is the upper limit for this trade.

I've noticed a curious difference in how people react to the 2% Rule. Poor beginners think this number is too low. Someone asked me at a recent conference whether the 2% Rule could be increased for small accounts. I answered that when he goes bungee jumping, it doesn't pay to extend the cord.

Professionals, on the other hand, often say 2% is too high and they try to risk less. A very successful hedge fund manager recently told me that his project for the next six months was to increase his trading size. He never risked more than 0.5% of equity on a trade—and was going to teach himself to risk 1%! Good traders tend to stay well below the 2% limit. Whenever amateurs and professionals are on the opposite sides of an argument, you know which side to choose. Try to risk less than 2%—it is simply the maximum level.

Whenever you look at a potential trade, check whether a logical stop on a round lot or a single contract would keep you on the right side of the 2% Rule. If it would put more money at risk, pass that trade.

Measure your account equity on the first of each month. If you start the month with $100,000 in your account, the 2% Rule allows you to risk a maximum of $2,000 per trade. If you have a good month and your equity rises to $105,000, then your 2% limit for the next month is—how much? Quick! Remember, a good trader can count! If you have $105,000 in your account, the 2% Rule allows you to risk $2,100 and trade a slightly bigger size. If, on the other hand, you have a bad month and your equity falls to $95,000, the 2% Rule sets your maximum permitted risk at $1,900 per trade for the following month. The 2% Rule lets you expand when you are ahead and forces you to pull in your horns when you do poorly; it links your trading size to your performance. What if you have several trading accounts, for example, one for stocks and another for futures? In that case, apply the 2% Rule to each account separately.

Futures—OK to Trade Spreadsheet

Imagine two traders, Mr. Hare and Mr. Turtle, both with $50,000 accounts, who are looking at two futures markets—S&P 500 and corn. The agile Mr. Hare notices that the average daily range in the S&P is about 5 points, worth $250 each. The daily range in corn is about 5 cents, worth $50 each. He quickly figures that if he catches just a half of a day's range, he'll make over $500 per contract in the S&P, whereas the same level of skill will bring him just a little over $100 in corn. Mr. Hare calls his broker and buys two contracts of the S&P.

The cautious Mr. Turtle has a different arithmetic. He begins by setting the maximum risk in his account at 2% or $1,000. Trading the S&P, moving over $1,000 a day with such a small account, is like grabbing a very large tiger by a very short tail. If, on the other hand, he trades corn, he'll have a lot more staying power. That tiger is smaller and has a longer tail, which he can wrap around his wrist. Mr. Turtle buys a contract of corn. Who is more likely to win in the long run, Mr. Hare or Mr. Turtle?

To find out which futures markets you may or may not trade, measure your equity against the recent level of market noise. Begin by calculating 2% of your account. Measure the level of noise with the SafeZone indicator, calculate its 22-day EMA, and translate that into dollars. Do not trade any market whose average noise level is more than 1% of your equity. If you follow this rule, you'll trade relatively sedate markets where you can safely place your stops. Why 1% and not 2%? Because your 2% stop will have to be more than the average noise level away from the market.

The first column in the spreadsheet in Table 7.1 lists the market, the second the value of one contract, the third the current SafeZone indicator, and the fourth multiplies SafeZone by two. The fifth column lists 2% of the account value, in this case $30,000. The last column compares the value of SafeZone multiplied by two to 2% of the account. If the latter is greater than the former, that market is OK to trade.

The values in Table 7.1 are current as this is being written, but have to be updated monthly because volatility changes and SafeZone with it. The exchanges occasionally modify contracts and change unit values. Use this table only as an example and a starting point. Do your homework, plug in the current numbers, and find out which contracts you may or may not trade.

If you cannot afford to trade a certain market, you can still download it, do your homework, and paper trade it as if you were doing it with

Table 7.1 OK to Trade Spreadsheet

Future	Unit value	SafeZone	SafeZone•2	2% of $30,000	OK to trade?
Bonds	$1,000	0.33	$660	$600	No
Euro$	$2,500	0.09	$450	$600	Yes
S&P	$250	10.00	$5,000	$600	No
SF	$1,250	0.40	$1,000	$600	No
JY	$1,250	0.38	$950	$600	No
DM	$1,250	0.26	$650	$600	No
C$	$1,000	0.21	$420	$600	Yes
Sugar	$1,120	0.11	$246	$600	Yes
Cotton	$500	0.63	$630	$600	No
Coffee	$375	1.70	$1,275	$600	No
Cocoa	$10	24.00	$480	$600	Yes
Unleaded	$420	1.84	$1,546	$600	No
Heating	$420	2.11	$1,772	$600	No
Crude Oil	$420	0.76	$638	$600	No
Silver	$5,000	0.09	$900	$600	No
Gold	$100	1.80	$360	$600	Yes
Copper	$250	1.05	$525	$600	Yes
Wheat	$50	2.60	$260	$600	Yes
Corn	$50	2.50	$250	$600	Yes
Beans	$50	6.50	$650	$600	No
Beanoil	$600	0.30	$360	$600	Yes
Beanmeal	$100	2.60	$520	$600	Yes

real money. This will prepare you for the day when your account grows big enough or the market grows quiet enough for you to jump in.

THE 6% RULE—PROTECTION FROM PIRANHAS

It used to puzzle me why institutional traders as a group performed so much better than private traders. An average private trader is a 50-year-old married, college-educated man, often a business owner or a professional. You would think this thoughtful, computer-literate, book-reading individual would run circles around some loud 25-year-old with minimal training who used to play ball in college and hasn't read a book since his junior year. In fact, the lifetime of most private traders is measured in months, while institutional traders continue to make money for their firms year after year. Is it because of their fast reflexes? Not really, because young private traders wash out just as fast as older ones. Nor do institutional traders win because of training, which is skimpy in most firms.

Institutional traders who make a lot of money sometimes decide to go out on their own. They quit the firm, lease the same gear, trade the same system, stay in touch with their contacts—and fail. A few months later, most cowboys are back in head-hunters' offices, looking for a trading job. How come they make money for the firms but not for themselves?

When an institutional trader quits his firm, he leaves behind his manager, the person in charge of discipline and risk control. That manager sets the maximum risk per trade for each trader. That is similar to what a private trader can do with the 2% Rule. Firms operate from huge capital bases, and the risk limit is much higher in dollar terms but tiny in percentage terms. A trader who violates that limit is fired. A private trader can break the 2% Rule and hide it, but a manager watches his traders like a hawk. A private trader can throw confirmation slips in a shoebox, but a trading manager quickly gets rid of impulsive people. He saves institutional traders from disastrous losses, which destroy many private accounts.

In addition, a trading manager sets the maximum allowed monthly drawdown for each trader. When an employee sinks to that level, his trading privileges are suspended for the rest of the month. We all go through cycles. Sometimes we're in gear with the markets, and everything we touch turns to gold. At other times we are out of sync, and everything we touch turns into a completely different substance. You may think you're hot, but when you keep losing, it is the market's way of saying you're cold.

Most private traders on a losing streak keep trying to trade their way out of a hole. A loser thinks a successful trade is just around the corner, and that his luck is about to turn. He keeps putting on more trades and increases his size, all the while digging himself a deeper hole in the ice. The sensible thing to do would be to reduce your trading size and then stop and review your system. A trading manager breaks his traders' losing streaks by forcing them to stop after they reach their monthly loss limit. Imagine being in a room with co-workers who are actively trading, while you sharpen pencils and run out for sandwiches. Traders do all in their power to avoid being in that spot. This social pressure creates a serious incentive not to lose.

A friend who used to manage a trading department in London had a woman on his team who was a very good trader. Once, she hit a losing streak and by the middle of the month was nearing her loss limit. My friend knew he would have to suspend her trading privileges, but she was very high-strung and he did not want to hurt her feelings. He found a course on treasury management in Washington, DC, and sent her there for the rest of the month. Most managers are not so gentle. Gentle or rough, the monthly loss limit saves traders from death by piranha bites— a nasty series of small losses that can add up to a disaster.

The piranha is a tropical river fish, not much bigger than a man's hand, but with a mean set of teeth. It doesn't look very dangerous, but if a dog, a person, or a donkey stumbles into a tropical stream, a pack of piranhas can attack him with such a mass of bites that the victim collapses. A bull can walk into a river, get attacked by piranhas, and a few minutes later only its skeleton will be bobbing in the water. A trader keeps sharks at bay with the 2% Rule, but he still needs protection from the piranhas. The 6% Rule will save you from being nibbled to death.

Whenever the value of your account dips 6% below its closing value at the end of last month, stop trading for the rest of this month. Calculate your equity each day, including cash, cash equivalents, and current market value of all open positions in your account. Stop trading as soon as your equity dips 6% below where it stood on the last day of the previous month. Close all positions that may still be open and spend the rest of that month on the sidelines. Continue to monitor the markets, keep track of your favorite stocks and indicators, and paper trade if you wish. Review your trading system. Was this losing streak just a fluke or did it expose a flaw in your system?

People who leave institutions know how to trade, but their discipline is external, not internal. They quickly lose money without their managers. Private traders have no managers. This is why you need your own system of discipline. The 2% Rule will save you from a disastrous loss, while the 6% Rule will save you from a series of losses. The 6% Rule forces you to do something most people cannot do on their own—stop losing streaks.

Using the 6% Rule, along with the 2% Rule, is like having your own trading manager. Let us review an example of trading using these rules.

For simplicity's sake, let us assume we'll risk 2% of equity on any given trade, even though in reality we try to risk less.

At the end of the month, a trader calculates his equity and finds that he has $100,000 and no open positions. He writes down his maximum risk levels for the month ahead: 2% or $2,000 per trade and 6% or $6,000 for the account as a whole.

Several days later the trader sees a very attractive stock, A, figures out where to put his stop, and buys a position that puts $2,000, or 2% of his equity, at risk.

A few days later he sees stock B and puts on a similar trade, risking another $2,000.

By the end of the week he sees stock C and buys it, risking another $2,000.

The next week he sees stock D, which is more attractive than any of the three above. Should he buy it? No, because his account is already exposed to 6% risk. He has three open trades, risking 2% on each, and he may lose 6% if the market goes against him. The 6% Rule prohibits him from risking any more at this time.

A few days later, stock A rallies and the trader moves his stop above breakeven. Stock D, which he was not allowed to trade just a few days ago, still looks very attractive. May he buy it now? Yes, he may, because his current risk is only 4% of his account. He is risking 2% in stock B and another 2% in stock C, but nothing in stock A, because its stop is above breakeven. The trader buys stock D, risking another $2,000, or 2%.

Later in the week, the trader sees stock E, and it looks very bullish. May he buy it? Not according to the 6% Rule, because his account is already exposed to a 6% risk in stocks B, C, and D (he is no longer risking any equity in stock A). He must pass up stock E.

A few days later stock B falls and hits its stop. Stock E still looks attractive. May he buy it? No, since he already lost 2% on stock B and has a 4% exposure to risk in stocks C and D. Adding another position at this time would expose him to more than 6% risk per month.

The 6% Rule protects you from the piranhas. When they start biting you, get out of the water, and do not let the nasty fish nibble you to death. You may have more than three positions at once if you risk less than 2% per trade. If you risk only 1% of your account equity, you may open six positions before maxing out at the 6% limit. The 6% Rule protects your equity, based on last month's closing value and not taking into account any additional profits you may have made this month.

If you come into a new month with a big open profit, you have to re-calibrate your stops and sizes so that no more than 2% of your new total equity level is exposed to risk on any given trade and no more than 6% on all open trades combined. Whenever you do well and the value of your account rises by the end of the month, the 6% Rule will allow you to trade a bigger size the following month. If you do poorly and the size of your account shrinks, it will reduce your trading size the next month.

The 6% Rule encourages you to increase your size when you're on a winning streak and stop trading early in a losing streak. If the markets move in your favor, you will move your stops beyond breakeven and put on more positions. If your stocks or futures start going against you and hitting stops, you will lose your maximum permitted amount for the month and stop, saving the bulk of your account to trade the next month.

The 2% Rule and the 6% Rule provide guidelines for pyramiding—adding to winning positions. If you buy a stock, it rises, and you move the stop above breakeven, then you may buy more of the same stock, as long as the risk on the new position is no more than 2% of your account equity and your total account risk is less than 6%. Handle each addition as a separate trade.

Most traders go through emotional swings, feeling elated at the highs and gloomy at the lows. If you want to be a disciplined trader, the 2% and the 6% Rules will convert your good intentions into the reality of safer trading.

POSITION SIZING

A few years ago the owner of a local stock trading firm asked me to run a psychological training group for his traders. They were shocked to hear a psychiatrist was coming and loudly insisted they "weren't crazy." The group got off the ground only after the manager told his worst performers that they had to join—or else. Once we began to meet and focus on psychology and money management, the results were such that six weeks later we had a waiting list for the second group.

The firm used a proprietary day-trading system. It worked so well that its two top traders took in more than a million dollars each month. Others who used the same system made less, and quite a few lost money.

In one of our first meetings a trader complained that he had lost money each day for the past 13 days. His manager, who sat in on the meeting, confirmed that the fellow was following the firm's system but could not make any money. I began by saying that I would take my hat off for anyone who could lose for 13 days in a row and have the intestinal fortitude to come in and trade the next morning. I then asked how many shares he traded, since the firm set a maximum for each trader. He was permitted to buy or sell 700 shares at a clip, but voluntarily reduced it to 500 while on his losing streak.

I told him to drop down to 100 shares until he had two weeks during which he had more winning days than losing and was profitable overall. Once he cleared that hurdle, he could go up to 200 shares. Then, after another two-week profitable period, he could go up to 300 shares, and so on. He was allowed a 100-share increment after two weeks of profitable trading. If he had a single losing week, he'd have to drop back to the previous level until he had a new profitable two-week period. In other words, he had to start small, go up in size slowly, and drop down fast in case of trouble.

The trader loudly objected that 100 shares weren't enough, and he wouldn't be able to make any money. I told him to stop kidding himself since trading a bigger size made him no money either, and he reluctantly agreed to my plan. When we met a week later he reported that he had four profitable days out of five and was profitable overall. He made very little money because his trading size was so small, but he was ahead of the game. He continued to make money during the next week and then stepped up to 200 shares. In our next meeting he asked, "Do you think it could be psychological?" The group roared. Why would a man lose while trading 500 shares, but make money trading 100 or 200?

I took a $10 bill out of my pocket and asked whether anyone in that group would like to earn it by climbing on top of our long narrow conference table and walking from one end to the other. Several hands went up. Wait, I said, I have a better offer. I'll give $1,000 cash to anyone who comes up with me up to the roof of our 10-story office building and uses a board as wide as the table to walk to the roof of another 10-story building across the boulevard. No volunteers.

I started egging on the group. "The board will be as wide and sturdy as our conference table, we'll do it on a windless day, and I'll pay $1,000 cash on the spot. The technical challenge is no harder than walking on the conference table, but the reward is much greater." Still no takers. Why? Because if you lose your balance on the conference table, you jump down a couple of feet and land on the carpet. If you lose your balance between two rooftops, you would be splattered on the asphalt.

When the level of risk goes up, our ability to perform goes down.

Beginners often make money on small trades. They gain a little experience and confidence, increase their trading size—and start losing. Their system hasn't changed, but bigger size makes them a little stiffer and less nimble. Most beginners are in a hurry to make a killing, and guess who gets killed.

Overtrading means, among other things, trading a size that is too large for you. Poor futures traders look for brokers with the lowest margin requirements. If the minimum margin in gold is $2,000, an eager beaver with $10,000 may buy five contracts. Each includes 100 oz. of gold, making his account swing $500 for every $1 move in gold. If gold goes against him, he is cooked. If it goes his way, that beginner will be convinced he has discovered a great new way of making money, continue to trade recklessly, and bust out on the next trade.

Unscrupulous brokers promote overtrading because it generates big commissions. Some stockbrokers outside the United States offer a "shoulder" of 10:1, allowing you to buy $10 worth of stock for every $1 you deposit with the firm. Some currency houses offer a shoulder of 100:1.

When a scuba diver jumps off a boat, he has a device called an *octopus* attached to his air tank. It consists of several tubes, one leading to his mouthpiece, another to his flotation vest, and yet another to an instrument that shows how much air he has left in his tank. If it falls too low, he may not have enough to get back to the surface, which is why scuba is such a deadly sport for illiterates and hotheads.

Putting on a trade is like diving for treasure. There is gold below the rocks on the ocean floor. As you scoop it up, remember to glance at your air gauge. How much gold can you take without endangering your survival? The ocean floor is littered with the remains of divers who saw great opportunities.

A professional diver thinks about his air supply first. If he doesn't get any gold today, he'll go for it tomorrow. All he needs to do is survive and dive again. Beginners kill themselves by running out of air. The lure of free gold is too strong. Free gold! It reminds me of a Russian saying—the only free thing is the cheese in a mousetrap.

There are tribes in Africa that catch monkeys by putting tidbits of food into jars with narrow necks, tied to stakes in the ground.

A monkey wiggles its hand into a jar, grabs a tidbit, but cannot pull it out because only an open hand can go through the narrow neck. The monkey still tugs at the bait when the hunters come to pick it up. Monkeys lose because of greed, grabbing and refusing to let go. Think of this when you feel tempted to put on a large trade with no stop.

A professional trader needs strong money management skills. All successful traders survive and prosper thanks to their discipline. The 2% Rule will keep you safe from the sharks, the 6% Rule from the piranhas. Then, if you have a half-way decent trading system, you'll be far ahead of the game.

MONEY MANAGEMENT STEPS

Overtrading—putting on trades that are too large for your account—is a deadly mistake. Beginners are in a hurry to make money, whereas serious traders begin by measuring risks. If you start small and concentrate on quality, you'll become a better trader. Once you've learned to trade—find trades, enter, set stops and profit targets, and exit—you can start increasing your trading size to the point where your account starts generating a meaningful income.

A new trader came to see me recently, a 42-year-old businessman tired of the rat race. His wife continued to run their business, while he put all his time and energy into the market. He kept bobbing around breakeven, trading anywhere from 100 to 1,000 shares at a clip. Often, he'd make money on several trades in a row trading small lots and then give back everything on a single large trade.

I told him he was ahead of the game because, unlike most beginners, he hadn't lost money. I then gave him the standard prescription— begin by trading 100 shares, the smallest round lot, until you have a profitable period during which you have more winners than losers and are profitable overall. That period should be two weeks for a day-trader or two months for a longer-term swing trader. Once you have had a profitable period, bump up your size by 100 shares and start trading 200. After another profitable period, go up another 100 shares and start trading 300. If you have a losing half-period (a week for a day-trader, a month for a swing trader), go back down to your previous trade size and start counting again. If you trade futures, substitute one contract for 100 shares. Advance slowly, retreat fast.

In his ground-breaking book *Portfolio Management Formulas*, Ralph Vince introduced the concept of the optimal *f*—the optimal fraction of your account to risk in any given trade for maximum long-term gains. His book is mathematically demanding, but it boils down to a few key concepts: there is an optimal *f* for every trade; if you bet less, your risk decreases arithmetically while profit decreases geometrically; if you keep betting more than the optimal *f*, you are guaranteed to go broke.

The optimal *f* keeps shifting with every trade and is hard to calculate. It provides the highest returns in the long run, but it also leads to vicious drawdowns that may exceed 90% of the account. Who has the fortitude to continue trading a system that has brought his account down from $100,000 to $9,000? The main value of the optimal *f* is simply to remind us that if we trade a size that's too large, we'll destroy our account. The optimal *f* marks the zone beyond which you walk into a minefield. Stay away from it, trade less than the optimal *f*.

Beginners who count profits put their cart before the horse. Reverse that approach and begin by counting risks. Ask yourself what your maximum permitted risk is if you follow the 2% and 6% Rules.

These are the steps of proper money management:

1. Measure your account value on the first of the month—the total of cash, cash equivalents, and open positions.
2. Calculate 2% of your equity. This is the maximum you may risk on any given trade.
3. Calculate 6% of your equity. This is the maximum you are permitted to lose in any given month, after which you must close out all trades and stop trading for the rest of that month.
4. For every trade, decide on your entry point and a stop; express your risk per share or per contract in dollars.
5. Divide 2% of your equity by your risk per share to find how many shares or contracts you may trade. To get a round number, round it down.
6. Calculate your risk on all open positions by multiplying the distance from the entry point to the current stop by the number of shares or contracts. If the total risk is 4% of your account or less, you may add another position, since you'll be adding 2% with your current trade, bringing the total to 6%. Remember, you do not have to risk 2% per trade; you may risk less if you like.
7. Put on a trade only after meeting all of the above conditions.

Establish the size of your trades on the basis of how much money you can afford to risk, not how much you want to make. Follow the 2% and the 6% Rules. If you are having a good month, with most trades going your way, you will move your stops beyond breakeven and will be allowed to put on more positions. You may even go on margin. The beauty of this money management system is that it clips your losses when you are cold and lets you go forward at full throttle when you're hot.

On the first of the month, if you have no open positions, the 2% and 6% levels are easy to calculate. If you approach the first of the month with some open positions, calculate your account equity—the value of all open trades at the latest market price plus all cash or money market funds. Calculate the 2% and 6% levels on the basis of that number. If you have moved stops beyond breakeven in open trades, you have no capital at risk and may look for new trades. If your stops are not yet at breakeven, find the percentage of your equity you have exposed to risk and count it against the 6%. Once you deduct that number from 6%, the result will let you know whether you may put on new trades.

How should you apply the 2% and 6% Rules if you trade futures, stocks, and options all at the same time? First of all, a beginner should concentrate on a single market. Diversify only after you succeed. If you are trading more than one market, open separate accounts and treat each as a separate trading enterprise. For example, if you have $60,000 in stocks and $40,000 in futures, calculate the 2% and 6% Rules for the $60,000 and apply them to stocks, and then calculate the 2% and 6% Rules for the $40,000 and apply them to futures. If you have more than one account, allocate trading-related expenses in proportion to their sizes.

Remember, both your trading system and your money management must be good in order to win in the markets.

PART THREE

COME INTO MY TRADING ROOM

Traders go through several stages of development. Many beginners view trading as a mechanical pursuit. They think that if only they could find the right parameters for the Stochastic or the proper length for a moving average, success would be theirs. They become easy prey for gurus selling mechanical systems.

Survivors realize that psychological factors, such as optimism or doubt, greed or the fear of pulling the trigger are much more important than any technical indicator. They start developing a feel for the importance of risk control. I keep running into folks at conferences who have a good grip on technical analysis and some understanding of psychology, but who know that something is missing because they cannot win consistently and must keep their day jobs. What should they do next?

Once you have a decent understanding of technical analysis, follow money management rules, and know the value of trading psychology, you need to develop new organizational skills. You already possess the building blocks of success—now is the time to erect the structure of successful trading.

There is no magic trick for converting a serious amateur into a professional trader. What I offer you here is a recipe for intense and focused work which will enable you to move up to the ultimate stage of professional trading.

THE ORGANIZED TRADER

What is the single most important trait of a successful trader? High intelligence? Not really, even though some basic level of performance is required. Good education? Not quite, since many of the best traders haven't gone past high school. The trait that all winners have in common is a very high level of discipline. How can you measure your level and then increase it? You do it by maintaining and learning from several sets of trading records.

Keeping good records is the single most important contribution to your success. If you maintain scrupulous records, review them, and learn from them, your performance will improve. If your money management is in place to ensure survival during the learning process, you're sure to become a success.

These are strong words, but my experience confirms them. In the years of teaching Traders' Camps, whenever I saw a person with good records, he was either a successful trader or soon became one. I have found that women tend to keep better records than men, which is one of the reasons the percentage of winners among them is higher.

Records are more important to your success than any indicator, system, or technical tool. Even the best system is bound to have some holes, but good records will allow you to find them and plug them up. A person who keeps detailed records makes a huge leap in his development as a trader.

Show me a trader with good records, and I'll show you a good trader.

Bad traders keep bad records. People who do not learn from the past are doomed to repeat it. "I've been hit, insulted, spat upon, and abused—the only reason I stick around is to see what happens next."

Good records let you learn from the past instead of struggling from day to day. When the market hits you, good records show from where that blow came. The next time, you'll take a different path and avoid trouble. You may run into a different sort of trouble the next time around, but keep at it long enough and you'll run out of mistakes. Just be sure your money management is in place, so that your money doesn't run out while you are learning. When you start making profits, your records will show how they came about, helping you repeat that experience. Good records reduce guesswork and make trading a much more professional exercise.

Remember the extensive notes you kept in college? Educators agree that keeping notes is an essential part of the learning process. If you are struggling, you must start keeping notes. Once you become a winner, you'll continue to keep them, because they will have become a key part of your trading process. Keeping records is time-consuming. If you get tired or bored and give them up, take that as a sure sign that you are gambling rather than trading. Your records are a litmus test of your seriousness as a trader.

A trader needs four types of records. Three of them look back, and one forward. The trader's spreadsheet, his equity curve, and his trading diary help review past performance. The spreadsheet rates each individual trade, the equity curve tracks your account as a whole, and the diary reflects your decision-making process. The fourth record is a trading plan for the day ahead. Maintaining these four records puts you on the road toward responsible, professional, successful trading.

TRADER'S SPREADSHEET

The first step of proper record keeping is setting up a spreadsheet that lists all your trades. Each horizontal line describes a new trade. Each vertical column contains a certain detail of each trade or rates an aspect of your performance. These columns belong in any workable trader's spreadsheet:

1. Trade number (list all trades in the order of entry)
2. Entry date
3. Long or short
4. Ticker (stock symbol)

5. Size (how many shares)
6. Entry price
7. Commission
8. Fee
9. Total (Entry price × size + commission + fee)
10. Channel (record the height of the channel on the daily chart or whatever chart you use for your intermediate timeframe; you'll use it to rate your trade after exiting)
11 Exit date
12. Exit price
13. Commission
14. Fee
15. Total (Exit price × size − commission − fee)
16. P/L (profit or loss—column 15 minus column 9 for longs or the opposite for shorts)
17. Entry grade (see below)
18. Exit grade (see below)
19. Trade grade (see below)

You may include several additional columns. For example, you may want to record the name of the system that prompted that trade, the initial stop, and slippage, if any. You can make your spreadsheet reflect multiple exits as well as record the reasons for exits, such as hitting price targets or stops, or impatience. You can make your spreadsheet give you quick summaries of profit and loss or the number of winning and losing trades per market and per system. You can make it show the average, the smallest, and the greatest profit or loss per trade in each market and each system.

The entry grade (17) rates the quality of your entry by expressing it as a percentage of that day's range. For example, if the high of the day was 80, the low 76, and you bought at 77, then your entry grade is 25, meaning you bought within the lower 25% of the day's range. Had you bought at 78, your grade would have been 50. The lower the percentage while buying, the better. Consistently buying at high numbers can be ruinous. Try to keep your entry rating below 50. This may not seem like much, but can be surprisingly difficult to accomplish.

The exit grade (18) rates the quality of your exit by expressing it as a percentage of that day's range. For example, if the high of the day was 88, the low 84, and you sold at 87, your exit grade is 75. It means you captured 75% of that day's range. Had you sold at 86, your grade would have been 50. The higher the percentage, the better for the seller. Selling at high numbers is good, while selling at low numbers amounts to charity. Work to get your exit rating above 50.

These ratings are important for position traders but even more so for day-traders. Just keep in mind that when shorting, you open a trade by selling and close it by buying. Similar ratings apply, as long as you keep in mind that the sequence of buying and selling is reversed.

The trade grade (19) expresses your profit as a percentage of the channel you've captured. It is the single most important rating of a completed trade, much more important than the amount of profit. Subtract column 6 (entry price) from column 12 (exit price) and divide the result by column 10 (channel width), displaying the result in percentage format. Reverse the formula when you go short—column 6 minus column 12 divided by column 10.

Rating your profit as a percentage of the channel provides an objective yardstick of your performance. You can make a lot of money in a big sloppy trade or just a little money in a finely executed trade in a difficult market. Rating each trade on the basis of its channel reflects your skill as a trader. If you can capture between 10% and 20% of the channel, your grade is a C. If your profit exceeds 20% of the channel width, you earn a B. And when you take 30% or more out of a channel, you make an A trade!

Add an extra column following each rating to calculate your average grades for entries, exits, and completed trades. Graph those numbers and keep doing everything you can to make them trend higher. A scrupulously maintained trader's spreadsheet is an active learning tool. It puts you in touch with your successes and failures, creating an island of stability and responsibility in the ocean of market chaos.

THE EQUITY CURVE

Are you disciplined enough to succeed in trading? Few people can definitely answer yes or no. Many traders are somewhere in the middle of the scale. There is a gauge, a meter that shows whether you're moving up or down as a trader. That gauge is your account equity. Whenever you act responsibly, it turns up, but ticks down with almost every lapse of judgment.

Most traders look at charts, but very few look at themselves. That is an oversight, since personality is a hugely important part of trading. An equity curve holds up a mirror to your performance. Professionals keep equity charts for themselves and their clients. When you start tracking your equity curve, you make a big step toward joining the pros.

Use a spreadsheet to track your equity curve. Each horizontal line reflects one unit of time, in this case a month. These columns belong in the spreadsheet:

1. Date
2. Account equity
3. 2%
4. 6%

Find your account equity on the last day of each month and type in that figure. Account equity equals all cash and cash equivalents in the account, plus the value of all open positions. Mark your account to market; your account equity is the liquidation value of your account. Repeat this procedure every month. After accumulating this data for several months, begin plotting your equity on a chart. The goal of every professional trader is a smoothly rising equity curve, flowing from the lower left to the upper right with only occasional shallow drawdowns.

Once you have accumulated a year's worth of equity data, add a moving average to your curve. A six-month simple MA will identify the trend of your equity. It will also answer an important question—when to add money to your account.

Most people add capital either after damaging losses or when they feel very confident after a string of successes. Adding money after your equity reaches a new high is emotionally understandable, but it happens to be a bad time to add money. We all go through cycles, and a trader who has just reached a new equity high is due for a pause or a pullback. If the moving average of your equity is rising, the best time to add money is on a pullback to the rising MA. The uptrend of the moving average of your equity confirms that you are a good trader, and a pullback shows a return to value. You buy stocks and futures on pullbacks to their EMAs, so why not use the same tactic when you want to give yourself more money to trade?

Program your spreadsheet to return two important numbers after you type in that month's equity—the 2% and 6% values. They set two safety nets for your account for the month ahead. The 2% Rule limits your risk on any single trade. Once you find a trade and decide where to put a stop, the 2% Rule will give you the maximum number of shares or contracts you may trade (try to risk less if you can). The 6% Rule takes away your trading privileges for the balance of the month if your account value drops to 94% of its previous month-end level.

You may enhance this spreadsheet, depending on what you want to know and how good you are at programming. You can use it to calculate the monthly curve with and without interest. You can calculate your curve both before and after trading expenses. You need to recalculate your curve whenever you add or subtract trading capital without mixing up past percentages. The key message—start plotting your equity curve now!

Your equity curve is the yardstick of your performance. An orderly uptrend is better than a steep uptrend with deep drawdowns. Your equity curve should keep rising, and if it turns down, you have to become much more defensive in your trading.

Trading Diary

A civilized person is in touch with his past. Understanding what has gone before helps you deal with the present and face the future. A trader who keeps a diary can learn from the past instead of mindlessly repeating mistakes. A trading diary provides a private mirror, a valuable feedback loop. It is probably the single best learning tool available to traders.

A trading diary is both a visual and written record of your trades. You can keep it on paper or in electronic form. I started keeping mine such a long time ago that I still do it on paper, using scissors and double-stick tape to paste up charts. You can follow these instructions or adjust them and convert your diary into electronic format.

A trading diary is an album, 11 × 14 inches or bigger. Assign each two-page spread to a single trade. Whenever you enter a trade, print out the charts that led to that trade, and paste them on the left page. Each chart is about 3 × 5 inches, with the weekly on top, followed by one or two dailies and sometimes an intraday chart. Write down the name of the stock, the date, and the number of shares bought or shorted. Add a note on the fundamentals if they had anything to do with that trade. Comment on how you first became aware of that stock—a scan of the database, a tip from a friend, or an article in a magazine or a newsletter. This allows you to track the sources of your information. Use a pen to mark indicator signals and chart patterns that led you into that trade. Write a few words about your feelings entering that trade (anxious, happy, confident, unsure) and note any unusual factors and circumstances.

I keep my diary at home, and if I trade at the office, I bring my printouts with me and paste them up in the evening. It takes time to clip the charts, tape them into my album, mark them up, and write the commentary. This discipline reminds me that trading is what I do, and trading takes priority over almost all other activities.

Repeat this process after exiting a trade—print out the charts and paste them up on the right page of the album. There are usually fewer charts on the right, as the weekly chart does not always figure in the exit. Mark up trading signals and write down your comments on the circumstances of the exit, including your feelings about it.

As your diary grows thicker, this visual record of your trades becomes more and more valuable. Keep going back, leafing through your diary. How do those signals look now? What are you happy with, what would you have done differently, what lessons have you learned? Most traders never ask themselves these questions. When they make money, they swell with pride, and when they lose, they feel angry or ashamed. Wallowing in feelings will not make you a better trader. Our losses can teach us more than our gains. A trading diary helps you put aside self-kicking or self-congratulation and pay attention to the facts. It helps you learn and succeed, helps you become free.

Nobody can give you a trading diary. You have to create it yourself, and your ability to maintain it will provide a running check of your discipline. Whenever you make some money, leaf through your diary and ask whether you could have done any past trades differently in light of what you have just learned. When you lose, do not kick yourself but write a good note on that trade, go back to review past trades, and think how to avoid such losses in the future. Learn from your profits and losses.

To learn even more, go back to each completed trade approximately three months after an exit and print out the current charts. Tape them to a sheet of paper, mark them up, and attach that flyleaf to your exit page. Now you can revisit your trades with the benefit of hindsight for an extra dose of trading education.

What if you are a very active trader or day-trader, making so many trades that a diary entry for each is simply impractical? In that case, have a diary entry for every fifth or every tenth trade listed in your Trader's Spreadsheet. You can add other trades to your diary if they are especially important, but be sure to maintain the discipline of every fifth or every tenth trade.

Keeping a diary and learning from your trades is as close as you can come to a guarantee of trading success. Be sure to strictly observe money management rules so that a string of freak losses doesn't toss you out of the game while you're still learning. Follow the rules, keep a spreadsheet, equity chart, and a trading diary, review them, learn from them, and you'll have everything it takes to become a successful trader.

ACTION PLAN

It is important to face each day knowing what and how you will trade. This is especially true for position traders, as day-traders must instantly react to quotes on their screens.

A pro does not squint at his charts. Good trades jump at you from the chart and scream—here I am, take me. If you have to squint, there is no trade and you should move on to the next stock. A good position trader, or any mature trader for that matter, looks not for the challenges but for the money.

The best time to search is in the evenings when markets are closed. You can review your markets in peace, think, check out other stocks and indicators, and then make your decision—to go long, short, or stand aside. Write down your decision and review it in the morning before the markets open.

Whenever you place an order, especially when you give it to the broker on the phone, it pays to read from a page instead of speaking from memory. Why? Because almost every trader I know has had the embarrassing experience, usually more than once, of accidentally reversing an order. You may want to sell short, but make a slip of the tongue, telling your broker to buy, and seconds later find yourself an owner of a collapsing stock. Even worse, there is a temptation to change your order at the last moment—buy more or less than you planned, or switch a limit to a market order. Putting a sheet of paper between yourself and your broker provides a useful layer of protection.

It is a good idea to write down some background for each order. My preferred format includes three lines: Weekly, Daily, and To Do. For example:

Weekly: EMA rising, MACD-H ticked down, deteriorating
Daily: MACD-H bearish divergence, pullback to the EMA in progress
To Do: Sell short at 71.30 with a stop at 73, target mid-60s

or

Weekly: EMA turning flat, MACD-H ticked up from a bullish divergence
Daily: EMA up, MACD-H rising, all in gear to the upside
To Do: Buy on a pullback to the EMA at 23.25, stop 22, target high 20s

I keep these notes in an Excel spreadsheet. It has a line for every stock that I track, with dates in vertical columns. Whenever I see a trade, I click on the cell for that date and stock, go to the Insert menu, and select Comment. Once I've written my three-line note, a tiny red triangle appears in the right upper corner of the cell. Whenever you move your cursor over it, the comment pops up on the screen. This record-keeping system makes it easy to sweep horizontally and review your entire analytic history of a stock or sweep vertically and review all your comments for that day. I keep my records for the ABC rating system, described below, in the same spreadsheet.

Remember to keep your notes descriptive. If you write something like "weekly charts give a buy signal," that does not tell you anything specific about a stock and will be useless when you look at it a few days later. Begin by describing what you see on the weekly charts, move on to the dailies, and only after that write down your trading ideas on the action line.

Keeping an action plan increases your load of paperwork, but it makes trading more businesslike and less like a swing through a casino. This reminds me of the time I took a group of mostly American traders for a mock trading session on the floor of the Russian Exchange in Moscow. Each person was assigned an interpreter and given a paper bankroll. Everybody had a grand time, trading and taking pictures, except for a lone Dutchman in our group. That market maker from Amsterdam kept furiously scribbling on the back of an envelope as he watched prices on the display panel above the floor. When the session ended and we moved on to the executive dining room, they brought us printouts with our results. It turned out that the group as a whole lost a million rubles. The Dutchman made a little over 900,000 rubles, while the rest went up in slippage and commissions—a pretty common outcome. Good records help create good traders, which is why I encourage you to invest time and energy in keeping and following your action plan.

TRADING FOR A LIVING

Trading attracts us with its promise of freedom. If you can trade, you can live and work anywhere in the world, be independent from the routine, and not answer to anybody. You can trade from a beach bungalow or a mountaintop chalet, as long as you have a good Internet connection. You have no boss, no customers, no alarm clock. You are your own person.

People pay lip service to their dreams of freedom, but many feel frightened by it. If I stop making money for any reason whatsoever, no corporate parent will take care of me. This a frightening thought for most people. No wonder so many of us have grown used to the security of our corporate cages.

Caged animals develop all sorts of neurotic behaviors. A common neurosis is an addiction to the earn-and-spend cycle. We are taught since childhood that our place in society is defined by what we consume. If you drive a $50,000 car, you are a better, more successful person than someone who drives a $15,000 auto, whereas a neighbor who drives a $120,000 car is a very special winner altogether. The man who dresses at an Armani boutique is a more refined individual than someone who buys his pants and shirts at the corner store. Society waves countless carrots in our faces. The ads sell not food, shelter, or transportation, but a boost of self-esteem. An addict feels revived by a fix for only a short time. People spend their entire lives straining to keep up with the Joneses. Those dastardly Joneses do not have the decency to stay in place, and as they climb the ladder, we must climb also.

Freedom begins in our minds, not in our bank accounts. To liberate yourself, start becoming conscious of your spending. You are likely to see that you need much less than you thought, making freedom that much closer.

There was a Wall Street analyst by the name of Joe Dominguez who saved enough money to retire at 31. He spent the rest of his life enjoying himself, doing volunteer work, and writing a book called *Your Money or Your Life*.

> We aren't making a living, we are making a dying. Consider the average American worker. The alarm rings at 6:45 and our working man or woman is up and running. Shower. Dress in the professional uniform—suits or dresses for some, overalls for others, whites for the medical professionals, jeans and flannel shirts for construction workers. Breakfast, if there's time. Grab commuter mug and briefcase (or lunch box) and hop in the car for the daily punishment called rush hour. On the job from nine to five. Deal with the boss. Deal with the coworker sent by the devil to rub you the wrong way. Deal with suppliers. Deal with clients/customers/patients. Act busy. Hide mistakes. Smile when handed impossible deadlines. Give a sigh of relief when the ax known as 'restructuring' or 'downsizing'—or just plain getting laid off—falls on other heads. Shoulder the added workload. Watch the clock. Argue with your conscience but agree with the boss. Smile again. Five o'clock. Back in the car and onto the freeway for the evening commute. Home. Act human with mates, kids or roommates. Eat. Watch TV. Bed. Eight hours of blessed oblivion.
>
> And they call this making a living? Think about it. How many people have you seen who are more alive at the end of the work day than they were at the beginning? . . . Aren't we killing ourselves—our health, our relationships, our sense of joy and wonder—for our jobs? We are sacrificing our lives for money—but it's happening so slowly that we barely notice.

Pull out your old tax returns or cash income books and add up all earnings since your first job. You're likely to find that even a moderately successful person has earned a million dollars or more. And spent it! Have you ever seen hamsters racing on a treadmill? Wouldn't it be nice to hop off, go for a walk, stop by some flowers and inhale? Most people cannot relax because they are hooked on spending. When they begin to trade, they set impossible goals. Fifty percent in the first year is not enough when you crave a downpayment on a Ferrari.

There is nothing wrong with owning a Ferrari or any other luxury, provided you have given it a lot of thought and are buying it for a true personal need rather than responding to advertising propaganda. People keep buying things to shut out their feelings of emptiness and dissatisfaction. A person who uses money to stuff up his sense of emptiness can hardly focus on finding the best quality trades.

Find the minimal level of spending which feels comfortable to you. To quote Dominguez again,

> You have enough for your survival, enough for your comforts, and even some special luxuries, with no excess to burden you un-necessarily. Enough is a powerful and free place. A confident and flexible place.

Become conscious of your expenditures. Use cash instead of plastic whenever possible. Stop trying to impress people with your posses-sions. They are not paying attention because they are too busy trying to impress you. Pay off all your debts, including your mortgage. That's not too hard once you reduce your expenses. Set aside enough money to live for 6 to 12 months and loosen the link between work and income. Trading should be a high-paying, high-integrity self-employ-ment. Once your living expenses are covered, start putting extra prof-its into tax-free bonds so that eventually you'll have enough income to take care of your normal needs in perpetuity. If tax-free municipals yield 5%, then $1 million worth of them will bring you $50,000 a year, free and clear. Will that be enough? Will you need twice that much? Three times? Five? The sooner you lower your expenses, the sooner you'll reach the moment of liberation. Rationally managing your per-sonal finances prepares you to rationally manage your trading account.

You probably did not expect a discussion of personal spending in a book on trading. If it has caught your attention, follow up by reading the Dominguez book. The key idea for traders is to approach the mar-ket in a sober and rational manner, maximizing gains, minimizing losses, and being accountable for every step that they take.

DISCIPLINE AND HUMILITY

A friend started out as a floor clerk and struggled for eight years before his trading took off. Now he is a world-famous money manager, and many of those who knew him when he was a beginner like to remi-nisce about how he clerked on one of the smaller exchanges in New York, taught classes, and struggled to make ends meet. An old trader said to me, "I knew him then, and I thought he would succeed. He had the right combination of being very careful and having this optimism you need to get up in the morning and believe you're going to make money trading the markets."

To succeed in trading, you need both confidence and caution. Having only one is dangerous. If you're confident but not cautious, you'll be arrogant, and that's a deadly trait for traders. If, on the other hand, you are cautious but have no confidence, you will not be able to pull the trigger.

You need confidence to say, "This stock is going up, my indicators say it will continue to rise, I am going to get long and ride this trend." At the same time, you need to be humble enough to put on trades whose size will not endanger your account. You have to accept the uncertainty of the markets and be ready to take a small loss without quibbling.

When you feel a surge of confidence in a new trade, it is hard to think of the downside risk, but if you don't do it, you cannot protect yourself. When the market goes against you and hits your predefined exit level, you have to humbly exit, no matter how confident you feel about that trade. You need both confidence and humility. The ability to be aware of two conflicting feelings at the same time is one of the hallmarks of emotional maturity.

I have a client in New York who came to several seminars and bought books and videos from my firm but kept struggling for years as a trader. He'd get ahead, fall behind, get ahead again, then lose money and get a job to make ends meet. He often seemed on the verge of success, but kept bouncing around breakeven. Then one day, I ran into him at a conference and saw a changed man. He was doing supremely well, managing about $80 million, with terrific grades from the rating agencies. A few weeks later I stopped by his office.

He had continued using the same trading system, developed years ago and derived from Triple Screen. He had made only one change. Instead of second-guessing the system, he came to see himself as a clerk. He imagined he had a boss who went to Tahiti and left him to trade the system. The boss will return and give him a bonus, depending not on profits, but on how faithfully he followed the system. My client stopped trying to be a hot-shot trader and moved into a position of humility and discipline. That's when he rose to sweeping success.

Second-guessing a system is a terrible error that creates a huge level of uncertainty. Tom Basso, a prominent money manager, says that it is

hard enough to figure out what the market is going to do; if you do
not know what you're going to do, the game is lost.

Choose your system, set up your money management rules, test
everything. Run the system each night, write down its signals, and read
those messages to your broker in the morning. Do not improvise when
quotes flash in front of your face because they hypnotize you and
prompt you to put on impulsive trades.

What if the markets change and your system starts missing good
moves or chewing up equity? Well, you should have tested it over a
long enough stretch of data to feel confident about its long-term performance. Your money management rules will help you ride out a rough
stretch. Be very conservative with an existing system. If you're feeling
restless, design a new system and trade it in a different account—leave
what works alone.

Trading demands discipline, but, paradoxically, attracts impulsive
people. Trading requires practice, humility, and perseverance. Successful traders are strong but humble people, open to new ideas. Beginners
like to brag, experts like to listen.

Ten Points

When a beginner puts on a trade too big for his account, and it starts
to swing, it floods him with adrenaline. An upswing gives him enough
money to dream about moving to easy street. Feeling elated, he misses
the signals of a top and gets caught in a downside reversal. A downswing puts him into such a state of fear that he misses the signals of a
bottom and sells out right near the lows. Beginners pay more attention
to their emotions than to the reality of the markets.

Once you begin to develop discipline, you start seeing much more
clearly what happens outside of your little account and in the great big
market out there. When you see the market freeze in a flat trading
range or explode in a vertical rally, you know what the masses of
traders feel, because you have been there. When a market goes flat,
and amateurs lose interest, you know that a breakout is coming. You
were once that amateur, you overlooked breakouts because you got
bored and stopped watching the markets. Now, when the market goes
flat, you recognize the way you used to be, and are ready to act.

The market surges to a new high, pauses for a day, and goes vertical. The newspapers, radio, and TV are screaming about the new bull

market. If you are a disciplined trader, you remember how, years ago, you bought within a few ticks of the top. This time is different. You reach for the phone and start taking profits on positions acquired when the market looked boring and flat. Understanding yourself and the path you have traveled allows you to read the market and beat your competitors.

How do you know that you are becoming a disciplined trader?

You keep accurate records. You maintain the minimum of four records—a trader's spreadsheet, an equity curve, a trader's diary, and an action plan. You scrupulously keep your records up to date and study them to learn from your experiences.

Your equity curve shows a steady uptrend with shallow drawdowns. The performance standard for professional money managers is 25% annual gain on the account, with no drawdowns of more than 10% from peak equity. If you can match or exceed that, you are far ahead of the game.

You make your own trading plans. Even when you get a terrific-sounding tip from a friend, you do not get swept up in the excitement. You either ignore it or put it through your own decision-making screens.

You do not chat about your trading. You may discuss a technical point or a closed trade with a trusted friend, but you never ask for advice on an open trade. You do not disclose your positions so as not to expose yourself to unwanted advice or tie up your ego in the process.

You learn all you can about the market you're trading. You have a good grasp of the main technical, fundamental, intermarket, and political factors that may impact your stock or a future.

You grade yourself on the adherence to your written plan. Imagine you are an employee, and the boss has left on an extended vacation, leaving you to manage his money by following his plan. When he returns he will reward or punish you based on how faithfully you followed his plan.

You allot a certain amount of time to the markets each day. You download data each day, put it through your battery of tests and screens, and write down the results and plans for tomorrow. You allocate time in your daily schedule to make trading a regular activity and not something you do catch as catch can.

You monitor selected markets daily, regardless of their activity. You avoid the typical beginners' error of monitoring markets only when they are active and "interesting." You know that strong moves spring from periods of relative inactivity.

You learn and are open to new ideas, but are skeptical of claims. You read market books and magazines, attend conferences, participate in online forums, but you do not accept any ideas without testing them on your own data.

You follow your money management rules as if your life depended on them—because your financial life does. If you have good money management, most decent trading systems will make you money in the long run.

HAVE YOU GOT THE TIME?

All traders pay attention to money but few are aware of the importance of time. Time is just as crucial as money—the more you have, the more likely you are to win.

Most people start out with too little money, and most traders do not give themselves enough time to learn. Trading is very different from physics or mathematics, where genius reveals itself early. In science, if you're not a star by the time you're 25, you'll never be one. Trading, on the contrary, is an old man's game, and now increasingly a woman's. Patience is a virtue and memory a great asset. If you slightly improve each year, you can grow into a brilliant trader.

My friend Lou Taylor, to whom *Trading for a Living* was dedicated, used to say, "if I become half a percent smarter each year, I'll be a genius by the time I die." As always with him, there was a great deal of wisdom in his joke.

Raise your eyes from the keyboard and think about two goals—to learn to trade and to make money. Which comes first and which comes second? Stop killing yourself trying to make a lot of money in a hurry. Learn to trade, and the money will follow. An intelligent horse trainer does not overload a young horse. Training comes first, pulling heavy loads comes later.

You learn best by making many small trades and analyzing your performance. The more you trade, the more you learn. Play for small stakes to reduce the pressure and concentrate on quality. You can always increase your size later. The goal is to acquire enough experience so that most actions become nearly automatic. A trader whose experience has taught him a lot of practical skills can focus on strategy—what he wants to do—instead of worrying about his next step.

If you are serious about trading, you have got to put time into it. Markets have to be studied, trading methods dissected and rated, systems designed and applied, decisions made and recorded. All of this adds up to a fair bit of work. What is a fair bit? Two examples come to mind, at opposite ends of the spectrum.

At the hard-working end, I think of a top-rated American futures money manager in whose apartment I once stayed. We lived under the same roof, but I hardly ever saw him. He would leave for the office before 7 A.M., return after 10 P.M., and fall asleep in his clothes in the living room. He worked like that six days a week, but on a Sunday he took it easy. In the morning he would go for a game of squash at a club before running back to the office to prepare for the opening on Monday. No wife, no girlfriend, no pastimes, and no friends—but man, was he raking in millions!

At the relaxed, but still very disciplined end, I think of a middle-aged Chinese trader whom I visited in his mansion when the stock markets were reeling throughout Asia. He had made a fortune in the two bull markets of the previous 10 years and told me that he needed just one more Asian bull market to make all the money he wanted. He was prepared to wait for several years for the next one, but meanwhile looked after his family, collected art, and played a lot of golf. He spent a few hours a week downloading the data and watching his indicators.

How much time should you spend analyzing markets and doing your homework? A beginner must spend every minute of his waking hours learning the basics. How much time will you need at the next stage, once you've become a competent semiprofessional trader? We are talking about position trading and not day-trading, which forces one to stay in front of the screen all day. The answer depends on how fast you work and how many markets you trade.

You must dedicate a certain amount of time to the markets each day. Amateurs and gamblers make a typical mistake. When markets are inactive, they stop watching and lose touch. They wake up after hearing the news of a runaway move. By that time, the markets are running—the amateurs have missed yet another train and now they chase it, hoping to hop aboard a runaway trend.

An organized trader tracks his markets, whether he trades them at the moment or not. He notices when a listless range starts rubbing against a resistance, buys early, and when amateurs start piling into the rally, he takes profits, selling to lazy latecomers. A serious trader is ahead of the game because he does his homework day in and day out.

How much time will you need? For every stock you must get a handle on its key fundamentals, including its industry group. For futures, there are the additional factors of supply and demand, seasonals, and spreads between delivery months. You need to make a calendar of events that may impact your market, such as Federal Reserve announcements or earnings reports. You need to study weekly charts for the past several years and daily charts for at least a year. You need to apply indicators, learn which work best with that market, and test their parameters.

Unless you are a genius or a speed demon, it is hard to accomplish this in less than two hours. And that is just an entry fee into any trading vehicle. Afterward the daily grind begins. A serious trader reviews weekly and daily charts each day. You have to compare your market with other related ones. You have to make daily notes and write down your plans for the day ahead. To do this properly, you'll need at least 15 minutes per stock or future.

And this is in a fairly routine day. What about the day when your market hits support or resistance, or breaks out of its trading range, and a trade seems imminent? Then you might spend closer to an hour analyzing it, measuring risk and reward, and deciding on your entry points and profit targets.

So let us turn the question around: If you have an hour a day for analysis, how many markets should you follow? Three, maybe four. If you have two hours, you may be able to follow six, eight, or even ten. The ABC system for organizing homework may allow you to double the number of markets. Whatever you do, remember, quality is more important than quantity.

Before you add a stock to your list, decide whether you have enough time to track it, day in and day out. You may skip a day once in a while, but even then you should at least glance at your markets. Daily homework is essential, and the number of markets you may follow depends on how much time you have each day. When we get out of touch, we grow cold. Even professionals take a few days to get back in touch with their markets after a vacation. These are the stages of development:

Beginner: At the start, track approximately six, but no more than 10 trading vehicles. You can always add more later. It is better to start with fewer markets and follow them well than to start with a lot and fall behind.

Daily homework is essential for developing a feel for the markets. Allocate time to study your markets each day. Even if you come home late at night from your job or a party, you can still find 10 minutes to download the data and glance at your five or six stocks. You can update your mental picture of them even if you don't plan to trade them tomorrow. A beginner who follows too many stocks bites off more than he can chew, falls behind, and becomes demoralized. Better to follow a small number, get to know them well, and add more later.

Intermediate: You may track several dozen stocks or futures at this stage. Analyzing each will take just as much time as it did when you were a beginner, but you'll analyze them more deeply. A serious amateur or a semiprofessional trader can use his time more efficiently with the help of the ABC Rating System (see next page).

Some good traders choose not to expand the number of stocks or futures they trade. A person might concentrate only on soybeans and their products, or only currencies, or only five or six technology stocks. In addition to analyzing your markets, expect to spend a minimum of five to six hours a week reading books and articles and interacting with other traders on the Internet.

After about a year or longer at this stage you will face an important choice: to treat trading as a mildly profitable hobby or to try to rise to the professional level. In that case, you will need to dedicate more time to trading. You will have to make sacrifices in other areas of your life and spend at least four to six hours a day working in the markets.

Professional: people who trade for a living tend to drop other professional interests. The markets demand time and attention, and money management is more challenging because the account is much bigger.

A professional trader almost always uses some version of the ABC Rating System, unless he chooses to trade just a handful of markets. He spends more time researching the markets. At the same time, he reviews them faster, thanks to his greater level of expertise. He spends several hours each week reading, deepening his analysis and improving his money management, and also keeping track of new developments on the Internet.

The rewards are very good at this stage, but a professional who has put years into getting there does not become intoxicated with the results. He lives very well, but continues to work harder than most beginners. Traders at this level love the markets and derive a great deal of satisfaction from them, like skiers enjoy tall mountains.

Managing Time with the ABC Rating System

Markets generate colossal volumes of information. No human can process all the available data. No one can have in mind all the fundamental values, the economic trends, the technical indicators, the intraday action, and the buying and selling by insiders and market makers while making a trading decision. We want to be thorough in our research, but it can never be complete. We need to select a relatively small number of markets and design a trading plan in order to channel the incoming information into a more manageable stream.

Trading is not about being brilliant, not about making forecasts, and not about scanning a huge universe of trading vehicles. Trading is about managing—our capital, our time, our analysis, and ourselves. If we manage right, we'll grind out profits.

Managing time is an important aspect of success. Find out how much time you need, depending on your personal style, to research a new market and track it daily. The ABC Rating System is designed to deliver major time savings, allowing you to track and trade more markets in the same time. This system is not for beginners, but an intermediate or expert trader can definitely benefit from it.

The ABC Rating System, shown to me by D. Guppy, is a system for managing time. It helps us concentrate on the markets in which a trade seems imminent and spend less time in less promising markets. The ABC system calls for a quick weekly review of all stocks or futures that you track and sorting them into three groups: A for those you think you might trade tomorrow, B for those you think you may trade later in the week, and C for those you do not expect to trade in the coming week.

The best time to run the ABC system is on weekends, after you have downloaded all your data. Prepare a spreadsheet with a horizontal line for every stock or future you follow. Put their names in the left column. Use vertical columns to record your A, B, and C ratings, one column per day. Prepare the weekly and daily templates in your trading software. Drop the first market into the weekly template. Does it look like you might want to trade this stock tomorrow? For instance, if you only trade from the long side and the weekly chart is in a solid downtrend, you will not trade it next week. In that case, mark it with a C and move on. Drop the next market into your weekly template. If it looks like a possible trade, then drop it into your daily template. Does it look like you might want to trade it on Monday? If so, put an A into your spreadsheet. If it looks like an unlikely trade on Monday but possibly later that week, put a B in your spreadsheet. Now move to the next market and drop it into the weekly template. Repeat this process until you go through your entire list.

Keep a good pace, do not slow down. You should be done with each market in well under one minute. Remember, good trades should leap at you from the screen and grab you by the face—it's me, trade me! If you have to squint at a chart, there's probably no trade.

The real work begins after you have filled in your ABC spreadsheet. Now you must study each stock or future you have marked with an A. Apply your trading system, set up entry levels, stops, and profit targets, and write down your orders for the day ahead. Do this for every market you have rated an A, leaving aside all others. After the closing on Monday, go through all your A-rated markets. If you have entered them, fill in a page in your trading diary and continue to manage those trades according to your plan. If your entry orders have not been triggered, review those markets again—do you still want to enter on Tuesday? Filtering out B and C groups saves time and lets you concentrate on the most promising trades.

Repeat the procedure after the closing on Tuesday, but now also review the markets you rated B over the weekend. Now is the time to decide whether you can upgrade them to an A and start monitoring them daily or downgrade them to a C and leave them alone until the weekend.

Earlier, we reviewed the action plan, a spreadsheet for recording your orders for the day ahead. That and the ABC system lend themselves to being combined into a single spreadsheet. Each horizontal line holds a trading vehicle, and each vertical column one trading day. The cells are filled with the letters A, B, or C, indicating your rating for that stock or future for the day ahead. Red triangles in the corners identify those cells in which you have inserted comments that tell you how to trade them.

Boredom is the trader's enemy. It is hard to watch a market day after day while it goes nowhere. A professional must track his markets, but no one enjoys watching paint dry. The ABC system provides an elegant solution. It lets you monitor all your markets in a quick and efficient manner, while dedicating most of your time and attention to the most promising trades. Once you get used to applying the ABC system, you can easily double the number of markets you follow and increase your trading opportunities.

THE DECISION-MAKING TREE

A professional trader takes the markets seriously and gives them the time and attention they deserve. If you have read this far, you are probably more dedicated than the average person. Now is the time to zero in on your plan of action.

You need to allocate a certain time to market work each day; keeping in close touch with the market is essential for success. You have to decide what markets to trade and focus on a select few to be successful. You need to design a plan for your education. Last but not least, you need to design your trading plan; a written plan is the hallmark of a serious trader.

Designing a Trading Plan

Traders go through three stages of development. We all start out as beginners. Some of us survive long enough to become serious amateurs or semipros, and a few rise to the expert level. A trader with a good written plan shows a rising level of development.

A beginner never writes down a plan because he has nothing to write. He is having too much fun chasing hot tips and trying to make a quick killing. Even if he wanted to write, he wouldn't know where to begin. A serious amateur or a semipro who writes down a plan, including money management rules, is on his way toward the expert level.

The main difference between a trading plan and a mechanical system is the degree of freedom it allows traders. Trading systems are rigid, whereas plans lay down the main rules but leave you free to use your judgment.

Some beginners gain a false sense of security from pouring tons of data into mechanical systems and finding sets of rules that would have worked in the past. The markets are live social organisms that develop, grow, and change. Rigid rules fitted to past data are not likely to perform well in the future. If mechanical systems could work, the best programmers would have owned the markets by now. All mechanical trading systems, left alone, self-destruct with the passage of time. Promoters keep selling them because the public loves marketing gimmicks.

A trading plan includes a few unbreakable rules along with more flexible recommendations that call for an exercise of judgment. Your judgment grows with experience. A trading plan includes the principles for selecting markets, defines the types of trades, generates buy and sell signals, and allocates trading capital. When you write a plan, avoid the temptation to make it all-encompassing. Know when to stop. Write down your rules but indicate where you will use your judgment at the moment of decision.

You must know what type of trading appeals to you. A general idea—to make money buying and selling—is not specific enough. Winners make money in different ways, while all losers fall into the same wastebasket of impulsivity. A long-term fundamental investor, like Peter Lynch, searching for his elusive "10-bagger"—a stock that rises 10-fold—acts differently from a successful short-term trader who goes short to sell him that stock. Both may succeed in the long run, but the floor trader with a 30-minute time horizon will close his shorts on a tiny but profitable dip before the end of the day, just as surely as the long-term investor will hold on to his longs.

A trading plan reflects your interests in specific markets and techniques, your experience, and the size of your account. It reflects your personality as well as the behavior of your markets. If two friends with equal capital and similar experience traded the same market and wrote down their plans, they would come up with different outlines. You may create more than one plan if you like different types of trading.

If you do not have a plan, start working on one. Drafting an intelligent plan requires a huge amount of work. The first time I tried to do it was on a flight from New York to Los Angeles. I thought that five hours in the air would be enough. A month later I was still at it.

Here are two fairly basic outlines of trading plans to illustrate their basic structure and provide starting points for developing your own. Reading someone's trading plan is like reading a guide to lovemaking. That manual may open your eyes to a few new positions, but ultimately you'll have to do what suits your temperament and environment to enjoy the results.

Trading Plan A   Trader A has $50,000 in his account and is interested in the stock market. He has been tracking it for a while and has observed that large-capitalization stocks (Dow-type stocks) tend to move in steady trends but swing above and below their central tendencies several times a year.

A trading plan takes a concept of market behavior—that prices oscillate above and below their average value—and translates it into a plan of action. It identifies the trend and the deviations, selects the tools for catching them, and includes money management rules, profit targets, and stops.

RESEARCH

1. Download four years' worth of data for 30 stocks in the Dow Jones Industrial Average.

2. Use weekly charts with a 26-week EMA to identify their long-term trends.

    A serious trader will test other approaches such as a longer or a shorter EMA, different EMAs for different stocks, or another trend-following tool, such as a least regression trendline. Finding the best tools for tracking the average consensus of value in your market forces you to do a lot of research before putting on the first trade.

3. Determine the average deviation from value for each stock you plan to trade.

    Measure how high a stock rises above or falls below its weekly EMA before swinging back. Channels can help, or you can put the numbers into a spreadsheet. Find out how far from the EMA the reversals occur, both in terms of price and percentages, as well as the average duration of those deviations.

WEEKLY ACTIONS

Review the weekly charts of all stocks you follow. Mark those that have deviated from their central tendencies by more than 75% of their average deviation and place them on your daily monitoring list.

DAILY ACTIONS

To streamline our discussion, we will consider only buying even though a complete trading plan is also likely to spell out steps for shorting.

1. Apply a 22-day EMA to stocks on your daily monitoring list to define their short-term trends. Research whether a longer or a shorter EMA would do a better job. When a stock is deviating on the weekly chart but its daily EMA stops moving and turns flat, it becomes a buy candidate.

   Here is another research idea: Is buying more profitable when the broad market rises? How will you define the trend of the broad market? The EMA of an index, such as the S&P or NASDAQ, or an indicator, such as a new-high–new-low Index*? If your stocks march to their own drummer, then ignore the broad market; otherwise, you may buy more when the broad market rises and less when it falls.

2. When the weekly chart shows a downside deviation, buy the first uptick of the daily EMA. Research types of entries—below the EMA, in its vicinity, at the market, or on a breakout above the previous day's high.

3. Place a stop using the SafeZone indicator on the daily chart and set a profit target at the weekly EMA. Recalculate your orders daily.

Calculate your dollar risk per share and decide how many shares to buy while observing the 2% Rule. A trader with $50,000 in his account may not risk more than $1,000 per trade, including slippage and commissions. Do not enter a trade if 6% of your account is already exposed to risk in other trades.

This plan includes several inviolate rules: buy only when prices are below the weekly EMA; buy only when the daily EMA is rising; do your homework, recalculate your stops daily, and never risk more than 2% of your account equity; do not expose more than 6% of your account to risk. This plan also makes you exercise your judgment about exactly where to enter, where to set profit targets, and what size to trade (as

---

*This simple indicator, which can easily be calculated for any exchange, is the best gauge of the power of bulls and bears in the stock market. New highs are the stocks that are making a new high for the year—the leaders in strength. New lows are the stocks that are making a new low for the year—the leaders in weakness. If you compare their number each day, you will see whether the upside or the downside leadership is stronger. This indicator shows you what the leaders are doing, and you can usually expect the crowds to follow the leaders. I have described this indicator at length in *Trading for a Living*.

long as you follow the 2% and the 6% Rules). It goes without saying that you have to back up your written plan by keeping good records.

Your plan is likely to grow more elaborate with the passage of time. The market will throw several curves at you, which will lead you to adjust your plan and make it longer. The plan above ties Triple Screen analysis (multiple timeframes and indicators) with money management, entries, and exits.

Trading Plan B   Trader B has $30,000 of risk capital and wants to trade futures. He has noticed that those markets tend to spend a lot of time in flat trading ranges, punctuated by relatively brief but fast trends. He wants to take advantage of those short-term impulse moves.

RESEARCH

This trader has relatively little money, but doesn't want to trade mini-contracts. Therefore, he should focus on inexpensive markets whose normal levels of noise will not overwhelm his money management rules.

For example, a 1-point change in the S&P 500 translates into $250 in the S&P futures. A normal 5-point move on an ordinary day will lead to a $1,250 change in equity, exposing a trader with a $30,000 account to a 4% loss. The 2% Rule puts many volatile and expensive markets off limits for small accounts. Coffee, soybeans, currencies, and many others have to be left alone until your account grows much larger.

1. Download two years' history in corn, sugar, and copper. Corn is the least volatile of grains, and sugar is the least volatile tropical. Both are very liquid, permitting easy entries and exits, unlike other inexpensive markets, such as orange juice, whose thin volume exposes traders to bad slippage. Copper is liquid and tends to be relatively quiet, except during economic booms. E-minis, electronically traded index futures, are good for futures traders interested in the stock market. Download two data series for each contract: at least two years of continuous data for weekly charts and six months of the front month data for daily charts.

2. Test several EMAs to determine which does the best job of tracking trends on the weekly charts. Do a similar job with the daily charts. Find the best channels for each market, especially for the past three

months on the daily charts. Those channels must contain 90 to 95 percent of recent market action. The past three months are the most relevant, but it is a good idea to go back two years in your channel research to prepare yourself for their dramatic expansions and contractions. Many traders lose their bearings when markets change. If you know your history, you'll feel less surprised.

WEEKLY ACTIONS

Review the weekly charts of your markets and determine their trends. When the weekly trend is up, proceed to the daily charts and look for buying opportunities. When the weekly is down, look for shorting opportunities. If the weekly trend is unclear, either leave that market alone or go directly to the daily charts.

You can define weekly trends by using the slope of an EMA, or you can be more inventive, especially if you track just a few markets. For example, you can use both the EMA and the MACD-Histogram to identify trends. When both indicators move in the same direction, they signal extra strong moves.

DAILY ACTIONS

Again, to streamline our discussion, we will only discuss buying, but the same logic applies to shorting. Every futures trader must be comfortable with shorting. These markets have no uptick rule, and the number of short positions always equals that of longs.

1. Apply the Impulse System. When both the EMA and MACD-Histogram rise, they give a strong buy signal.

2. Go long the following day, but do not buy above the upper channel line.

   This aggressive entry aims to capture high-speed impulse moves. You will have to research and test this idea in the market you want to trade at the moment. Avoid the trap of mechanical systems that people trade long after the markets have changed.

   Before you enter a trade, calculate where to put your stop. See what percentage of capital you will risk in that trade. Decide whether your money management rules allow you to take it. Does the 6% Rule allow you to trade? For example, if you've lost 3.5% of your account this month and have an open trade with 2% of equity at risk, no new trade may be opened because it would risk more than 6% of your equity.

3. Set a stop using the SafeZone indicator on the daily chart.

If your stop placement allows you to take the trade, place the buy order. As soon as you have your confirmation, place your stop. Recalculate your stop and place a new one each day. Don't allow a sudden violent move to blow through a mental stop while you're not watching.

Take your profit before the close of the day during which the daily screen goes off its buy signal. This means you have to calculate your formula a few minutes before the close. The upper channel line on the daily chart is too modest a target when you are fishing for an impulse move. Stay with the trade as long as the buy signal stays in force. Be sure to test this approach.

This plan combines inviolate rules with recommendations that encourage you to use your judgment. Using multiple timeframes, following money management rules, using stops, and scrupulously keeping records are non-negotiable. Choosing the markets, the entry points, and the profit targets and deciding what size to trade—these all depend on your judgment.

Expect to modify your plan as you continue to research the markets and as your expertise grows. Remember to write down any changes, and record your development as a trader. Be sure to add short selling to your plan because this is an integral part of trading futures.

At some point you may want to design a flowchart of your decision-making process, along these lines:

Does the 6% Rule allow me to trade?
If No, stand aside; if Yes:

Is the weekly chart giving a signal?
If No, move to the next market; if Yes:

Is the daily chart giving me a signal to trade in the same direction?
If No, skip that market; if Yes:

Where will I put my profit target and stop; is the risk-reward ratio worth trading?
If No, skip that trade, if Yes:

What size does the 2% Rule allow me to trade and how much will
I trade?

One could draw an extensive flowchart for every trade, but the key
point is to observe several inviolate rules, mostly having to do with
money management and multiple timeframes. As long as you observe
those rules, you have a wide choice of analytic and trading techniques.
Just be sure to keep good records and continue to learn from your
experience if you want to trade like a pro.

BEGINNER, SEMIPRO, PRO

Traders' questions reveal their stages of development. Beginners always
ask about trading methods—what indicators to use, what systems to
choose. They want to know the right Stochastic parameters and the
best length of a moving average. Most newbies are so excited about
profits and so clueless about risk that no fancy tools can save them
from disasters.

Those who survive the stage of original innocence move on, thanks
to a combination of luck, work, or an inborn sense of caution. They
learn to select trades and find where to buy and sell. They start asking
why their profits are so inconsistent, if they know so much. How come
their account is up 20% one month and down 25% the next? How come
they can make money but not grow equity?

Traders at the second stage often grab a profit and spend it before
that money evaporates. They feel insecure about their ability to
make money. I remember ages ago taking a penny profit from Swiss
franc futures and rushing to a jewelry store to buy my then-wife a
necklace. Another time, I used a little less than a cent profit to buy
my daughter an expensive Abyssinian cat. Those cats have long
lives and hers, named Swissie, used to remind me of my old impulsive trading days.

Traders who get stuck at that level keep bouncing up and down like
a flower in an ice hole. To move to the next stage, a trader must overcome the biggest obstacle to winning—the person he sees in the mirror.
He must recognize his role in putting on impulsive trades, undisciplined trades, trades without stops. No matter how clever his methods,
he is not a winner until his mind is in the right place. His personality,
with all its quirks, influences results more than any computer. Traders
at that stage ask: "Do I have to put in stops or can I use mental stops?"

"Why am I afraid to pull the trigger?" "How come the trades I don't take work out better than those I take?"

A trader who survives, succeeds, and moves up to the third stage feels relaxed and calm. When he asks questions, he is interested in money management. His trading system is in place, his discipline is good, and he puts a lot of time into thinking how to allocate his trading capital and reduce risk.

These three stages form a pyramid, a structure with a broad base and a narrow top. The journey has a high attrition rate. I wrote this book to help make your passage a little smoother, faster, less painful, and more profitable.

What are the reasonable profit targets for different stages? The numbers I'll give you may surprise you as low. You want to make more money, and you should feel free to reach higher and do better if you can. These guideposts should help you see whether you're meeting the minimum requirements. They help you recognize when you are in trouble so that you can stop, think, and adjust your methods. If you trade for a bank and keep missing profit targets, your manager will pull your trading privileges. A private trader has no manager and is in charge of his own discipline. If this book helps you stop, think, regroup, and move higher, I have not wasted my time writing.

1. **BEGINNER**

   A. *The minimal acceptable performance level for a beginner is a loss of 10% of trading capital in a year.* Traders are shocked when I give them this number. They forget that most beginners blow themselves out fast. Many lose 10% in a month if not in a week. If you can survive for a year, learn about trading, and lose less than 10%, your education is cheap and you are way ahead of the crowd.

   B. *The goal of a beginner is to cover trading expenses and generate annual return on his account equal to one and a half times the current rate on T-Bills or a comparable riskless instrument.* You have to charge the cost of software, data, classes, and books, including the one you're reading, against your trading account. Beginners often throw money at gurus who promise the keys to the kingdom. Charging your trading-related expenses against your account introduces a useful reality check. If you can cover them and then beat the Treasury bills, you' re no longer a beginner!

2. INTERMEDIATE (SERIOUS AMATEUR OR SEMIPROFESSIONAL)

A. *The minimum acceptable performance level for a serious amateur is return on equity twice the current rate on T-Bills.* Your improvement is evolutionary, not revolutionary. Cut some of your losses a little faster, grab some of your profits a little sooner, learn a few more tricks of the trade. Once you're covering your trading expenses and making double what you could get from riskless paper, you're miles ahead of the efficient market theorists.

B. *The goal of a serious amateur or a semiprofessional is to generate a 20% annual return on equity.* At this stage, the size of your trading capital becomes an important factor. If you are trading a million dollars, you may be able to start living off your profits. But what if you trade a relatively small account, say $50,000? You know you can trade, but 20% of $50,000 is not enough for a living. Most undercapitalized traders destroy themselves by overtrading, trying to squeeze unrealistic returns from their tiny accounts. Take crazy risks, and you'll have crazy results—both on the way up and on the way down. Better stick to your trading system and leverage your skills by trading other people's money (see "Going Pro" on the next page).

3. EXPERT

A. *The minimal performance targets are more flexible for experts. Their returns are steadier, but not necessarily higher than those of serious amateurs. You have to continue outperforming T-Bills—to fall behind them would be ridiculous.* An expert may grab a 100% return in a good year, but trading a serious amount of money year after year, just staying north of 20% is a very good performance. Certified geniuses such as George Soros maintain a lifetime average of nearly 30% per year.

B. *The goal of an expert trader is to put enough money into riskless investments to be able to maintain his current standard of living forever, even if he stops trading.* Trading at this stage becomes a game that you continue to play for your own enjoyment. Soros certainly doesn't need any more money for personal expenses but trades because he enjoys spending fortunes on political and charitable causes. Curiously enough, when you no longer have to stretch for the money, it starts flowing in faster than ever.

GOING PRO

A beginner is better off starting with a relatively small account. Someone who has moved up to a solid semiprofessional level needs to start pushing up his account size to increase profits. An expert with a large account has to be cautious not to impact thin markets with his trades. He has to watch out for a fall in performance, a frequent side effect of greater size.

The minimum size for a trading account is about $20,000 at this time. Once you've moved up to the level of a serious amateur or a semiprofessional trader, $80,000 will give you more freedom to diversify. Once you get your account up to $250,000, you may start thinking of moving up to professional trading. These are absolute minimums, and if you can increase them, your life will be easier. Starting with $50,000, having $120,000 at a semiprofessional level, and moving up to professional trading at $500,000 will improve your chances of success.

What if you do not have that much? Trading on a shoestring raises the pressure to a deadly level. A person with a tiny account cannot apply the essential 2% Rule. If he has only $5,000, his permitted risk is only $100 per trade, which guarantees that he will be stopped out by market noise. A desperate beginner swallows hard and puts on a trade without a stop. Most likely, he'll lose, but what if he wins, ends up with $7,000, then puts on another trade and goes up to $10,000? If he is smart, he will sharply reduce his trading size and start using the 2% Rule now. He was very lucky and should put his winnings into a sensible trading program. Most people become intoxicated by success and cannot stop. A beginner who has doubled his $5,000 stake usually feels that the game is easy and he's a genius. He feels he can walk on water, but soon drowns.

You might be able to start by getting a trading job, but corporate Wall Street will not hire someone over 25 for a paying job as a trader trainee. A more realistic option is to sharply cut expenses, get a moonlighting job, and save money as fast as you can, while paper trading the markets. This calls for discipline, and some of the best traders have started this way. The third option is to trade other people's money.

Trading your own capital reduces the level of stress. Having to raise money increases tension and interferes with trading. Taking a loan is not a sensible way to raise funds because the interest raises an insurmountable barrier to success. Borrowing money from family and friends has the added kicker of having to justify their trust and trying to show off.

Scared money is losing money. If you have to worry about paying it back, you cannot concentrate on trading. Companies that hire executives usually run credit checks on their candidates. A high level of debt kills a candidacy because a person who is worried about money cannot properly concentrate on his job. I know a chronic loser who received a quarter million from his mom as a wedding gift. She told him to buy an exchange seat as an investment, but he resented his financial dependency on the strong-willed lady and decided to show how good he really was. He took a loan against the seat and went to trade on the floor. His scheme had a predictable ending, and to this day his family talks of "the missing seat."

You are better off learning to trade with your own money. The time to use other people's money comes when you know what you are doing and want to leverage your skills. There are huge pools of capital sloshing through the financial system, looking for competent money managers. Show a good track record going back several years, and you will have all the money you care to manage.

I have a friend who earned an engineering degree but went to work as a floor clerk on a futures exchange. He spent several years learning to trade, saved $50,000, and then quit his job to trade full-time. He moonlighted by writing a book and teaching a few classes but continued to struggle despite his steady 50% annual returns. His profit was about $25,000 a year, but he had to pay rent, eat, and occasionally buy a new tennis racket and a pair of shoes. After a few years of this he had a bad year and broke even. That's when he had to eat his seed grain—dip into his trading capital for living expenses. Then he connected with a big money management firm.

The firm checked his track record and staked him out with an additional $50,000. He was to trade through that firm, at low commissions, and keep 20% of any profits on managed money. He kept delivering, and they kept giving him more money to manage. In a few years he was up to $11 million but then had another bad year, returning only 18% profit. In the old days he would be dipping into his capital, but now the math was different. Eighteen percent profit on $11 million came to almost $2 million, and his 20% share was $400,000. That's how much he earned in a bad year. He now has over $100 million under management. His performance as a trader has not changed much, but the size of his rewards went through the roof.

You can start trading other people's money informally, without a license, although you will have to register once the funds under management exceed a certain limit. The rules are different for stocks and futures because they have different regulators.

You can begin by asking people to give you the power of attorney over their accounts, allowing you to trade but not to withdraw the money. Once you become registered, it is not a good idea to have individual managed accounts because their owners receive confirmation slips for each trade and pepper you with questions. It is better to have all your accounts in a pool whose members receive a single statement at the end of the month telling them how much that pool is worth and what their share is.

Futures money managers are regulated by the National Futures Association (NFA). To become a Commodity Trading Advisor (CTA), you must pass an exam known as Series 3, unless you are a floor trader. Stock market money managers are regulated by the Securities and Exchange Commission (SEC). Their exam, called Series 7, is much harder and many people take months to prepare for it.

The more free-market NFA allows its members to charge performance fees, taking a share of profits, much as US lawyers work on contingency fees. It is not uncommon for a manager to take 20% of profits, but that is not how most of them make their money. Many charge 1% or 2% of assets as a management fee. If you collect 1% on $50 million, you are taking in half a million dollars a year just for being a nice guy. Any performance fees come on top of that as pure gravy.

The more blue-blood SEC does not allow performance fees, forcing its registrants to be satisfied with a small percentage of assets. Since the assets in the stock market are much greater than in the futures market, those fees are nothing to sneeze at. For all the mutual fund advertising hoopla, those fees are a key deciding factor in funds' long-term performance. The Vanguard Fund, which has always made low fees its key selling point, keeps outperforming most hot-shot managers in the long run.

Stock market money managers have found a way to run around the SEC regulation against performance fees. They set up vehicles known as hedge funds. Only so-called qualified investors who pass income and assets tests are allowed to invest in them. Hedge fund managers typically put their own money into the funds and receive performance fees comparable to those in futures markets. A hedge fund manager is trading his own money along with that of his clients, which is probably why hedge funds as a group outperform mutual funds. Tracking hedge fund managers and shifting funds between them offers an alternative to tracking the markets for wealthy investors. If you go this route, make sure you find out what percentage of their own assets they have in their funds.

Successful money managers go through three stages of development. Many begin by informally managing a few modest accounts. Then they become registered and the funds under management rise to millions of dollars. Those who accumulate a five-year track record of steady gains and low drawdowns can go after the key prize—pension funds and endowment money. Those who get to manage these assets are the true elite of professional money managers.

CHAPTER TEN

COME INTO
MY TRADING ROOM

Good trades begin and end with money management. The 6% Rule tells you whether you may put on a trade in the first place. Then, before you place an order, the 2% Rule tells you the maximum size allowed for that trade, based on the distance from your entry to the stop. Sandwiched between those rules is market analysis. Here, in this chapter, I want to illustrate the analytic process for you.

Shocking but true, most people who write books on trading do not trade. In putting together their books, they rely on the power of well-chosen hypothetical examples. The only people obligated to disclose their track records are money managers. I trade my own money and feel no need to lay my full accounting open to curiosity seekers. Still, you trusted me enough to buy this book. Since all trust is mutual, I want to reciprocate by showing you some of my trades.

Here are a few trades I executed in recent months. It is important that all of them have already been closed out. One of the worst things a trader can do is reveal his open trades, putting his ego on the line and gumming up the decision-making process. Completed trades are history, from which we may learn.

These charts show how one trader makes his buy and sell decisions. Mine are based primarily on Triple Screen trading system—making strategic decisions in the longer timeframe and tactical decisions in the shorter timeframe.

Whenever I put on a trade, I print out its charts and mark key signals that prompted me to act. Whenever I close a trade, I print out its charts again and mark up those signals that prompted me to exit. I may write a few lines on how I first became aware of a potential trade, how I felt entering and exiting, and so on. I try not to write a dissertation on every trade, and record only the key factors, aiming for speed and brevity.

My journal, a hard-cover spiral-bound album, sits on a bookshelf in my trading room. I sometimes come into that room in the evening, sprawl in an armchair, and review my trades, one after another. Some pages are pleasant, others painful, but all are educational.

As you go looking for trades, please do not feel as if you have to find the same patterns as shown here. This is just a brief excerpt from one man's diary—a few of the trades made in recent months. Also, trading is intensely personal, with different people reacting to different aspects of the game. There are many ways to make money in the markets and even more ways to lose it. My main purpose in showing you a few pages from my diary is to prompt you to begin documenting your trades in order to learn from your own experience.

EXCERPTS FROM THE DIARY

Charts in my trading diary are printed in color and marked up by hand. Comments, written on margins, are telegraphic and abbreviated. In preparing this manuscript for publication, I had to print those charts in black and white rather than color, while slightly expanding my comments to make them easier to understand.

Showing strangers your trading diary feels almost like inviting them into the bedroom during an intimate moment. As we grow older, we care less and less about what others think of us; I do not believe I could have shown you my diary just a few years ago.

The key question is, What are you going to do with it? Will you casually flip through the pages? Will you go through them slowly, evaluating each trading signal? Will you feel overwhelmed? Will you feel critical, especially of trades with less than perfect scores? Before I turn my records of six recent trades over to you, I have just one question. Will you be keeping your own diary? If my example has inspired you, I will have achieved my goal.

Trade 1—Long CSCO

The stock market has been falling for a year, accelerating in recent months. In a Traders' Camp a month prior to this trade I asked a guest instructor, a famous expert, what companies will be left standing at the bottom of a severe economic, as well as financial, decline, that is, what stocks to buy amid the ruins. His answer—BGEN, CSCO, and IBM. I included all three in my weekly scan of the market.

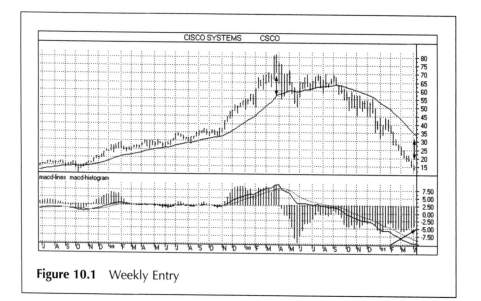

Figure 10.1   Weekly Entry

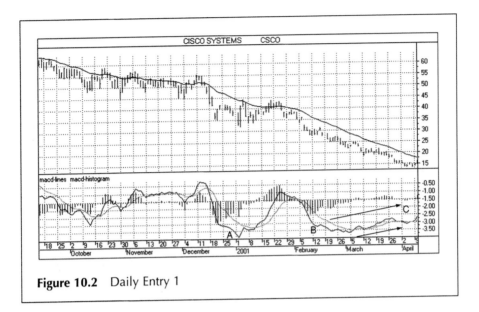

Figure 10.2   Daily Entry 1

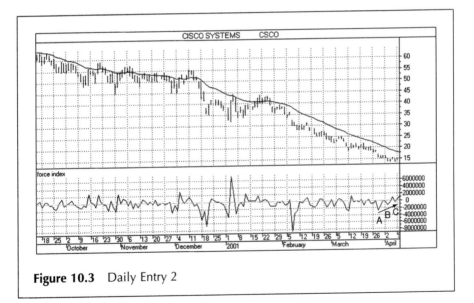

Figure 10.3   Daily Entry 2

ENTRY

Weekly: CSCO has lost over 85% of its value, but this company is not going to disappear like some silly dot-com. Weekly trading ranges have become narrow; the bars near the right edge are only a couple of dollars wide, compared with $10 bars a year ago. This is a sign that speculative excesses have been squeezed out. Weekly MACD-Histogram has been rising for the past six weeks at the right edge—bullish. Weekly price is as far below its EMA as it was above it at the top in 2000; the "rubber band" that connects price to the EMA is overextended, ready to snap back.

Daily: Massive bullish divergence between price and MACD-Histogram. See how strong bears were at bottom A, weaker at bottom B, and now, at C, with prices much lower, bears hardly have any power. Moreover, there is a rarely seen bullish divergence B-C between price and MACD-Lines. Triple bullish divergence A-B-C between two-day Force Index and price shows that each recent attempt to drive prices lower was weaker than before. This divergence is shouting to buy now because it reveals that bears are out of steam and bulls are about to seize control.

Action: Long on 4/9/2001 at 13.91, with a stop at 13.18, below the latest low.

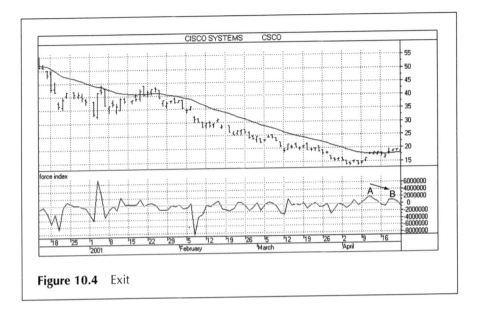

Figure 10.4 Exit

EXIT

Daily: Prices snapped back slightly above their EMA, working off the over-sold condition, and appear to have stalled. The two-day Force Index is tracing a bearish divergence A-B, showing that the rally of the past three days is weaker than during the previous week.

Action: Sold longs on 4/20/2001 at 18.85. Trade rating 55% (took 4.94 out of a 9-point channel).

Trade 2—Long GX

Different stocks often trace similar patterns within a few days of each other. If you figure out what the leaders are doing, you can start looking for similar patterns in the laggards. A friend drew my attention to GX when she called to ask my opinion on a handful of stocks that she liked. Its patterns looked remarkably similar to CSCO, which was already running in my favor.

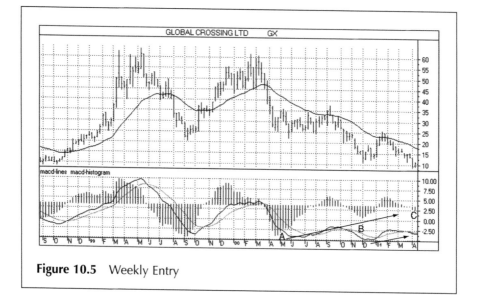

Figure 10.5   Weekly Entry

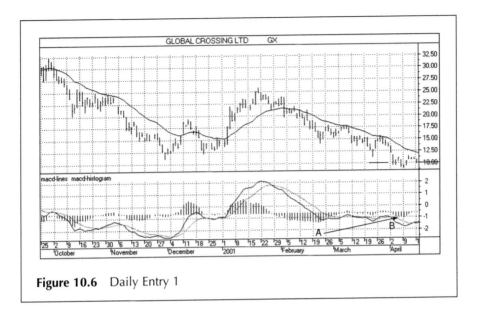

Figure 10.6 Daily Entry 1

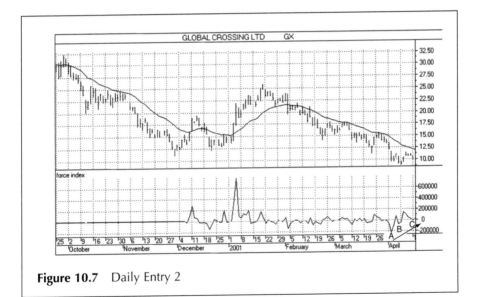

Figure 10.7 Daily Entry 2

ENTRY

Weekly: GX has lost over 80% of its value. Prices are as deep below their weekly EMA as they have ever been, just above the $10 psychological support level. Both MACD-Histogram and MACD-Lines are tracing massive bullish divergences (A-B-C and B-C, respectively).

Daily: Bullish divergence between MACD-Histogram and price A-B shows that bears are becoming weaker, prices are falling out of inertia, and no great selling pressure exists. Seven trading days ago there was a false breakout below 10, and the rightmost bar is declining to retest that level. The bottom of the previous week's break provides a logical stop-loss point. The two-day Force Index is tracing a triple bullish divergence A-B-C, showing that bears have no force—it is a screaming buy. Expect prices to snap above their EMA.

Action: Long on 4/16/2001 at 10.05, with a stop at 8.76, below the latest low.

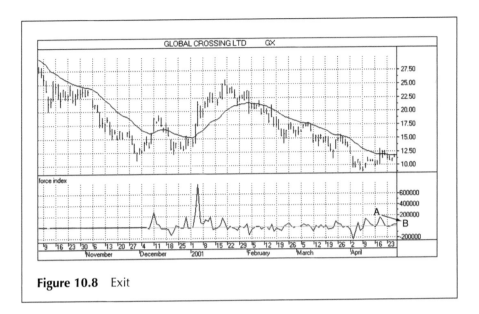

Figure 10.8 Exit

EXIT

Daily: The rally is stalling, as prices have snapped back slightly above their EMA. The two-day Force Index is tracing a bearish divergence A-B, showing that the rally at the right edge is running out of steam.

Action: Sold longs on 4/27/2001 at 11.47. Trade rating 24% (took 1.42 out of a 5.82-point channel).

Trade 3—Long PG

At the end of April 2001 I taught a weekend mini-Camp at a California resort. Once I presented my methods, we spent the bulk of the time applying them to stocks chosen by campers. Out of dozens of stocks we analyzed that weekend, none looked more appealing than PG. On Monday morning I went on-line and placed a buy order.

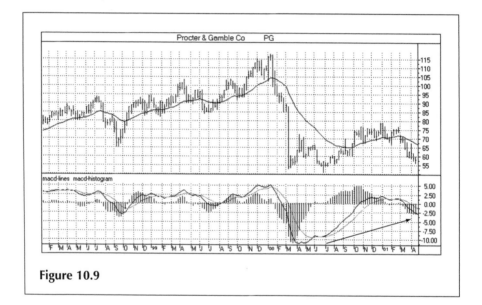

Figure 10.9

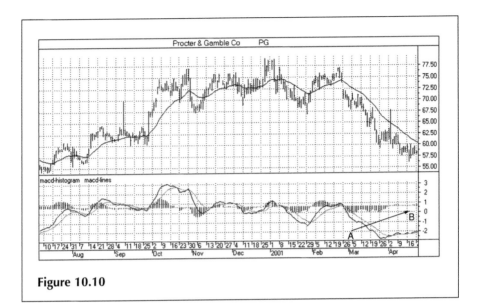

Figure 10.10

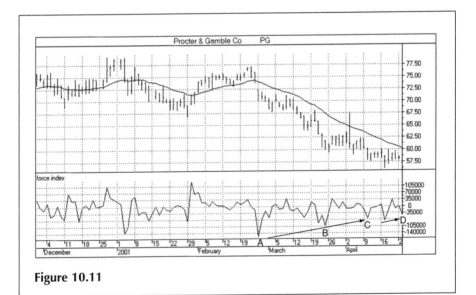

Figure 10.11

ENTRY

Weekly: Prices declining into support, weekly MACD-Histogram on the verge of completing a bullish divergence, while the broad market is rallying.

Daily: Bullish divergence of MACD-Histogram A-B with an extremely shallow second bottom B shows that bears are completely out of steam. The two-day Force Index shows both a longer-term bullish divergence A-B-C-D since February and a short-term C-D at the right edge, giving the final command to pull the trigger. Expect prices to snap above their EMA, at least as high as they are currently below that line.

Action: Long on 4/23/2001 at 58.02, with a stop at 55.95, below the latest low.

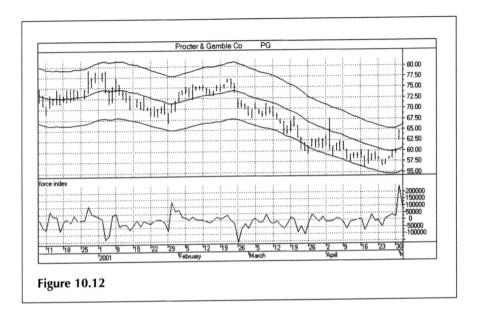

Figure 10.12

EXIT

Daily: At the right edge, prices gapped up on an earnings report; I had a standing order to sell at 62, which was filled at 63.

Action: Sold longs on 5/1/2001 at 63. Trade rating 45% (took 4.98 out of a 10.83-point channel).

Trade 4—Long IMPH

The same friend who called me about GX e-mailed and asked for my opinion on another dozen stocks that she liked, among them this one, which caught my attention.

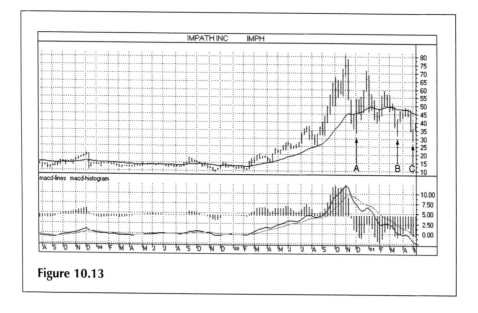

Figure 10.13

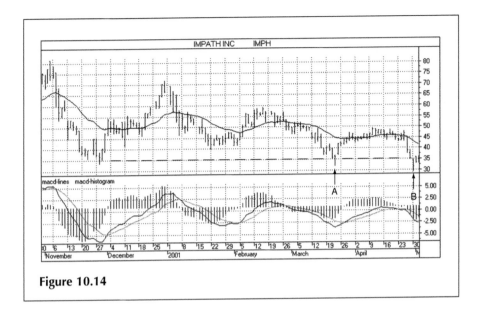

Figure 10.14

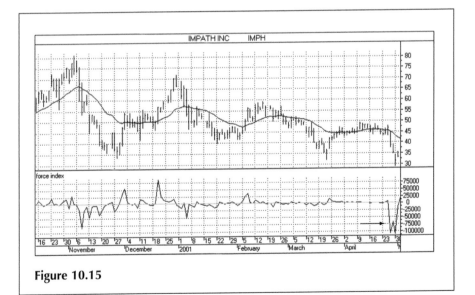

Figure 10.15

ENTRY

Weekly: There is a kangaroo tail C at the right edge of the chart, a formation rarely seen on weekly charts. Previous tails A and B led to big rallies. The overall market is bullish.

Daily: Prices are at the support level; a kangaroo tail B is also seen on the daily chart. A deep bottom of the two-day Force Index near the right edge reflects massive liquidation, which appears to be over, as prices rallied above support. Expect prices to snap back to their EMA.

Action: Long on 5/2/2001 at 33.86, with a stop at 30.50, half way down the tail.

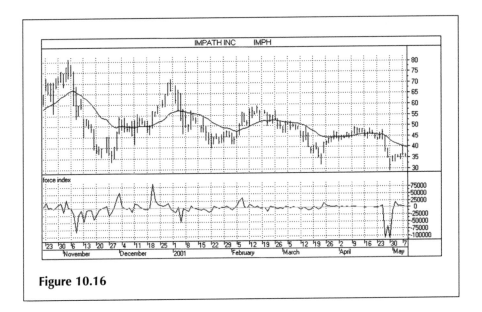

Figure 10.16

Exit

Daily: Another tail, this one pointing up. The expected rally to the EMA did take place; unfortunately, prices recoiled before profits could be taken at that level.

Action: Sold longs on 5/8/2001 at 36.39. Trade rating 16% (took 2.53 out of a 16-point channel).

Trade 5—Short OCA

A dentist friend asked me to take a look at a firm that was trying to take over his dental company. He was being offered its stock and did not know whether it was a good deal. It looked just the opposite to me.

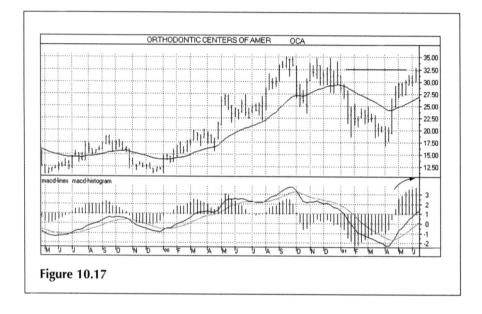

Figure 10.17

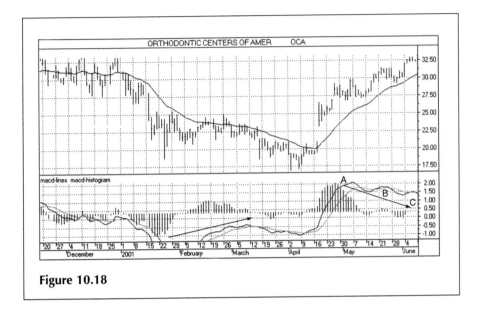

Figure 10.18

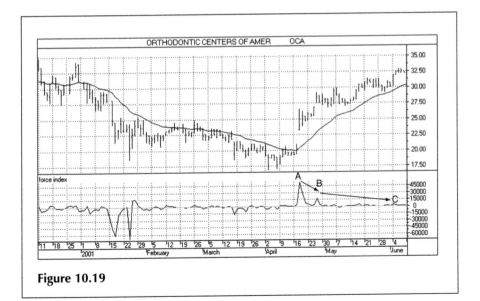

Figure 10.19

ENTRY

Weekly: The rally is running into heavy resistance, with weekly MACD-Histogram flattening at the right edge, indicating that the rally is near its end.

Daily: Massive bearish divergences on the dailies of MACD-Histogram and MACD-lines (A-B-C), as well as Force Index (A-B-C). The tiny daily ranges during the last week show that bulls have retreated from the market; resistance to this rally is overwhelming. The plan is to sell short with a SafeZone stop.

Action: Short on 6/11/2001 at 32.21, with a stop at 33.49.

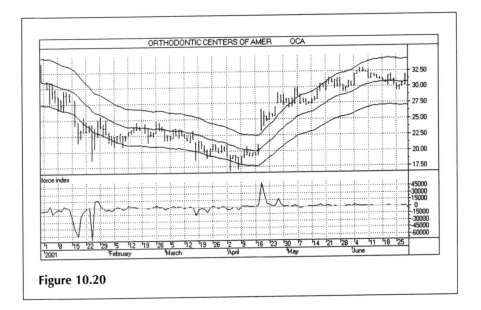

Figure 10.20

EXIT

Daily: Strong support near the EMA, prices not collapsing; the latest rally day at the right edge hit the SafeZone stop.

Action: Covered shorts on 6/28/2001 at 31.46. Trade rating 11% (took 0.75 out of a 7-point channel).

Trade 6—Short EBAY

As the market was becoming "heavier" in summer 2001, with many stocks breaking down, I found this trade in EBAY, which at that time was on my regular scanning list.

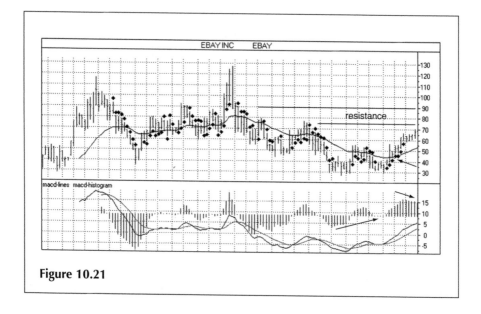

Figure 10.21

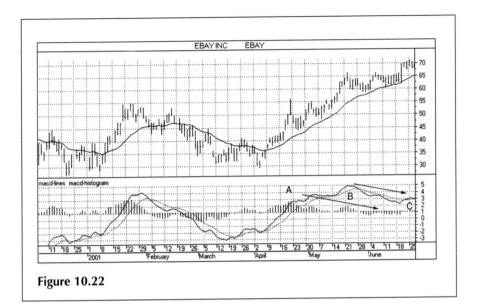

Figure 10.22

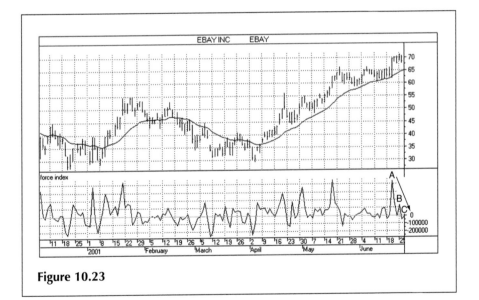

Figure 10.23

ENTRY

Weekly: The rally is running into resistance, and weekly MACD-Histogram headed down during the past four weeks. The Impulse System is no longer flashing its buy signal, as it last did at point A, permitting shorting.

Daily: Massive bearish divergences between prices and MACD-Histogram (A-B-C), as well as a rare bearish divergence with MACD-lines (B-C). The triple bearish divergence A-B-C between Force Index and price at the right edge gives a signal to pull the trigger. The plan is to sell short with a SafeZone stop.

Action: Short on 6/25/2001 at 69, with a stop at 72.51.

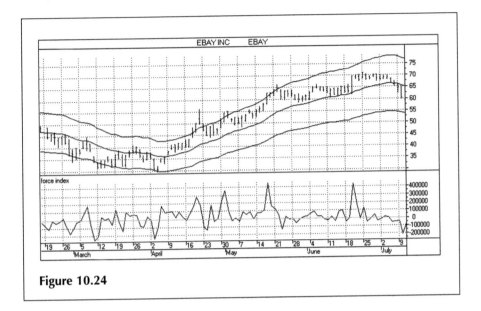

Figure 10.24

EXIT

Daily: Price collapses below the EMA, about as deeply below as it used to be above it. Force Index is about as low as it gets—time to cover shorts.

Action: Covered shorts on 7/11/2001 at 59.34. Trade rating 42% (took 9.79 out of a 23-point channel).

YOUR NEXT TRADE

It took me twenty years of trading and three years of writing to complete this book. The work was hard, but I enjoyed the journey. Reading must have been hard work for you, especially if you studied this book and did not just skim. I wrote on several levels, and it will probably take you more than one reading to grasp all its ideas and concepts. Expect to return and review sections of this book in the months and years ahead, as your expertise grows and new questions emerge.

We spent a lot of time together, but now our paths diverge.

I've accomplished what I wanted, summarized my ideas on trading. Liberated from the word processor, I am off to pursue my passions, especially trading and travel. I will spend more time in front of the screen, travel to faraway places, and if they have good Internet connections, I'll trade from there, combining my interests.

What will you do?

You had your lessons in psychology, technical analysis, money management, and record keeping. If you are serious about success, start applying what you've learned. You have your work cut out for you.

Your first task is to set up a record-keeping system. Keeping records is like looking in a mirror while shaving with a very sharp blade. You're safer if you look. Hammering on this topic reminds me how I once sent a patient to AA who told me that those meetings ruined him as an alcoholic. Getting drunk could never be fun again. Keeping records will do the same for you—it will immunize you against impulsive gambling.

Your next step is to set up a money management plan. Follow that by writing down your trading plan, a decision-making tree. Once you do that, you'll be moving in the direction opposite to the majority of the trading public. Test everything you read in this or any other book. Only testing can make any method your own.

Those who concentrate on the rewards, which are considerable, often push themselves too hard. It is better to trade small in order to be more relaxed and enjoy the learning process. Then you will emerge not only richer, but also more alert, aware, free, and at peace with yourself.

I have traveled this road, made my choices, and battled my demons, growing from a wide-eyed beginner into someone who knows what he is doing. The journey had many rough stretches, but both the trip and the rewards are worth it.

Closing this book does not mean having to say good-bye. If I continue to run my Traders' Camps, you may come to spend a week during which we'll work on trading together. All new ideas in this book have first been presented to my campers, to whom my work is dedicated.

In writing this book I gave you my best and did not hold anything back. I hope you will give all of yourself to becoming a good trader. I now return to my trading room and wish you success in yours.

Dr. Alexander Elder
New York
February 2002

ACKNOWLEDGMENTS

Writing this page is like having a dessert—after working on this book for more than three years, I get a chance to thank those who helped me along the way.

Thanks, first of all, to my campers, the people to whom this book is dedicated. For the past several years I have been running Traders' Camps, becoming friends with some of the sharpest, most inquisitive people in the markets. Their questions forced me to dig deeper and articulate my ideas more clearly. To this day, one of the highlights of each month is a meeting of campers in my apartment in Manhattan.

I want to thank my staff, especially my manager, Inna Feldman. I trust her to take good care of my clients while I am traveling or trading overseas.

Fred Schutzman, an old and loyal friend, found time in his busy schedule to read the entire manuscript, and his eagle eye caught several oversights. Fred did a similar review of my previous book, *Trading for a Living*. At its publication party I introduced him to the woman who was my assistant manager. They started dating, married, and last year had their third child. Fred has a beautiful family, an unexpected bonus for his hard work.

My best friend, Lou Taylor, to whom *Trading for a Living* was dedicated, died more than a year before the current book was completed. His sage advice was priceless and his absence at the next book party will feel like a huge void.

My older daughter Miriam, a journalist in Paris, helped edit this manuscript. It seems like just a few years ago I was correcting her homework, and now she takes a red pen to my pages. Her English and her style are impeccable; it looks like that homework paid off. My second daughter, Nika, an art historian in New York, another person with a razor-sharp sense of taste, developed the design for the jacket of the book. She also selected the fonts and made other suggestions to improve the look and feel of the book. Both girls, as well as my youngest child Danny, provided many cheerful distractions from business. I often took them on trips, and since they like to sleep late, I had the time to work on this book in the cafes of Venice, Fiji, New Zealand, and other locales, before a day of skiing or museum hopping.

My former manager, Carol Keegan Kayne, who edited all of my previous books, reviewed page proofs of this one. She convinced me once and for all that no book of mine is finished until she signs off on it.

My old friend Ted Bonanno insulated me from the most stressful part of writing a book—negotiating a publishing contract. Ted is an Olympic rowing coach (not long ago he went to the Sydney Olympics and I did not go near the gym for three blessed weeks). We work out together, and it was fun discussing business with Ted while running or between rounds of weight lifting.

Last but not least, I want to thank many friends around the world in whose beach, mountain, or city houses I sometimes stayed while writing this book. Since many of them are traders, I hope they benefited from the insights I shared with them as much as I enjoyed their hospitality.

Dr. Alexander Elder
New York
February 2002

SOURCES

Achelis, Steven. *Technical Analysis from A to Z* (New York: McGraw-Hill, 1995).

Appel, Gerald. *Day-Trading with Gerald Appel* (video) (New York: Financial Trading, 1989).

Basso, Thomas F. *Panic-Proof Investing* (New York: John Wiley & Sons, 1994).

Belveal, L. Dee. *Charting Commodity Market Price Behavior* (1969) (Homewood, IL: Dow Jones Irwin, 1989).

Bernstein, Peter L. *Against the Gods* (New York: John Wiley & Sons, 1996).

Bloom, Howard. *The Lucifer Principle* (New York: Atlantic Monthly Press, 1995).

Briese, Stephen E. *The Inside Track to Winning* (video) (New York: Financial Trading, 1993).

Brower, William. Personal communication.

Caplan, David. *Trade Like a Bookie* (Oxnard, CA: Com-Op Publishing, 1995).

Chande, Tushar S., and Stanley Kroll. *The New Technical Trader* (New York: John Wiley & Sons, 1994).

Dominguez, Joe, and Vicki Robin. *Your Money or Your Life* (New York: Penguin Books, 1992).

Douglas, Mark. *The Disciplined Trader* (New York: New York Institute of Finance, 1990).

Douglas, Mark. *Trading in the Zone* (Englewood Cliffs, NJ: Prentice-Hall, 2001).

Edwards, Robert D., & John Magee. *Technical Analysis of Stock Trends* (1948) (New York: New York Institute of Finance, 1992).

Ehlers, John. Personal communication.

Ehlers, John. *Rocket Science for Traders* (New York: John Wiley & Sons, 2001).

Elder, Alexander. *Rubles to Dollars* (New York: New York Institute of Finance, 1999).

Elder, Alexander. *Study Guide for Come Into My Trading Room* (New York: John Wiley & Sons, 2002).

Elder, Alexander. *Study Guide for Trading for a Living* (New York: John Wiley & Sons, 1993).

Elder, Alexander. *Trading at the Right Edge* (video) (New York: Financial Trading, 1996).

Elder, Alexander. *Trading for a Living* (New York: John Wiley & Sons, 1993).

Elder, Alexander. *Winning Psychology and Tactics* (video) (New York: Financial Trading, 1999).

Friedentag, Harvey Conrad. *Options—Investing without Fear* (Chicago: International Publishing, 1995).

Gleick, James. *Chaos* (New York: Viking Penguin, 1987).

Guppy, D. Personal communication.

Hagstrom, Robert G., Jr. *The Warren Buffett Way* (New York: John Wiley & Sons, 1995).

Hartle, Thom. *Talking with "Turtle" Russell Sands* (Stocks & Commodities. 1992; 10(12): 544–548).

Hieronymus, Thomas A. *Economics of Futures Trading* (New York: Commodity Research Bureau, 1971).

Hurst, J. M. *The Profit Magic of Stock Transaction Timing* (Englewood Cliffs, NJ: Prentice-Hall, 1970).

Kaufman, Perry J. *Smarter Trading* (New York: McGraw-Hill, 1995).

LeBeau, Charles. Personal communication.

LeBeau, Charles, and David W. Lucas. *Technical Traders Guide to Computer Analysis of the Futures Market* (New York: McGraw-Hill, 1991).

Leigh, Norman. *Thirteen against the Bank* (London: Weidenfeld, 1976).

LeFevre, Edwin. *Reminiscences of a Stock Operator* (New York: George H. Doran Company, 1923).

Lynch, Peter. *One Up on Wall Street* (New York: Simon & Schuster, 1989).

McMillan, Lawrence G. *Options as a Strategic Investment*, 3rd ed. (New York: New York Institute of Finance, 1999).

Murphy, John J. *Technical Analysis of the Financial Markets* (Englewood Cliffs, NJ: Prentice-Hall, 1999).

Natenberg, Sheldon. *Option Volatility and Pricing* (New York: McGraw-Hill, 1994).

Nison, Steve. *Japanese Candlestick Charting Techniques* (New York: New York Institute of Finance, 1991).

Perry, Roger. Personal communication.

Perry, Roger. RightLine Report—Stock Splits and Momentum Trading (a presentation in the Traders' Camp, January 2001).

Schabacker, Richard W. *Technical Analysis and Stock Market Profits* (London: Pearson Professional, 1997).

Schwager, Jack D. *Market Wizards* (New York: HarperBusiness, 1990).

Schwager, Jack D. *Technical Analysis of the Futures Markets* (New York: John Wiley & Sons, 1995).

Schwager, Jack D. *The New Market Wizards* (New York: HarperBusiness, 1992).

Steidlmyer, J. Peter, and Kevin Koy. *Markets & Market Logic* (Chicago: Porcupine Press, 1986).

Sweeney, John. *Campaign Trading* (New York: John Wiley & Sons, 1996).

Teweles, Richard J., and Frank J. Jones. *The Futures Game*, 3rd ed. (New York: McGraw-Hill, 1998).

Tharp, Van K. *Trade Your Way to Financial Freedom* (New York: McGraw Hill, 1998).

Thorp, Edward O. *Beat the Dealer* (New York: Vintage Books, 1966).

Vince, Ralph. *Portfolio Management Formulas* (New York: John Wiley & Sons, 1990).

Wilder, J. Welles, Jr. *New Concepts in Technical Trading Systems* (Greensboro, SC: Trend Research, 1976).

INDEX

ABOUT THE AUTHOR

Alexander Elder, M.D., is a professional trader, living in New York. He is the author of *Trading for a Living* and the *Study Guide for Trading for a Living*, considered modern classics among traders. First published in 1993, these international best-sellers have been translated into Chinese, Dutch, French, German, Greek, Japanese, Korean, Polish, and Russian. He also wrote *Rubles to Dollars*—a book about the transformation of Russia.

Dr. Elder was born in Leningrad and grew up in Estonia, where he entered medical school at the age of 16. At 23, while working as a ship's doctor, he jumped a Soviet ship in Africa and received political asylum in the United States. He worked as a psychiatrist in New York City and taught at Columbia University. His experience as a psychiatrist provided him with a unique insight into the psychology of trading. Dr. Elder's books, articles, and software reviews have established him as one of today's leading experts on trading.

Dr. Elder is a sought-after speaker at conferences and the originator of Traders' Camps—week-long classes for traders. Readers of *Come into My Trading Room* are welcome to request a free subscription to his electronic newsletter by writing or calling:

Financial Trading, Inc.
P.O. Box 20555, Columbus Circle Station
New York, NY 10023, USA
Tel. 718-507-1033; fax 718-639-8889
e-mail: info@elder.com
website: www.elder.com